SUPERNATURAL
Transformation

GUILLERMO MALDONADO

SUPERNATURAL
Transformation

WHITAKER
HOUSE

SUPERNATURAL TRANSFORMATION:
Change Your Heart into God's Heart

Guillermo Maldonado
13651 S.W. 143rd Ct., #101
Miami, FL 33186
http://kingjesusministry.org/
www.ERJPub.org

ISBN: 978-1-62911-195-7
eBook ISBN: 978-1-62911-196-4
Printed in the United States of America
© 2014 by Guillermo Maldonado

Whitaker House
1030 Hunt Valley Circle
New Kensington, PA 15068
www.whitakerhouse.com

Library of Congress Cataloging-in-Publication Data (pending)

1 2 3 4 5 6 7 8 9 10 11 12 ᴸᴶ 22 21 20 19 18 17 16 15 14

Contents

1

Matters of the Heart

What is the most important question you've ever been asked?

During Jesus' ministry on earth, one of the religious scribes asked Him to name the one commandment—of all God's commandments—that was *"first,"* or most significant. (See Mark 12:28.) Such a question is the equivalent of asking, "What is the most important thing in the world?"

Jesus answered, *"The first of all the commandments is:...'You shall love the LORD your God with all your heart, with all your soul, with all your mind, and with all your strength'"* (Mark 12:29–30). Then He immediately linked that commandment with another: *"And the second, like it, is this: 'You shall love your neighbor as yourself.' There is no other commandment greater than these"* (Mark 12:31).

Entrance to the Kingdom

The scribe who had asked this question replied that he agreed with Jesus' answer, saying that to love God wholeheartedly and to love your neighbor as yourself *"is more than all the whole burnt offerings and sacrifices"* (Mark 12:33). Jesus responded by telling him, *"You are not far from the kingdom of God"* (Mark 12:34).

From this exchange, we see that entering God's kingdom—and living according to that kingdom—is, at its essence, a matter of the heart. The most important thing we can do is to love God with our entire being.

What Is the Heart?

Physically speaking, the heart is the central organ of the human body. Its function is to circulate the blood throughout the whole bodily system, pumping oxygen and nutrients to the other organs and pulling toxins away from them. If the heart stops beating permanently, bodily life ends; obviously, the heart is indispensable. A human being's entire physiological system is designed to safeguard this organ, above all others. For example, in extremely cold conditions, the blood begins to retract from the extremities in order to maintain the integrity of the heart.

We have another "heart" that is the center of our spiritual being. The Scriptures say, *"Now may the God of peace Himself sanctify you completely; and may your whole **spirit, soul, and body** be preserved blameless at the coming of our Lord Jesus Christ"* (1 Thessalonians 5:23). A human being is a spirit that has a soul and lives in a physical body. The sense in which I use the term "heart" in this book is principally the spirit, but it also includes the spirit's interactions and connections with the soul—which is the moral seat of humanity and consists of the mind, the will, and the emotions.

The Foundation of Our Being and Character

The word *"heart"* appears hundreds of times in the Scriptures. In the Old Testament, the words most often translated *"heart"* are the related Hebrew terms *lebab* (H3824) and *leb* (H3820). *Lebab* means "the heart as the most interior organ," and this term is also used in the same sense as *leb*. *Leb* means "the heart; also used figuratively very widely for the feelings, the will and even the intellect."

So, figuratively, these terms refer to the inner being of humans—our very core, including our feelings, desires, will, and intellect. In the New Testament, the main word translated *"heart"* is *kardia*, which, in a figurative sense, indicates "the thoughts or feelings (mind)." Our heart is our true self, and it is the catalyst for our desires, motives, intentions, and actions. A *desire* is "a strong wish: a wish *for* something or *to do* something." A *motive* is "something (as a need or desire) that causes a person to act." An *intention* is "the thing that you plan to do or achieve: an aim or purpose."

Another term the Bible uses to refer to the heart, or spirit, is *"inner man"*: *"That* [God] *would grant you, according to the riches of His glory, to be strengthened with might through His Spirit in the **inner man***" (Ephesians 3:16). Again, the heart is the core, or identity, of the human being. It is the most complex, sacred, and intimate part of a person—the foundation of his whole being and character, from which his desires, designs, purposes, will, thoughts, and attitudes originate.

Accordingly, *the condition of our heart will be the condition of our life.* The state of our spiritual heart affects all aspects of our daily living. Every spiritual, mental, and emotional matter—and many physical ones—is rooted in the heart.

Becoming Spiritually Heart-Healthy

"Heart-healthy" is a popular phrase today. We hear it from doctors, nutritionists, fitness instructors, and food manufacturers who want to encourage us to pursue a lifestyle of "wellness" that will strengthen our cardiovascular endurance, prevent heart disease, and promote long life. We are encouraged to choose a healthy lifestyle through exercising regularly and by eating nutritious meals—making use of resources such as heart-healthy cookbooks, diets, and restaurant options. In the United States, the American Heart Association's symbol for an approved heart-healthy product is a red heart with a white check mark in it.

As we will explore further in chapter 2, every human being is faced with a spiritual health issue—we all have "heart disease" and need to become spiritually heart-healthy. The Scriptures say, *"The heart is deceitful above all things, and desperately wicked; who can know it?"* (Jeremiah 17:9). Although our heart is the center of our being, many people do not truly understand the heart and how it functions. Jesus Christ came to earth not only to reveal God the Father to us but also to reveal ourselves to us. He wants us to understand the nature of our heart and how it affects our relationship with our heavenly Father and other human beings, as well as the whole course of our life.

Even when we have been forgiven and reconciled to God through Jesus' sacrifice on the cross for us, we must actively focus on this matter of the heart and the spiritual laws God has "written" there (see, for example, Hebrews 8:10), so that we will know the fullness of life He desires for us. Heart issues often keep us from overcoming the problems and hindrances in our life. God wants us to experience a transformation of the heart that will make us whole again.

Every spiritual, mental, and emotional matter—and many physical ones—is rooted in the heart.

The Scriptures encourage us to have a heart-healthy spiritual lifestyle, gaining God's seal of approval for the state of our heart. A strong spiritual heart enables us to be all God created us to be and to fulfill His will in the momentous times in which we are living. Thus, we need to have a steady diet of God's Word and to exercise specific spiritual principles and commands related to our heart, for the welfare of our inner being. A healthy spiritual heart is our supernatural lifeline to God and His purposes.

What Comes Out of the Heart?

How would Jesus, the Great Physician, assess the current condition of your heart? The Scripture juxtaposes two fundamental conditions of the human heart—a heart that has *"good treasure"* in it, and a heart that has *"evil treasure"* in it:

> A good man out of the good treasure of his heart brings forth good; and
> an evil man out of the evil treasure of his heart brings forth evil. For out
> of the abundance of the heart his mouth speaks.   (Luke 6:45)

Let's compare these two kinds of "treasures":

- ✦ The heart with good treasure is full of kindness, humility, purity, obedience, righteousness, and spiritual strength. It has the ability to love, submit to, and surrender to God, in accordance with His purpose and will.

- ✦ The heart with evil treasure disbelieves God, is easily wounded, becomes offended, and refuses to forgive; it is full of disobedience, selfishness, ambition, and pride—it has become hardened.

Have you thought about what type of treasure you are storing up in your heart? Jesus said, *"For where your treasure is, there your heart will be also"* (Matthew 6:21).

Even as we grow in grace, we still manifest a mixture of good and evil treasures within us. At times, we reveal the good treasure that is within us through the Holy Spirit. Other times, we manifest an aspect of the evil treasure, demonstrating that we need the Spirit of Christ to reign in that area, removing the corruption and cleansing us, so that we may live in *"newness of life"* (Romans 6:4; see also 2 Peter 1:3–10).

The apostle James wrote about the spiritual incompatibility of a mixture of the two natures:

> *With* [our tongue] *we bless our God and Father, and with it we curse men, who have been made in the similitude of God. Out of the same mouth proceed blessing and cursing. My brethren, these things ought not to be so. Does a spring send forth fresh water and bitter from the same opening? Can a fig tree, my brethren, bear olives, or a grapevine bear figs? Thus no spring yields both salt water and fresh.*
>
> (James 3:9–12)

The words that we say, including the ways in which we express ourselves and communicate with others, reflect the nature of our heart in some way. *"For out of the abundance of the heart the mouth speaks"* (Matthew 12:34).

Similarly, any action we take, whether it is good or evil, comes from a motivation or intention of our heart. This means that all wrongdoing is conceived in the heart first. Jesus said, *"For from within, out of the heart of*

men, proceed evil thoughts, adulteries, fornications, murders, thefts, covetous-
ness, wickedness, deceit, lewdness, an evil eye, blasphemy, pride, foolishness. All
these evil things come from within and defile a man" (Mark 7:21–23). For
example, if you have an arrogant attitude, it means that your heart still har-
bors arrogance; it doesn't reflect its true identity in Christ, who is *"humble*
in heart" (Matthew 11:29 NIV). However, if you consistently exhibit an attitude of genuine humility, then you have a humble heart, reflecting the
nature of God in that area of your life.

Likewise, if you project an attitude of resentment or anger, you prove
that your heart is wounded and bitter; you may feel the need to protect
yourself from being hurt again, so you lash out at others. Or, if you are insensitive to the needs of your family and to the obvious human pain around
you, it shows that you have a hardened heart.

You may wonder, "How can I love God to the extent that I commit
my whole being—heart, soul, mind, and strength—when my heart is in
the condition you described?" On our own, none of us can. But our heart
will be transformed as we respond to God's deep love for us: *"We love Him*
because He first loved us" (1 John 4:19).

God is ready even now to change our heart to be like His heart
through a *supernatural* transformation. Only the work of God's Holy
Spirit within us can effect a total transformation of our heart. And our
heart is the key to our soul, mind, and strength, as well. God wants us to
yield to Him and actively cooperate in the process of transforming our
heart. That transformation begins with the new birth (see John 3:3–7)
and progresses throughout our life as we daily grow to be more like our
heavenly Father.

A woman named Victoria experienced a change in her heart that led to
an encounter with Jesus as her Savior and King. Here is her story:

"In early 1990, I arrived in New York as a refugee from Kiev, Ukraine.
Financially, I had always been blessed; however, relationally—specifically
in marriage—I had experienced destruction, and I was twice divorced. My
two daughters were without a father, so I began to look for answers from
above.

"I started exploring Eastern religions like Buddhism, but my life seemed to become more complicated than ever. One day, I cried out to God, saying, 'God, I haven't found You in the Jewish traditions, in Eastern religions, or in Russian Orthodox churches. Please tell me who You are. Change my life.' While visiting my father in the Czech Republic, I met a Russian couple who introduced themselves as Christian evangelists. They prayed for me, and when I got back to New York, everywhere I went, I received Bibles as gifts.

"On Christmas Day 2000, someone gave me recordings of the New Testament and told me, 'Victoria, when you drive in your car, please listen to those tapes.' I did, and something started happening—an atmosphere filled my car, and that atmosphere began to draw me to my vehicle to listen to the tapes. Day after day, I would cry in my car, without understanding what was going on with my heart.

"After I finished listening to the gospel of John, I felt like I was ready to give birth. When I heard the name of Jesus, I felt heat inside me. Later that day, I got a phone call from the person who had given me the tapes. He gave me the address of a church where a service would be held on that very day. I went to the service and liked what I heard on that first Thursday night of 2001. During the worship, the Lord opened my spiritual eyes, and I saw Jesus. I didn't see Him as on an icon but alive, as a King. And the Holy Spirit told me that He is the Messiah. I couldn't hear the preaching; I was crying so hard and repenting of my sin, for which I felt so dirty.

"I knew that I had come to the house of my Father and there was no turning back. I was born again—radically! As I progressed in my walk with the Lord, I began to seek healing and deliverance, elements that were missing in my church. There was a lot of knowledge there but very little demonstration of it. After years in the ministry, the Lord brought me to King Jesus International Ministry in October 2010.

"Today, I am a woman of purpose and destiny. I am single and completely fulfilled in the Lord. For the first time in my life, I feel like a daughter of the King. Before, I knew the Lord, but His kingdom wasn't a clear part of the picture to me. Now I have discovered the kingdom, and I am so grateful."

Monitoring Our Heart

We know that, generally, the condition of our physical heart determines the health of our body. Even in routine checkups at the doctor's office, medical personnel review our heart rate and blood pressure to help them determine our overall health. And, if they discover a problem—if our pulse is high, for example—they may advise us to make adjustments to our diet or get more regular exercise.

Moreover, when someone is admitted to the hospital, nurses and other medical technicians will continually record the patient's vital signs. Among other things, they monitor the electrical activity of his heart, determining whether the heart rate is consistent and within normal range. If not, medications and/or other treatments may be called for.

In a similar way, we need to regularly assess the condition of our spiritual heart. Maintaining a healthy heart before God is a matter of vigilance. We must monitor the operations of our inmost being and evaluate whether we are living according to the life and purposes of our heavenly Father.

An Ongoing Process

The verb *monitor* means "to watch, observe, listen to, or check (something) for a special purpose over a period of time." Again, monitoring our heart is an ongoing process. It is something we should do willingly, and always in conjunction with God's Holy Spirit within us, for the purpose of becoming more like the Father. No one except God can truly "see" and know our inner being. After stating, "*The heart is deceitful above all things, and desperately wicked; who can know it?*" (Jeremiah 17:9), the Scriptures say, "*I, the LORD, search the heart, I test the mind, even to give every man according to his ways, according to the fruit of his doings*" (Jeremiah 17:10).

God knows us completely. Therefore, when we become aware of a problem in our heart—whether that awareness comes through reading and studying God's Word or the direct prompting and conviction of the

Holy Spirit—we must address it so that we can lead joyful and productive lives before God and maintain a close relationship with Him. Only if we are spiritually healthy can we be alert and ready to respond to the moves of God's Spirit in our own lives and in His church.

The Issues of Life

The book of Proverbs tells us, "*Keep your heart with all diligence, for out of it spring the issues of life*" (Proverbs 4:23). Here is the same verse in two other translations: "*Above all else, guard your heart, for it is the wellspring of life*" (NIV). "*Watch over your heart with all diligence, for from it flow the springs of life*" (NASB).

The word translated "*keep*" or "*guard*" or "*watch over*" includes the idea of protecting or maintaining. The combined sense of these translations of Proverbs 4:23 is that our heart requires our diligent oversight, and it needs to be defended from attack by negative spiritual forces and anything else that would do it harm.

Let us now look at the larger context of the above verse:

> *My son, give attention to my words; incline your ear to my sayings. Do not let them depart from your eyes; **keep them in the midst of your heart; for they are life to those who find them, and health to all their flesh.*** Keep your heart with all diligence, for out of it spring the issues of life.* (Proverbs 4:20–23)

Note that there are specific criteria by which we are to oversee our heart. The speaker in Proverbs 4 encouraged his son to keep his father's words in his heart and to obtain "*wisdom*" and "*understanding*." (See Proverbs 4:4–6.) In that way, he would develop into a righteous man. It is only when we keep God's Word in our heart and follow His commandments and wisdom that our heart will produce a "*wellspring of life*."[1]

Proverbs 4 also says: "*The path of the just is like the shining sun, that shines ever brighter unto the perfect day. The way of the wicked is like darkness; they do not know what makes them stumble*" (Proverbs 4:18–19). Our heart

---

1. See *The Wycliffe Bible Commentary*, Charles F. Pfeiffer and Everett F. Harrison, eds. (Chicago: Moody Press, 1962), 561.

determines the path of our life; therefore, it is our most precious possession and our most crucial resource.

The condition of your heart will be the condition of your life.

Life Begins in the Heart

We know that wrongdoing begins in the heart. However, godly life also begins in the heart. All of us have areas in our life that we need to align with God's ways. That kind of change can occur only through God's supernatural transformation.

As I indicated earlier, the condition of our heart affects all aspects of our life. For instance, a person's physical ailment can sometimes be traced to unforgiveness in his heart. One time, when I was teaching about the topic of the spiritual heart during a service, the Lord led me to demonstrate that many infirmities, including those of the mind and emotions, are connected to a lack of forgiveness. I called forward anyone who had various maladies, such as physical affliction or depression, and I led them to repent of their sins, to forgive others, to ask for forgiveness, and to renounce any bitterness and unforgiveness they were harboring in their hearts. Without exaggeration, after they did this and offered a simple prayer to God, about 250 people were delivered—they were healed instantly of diabetes, arthritis, depression, and many other ailments!

Another clear example of this truth may be seen in the life of a businesswoman named Lesley who attended one of the Inner Healing and Deliverance Retreats that our ministry periodically hosts. She writes, "Before knowing Christ, I had resentment, doubt, and bitterness toward my family. It was so great that I even lost my sight in a matter of weeks. After consulting several doctors, I discovered there were no eye drops, eyeglasses, or operations that could help me, or anything else they could do for me. The blindness was chronic and without apparent cause! Then, I decided to surrender this situation to God. Even though I had received messages through my family and even strangers to forgive the family members with whom I had problems, I never thought that this had anything to do with my blindness. But, one day, my cousin Denise told me that the Lord had shown her there was nothing wrong with my eyes, that the only thing I had to do was forgive, because it was a spiritual matter. She invited me to attend a deliverance retreat, but I didn't want to go. Since the registration for the retreat was limited, I asked God that if it was His will for me to go, a spot would be opened for me, and it was! Reluctantly, I attended, and there I received revelation about unforgiveness and what curses are. I forgave, then renounced and canceled every curse in my life, and I was free. People prayed for me, and God gave me back my sight—immediately!"

Our attitudes are a projection of our heart.

Fresh Revelation About the Heart

This book is a journey into the human heart, exploring its purpose, motivations, and potential. We will come to understand and identify our true self and make key decisions with respect to our "inner man." Today, there is no place for being spiritually lukewarm; we cannot remain spiritually neutral. In this day and age, God is bringing fresh revelation to His people regarding the state of our heart. I believe the reason is that the return of Jesus Christ to the earth is near, and hard times will precede His coming—as foretold by the Bible.

The apostle Paul wrote to his spiritual son Timothy, *"But know this, that in the last days perilous times will come"* (2 Timothy 3:1). Why did Paul emphasize his statement by preceding it with *"Know this…"*? Paul understood human nature and its tendency toward degradation, incurring the judgment of God. In another Bible version, the phrase *"perilous times"* is translated *"terrible times"* (NIV). If there was ever a time in history for which that phrase was appropriate, it is this one. God's judgment will come upon the earth, even if many people think it will never happen. I believe it will take place in three stages—a preliminary judgment, an intermediate judgment, and the final judgment—and that we are now in the preliminary judgment stage.

God's grace has provided salvation and redemption in Christ, but the perpetual corruption and rebellion within humanity continue to provoke divine judgment. There is no need to blame governments, religions, or other factors for the judgment that our planet and the human race is now undergoing. The basic cause is the degradation of human character resulting from the iniquity entrenched in the human heart.

The apostle Paul listed eighteen character failings that would mark people in the end times. Again, they describe our present generation: "*lovers of themselves, lovers of money, boasters, proud, blasphemers, disobedient to parents, unthankful, unholy, unloving, unforgiving, slanderers, without self-control, brutal, despisers of good, traitors, headstrong, haughty, lovers of pleasure rather than lovers of God*" (2 Timothy 3:2–5).

These negative impulses will try to pull our heart away from our heavenly Father. We are entering a period when our heart will be weighed in the balance to see on which side we will end up. The situations in our life and the circumstances of the world will soon compel us to decide where our allegiance belongs—to God's interests or to selfish interests; to the "good treasure" or to the "evil treasure." Will we be prepared to make the right decision?

"*Sow for yourselves righteousness; reap in mercy; break up your fallow ground, for it is time to seek the* Lord, *till He comes and rains righteousness on you*" (Hosea 10:12). It is time to seek the Lord with all our heart. We must have a heart that God can trust to follow Him and obey what He calls us to do, so that we may participate in the manifestation of His coming glory and the last great harvest of souls upon the earth.

Radical and Permanent Transformation

God's plan is not to place patches over the "holes" in our heart caused by our spiritual, emotional, mental, or physical issues. He does not try to "fix" or "improve" the corruption of our heart, and He doesn't gloss over sin. As we will discuss in chapter 2, these are the approaches that various religions take. Instead, His plan involves a radical and permanent transformation of the heart.

In the coming chapters, therefore, we will examine the original nature of the human heart. We will learn what it means for our heart to be "circumcised," how to forgive others and thereby receive healing for an offended heart, and how to gain freedom from a heart of unbelief.

We will also discover the purpose for brokenness of heart, as well as how to surrender our heart completely to the Lord so it can be a true reflection of His own heart of love, justice, joy, and other divine qualities. And, we will learn how to experience transformation through the renewing of our mind in the presence of God (see Romans 12:2), so that we may experience both deep and far-reaching change in our life.

Do you want to change your life? Change your heart!

The psalmist wrote, "*Behold, You desire truth in the inward parts, and in the hidden part You will make me to know wisdom*" (Psalm 51:6). God has provided the only solution for the corruption of the human heart: repentance, identification with the death and resurrection of Jesus Christ, new birth through the Spirit of God, and ongoing transformation into the image of our Creator. "*Therefore, if anyone is in Christ, he is a new creation; old things have passed away; behold, all things have become new*" (2 Corinthians 5:17). You can become a new person, a new creation, through the supernatural transformation of your heart.

2

Understanding the Heart

From the beginning, it was God's desire and purpose for human beings to have a heart like His. The Scriptures tell us: *"Then God said, 'Let Us make man in Our image, according to Our likeness....' So God created man in His own image; in the image of God He created him; male and female He created them"* (Genesis 1:26–27). God also breathed into humanity His own Spirit: *"And the Lord God formed man of the dust of the ground, and breathed into his nostrils the breath of life; and man became a living being"* (Genesis 2:7).

Humans, therefore, were made with a heart, or spirit, fashioned after their Creator's. This heart was pure and complete, filled with God's nature and character.

A Devastating Change of Heart

But the first human beings, Adam and Eve, turned away from God's heart and the nature in which they had been created. Instead of cherishing God's instructions and wisdom, they willfully disobeyed Him. God had commanded them not to eat of the Tree of Knowledge of Good and Evil, warning them that if they did so, they would die. Tragically, they listened to the voice of God's enemy, Satan (the devil), who told them, *"You will not surely die. For God knows that in the day you eat of it your eyes will be opened, and you will be like God, knowing good and evil"* (Genesis 3:4).

Enticed by a promise of "being like God"—although they had already been made in His image—the first man and woman went against their Creator. Their rejection of God's heart resulted in a terrible change in the human heart, giving human beings an all-too-familiar knowledge of evil, because it was now within them. Their disobedience, or sin, resulted in their fall from their true selves and the loss of their innocence—it initiated the corruption of the human heart.

With their fall, human beings brought a difficult and cursed life on themselves. (See Genesis 3:1–19.) And they did experience death, for *the wages of sin is death*" (Romans 6:23). First, their hearts underwent spiritual death. And second, they eventually—and inevitably—experienced physical death. One of the most devastating results of the fall for humans was their removal from the immediate presence of God, no longer to enjoy direct fellowship with Him. (See Genesis 3:22–24.) Yet God never departed from His faithfulness to His beloved creation or His desire that they be restored to a close relationship with Him.

A Corrupt Inheritance

All human beings descend from the first man and woman who turned their hearts away from God, and therefore we have all inherited their corrupt nature. From the point of Adam and Eve's disobedience, humanity's corruption continued in human history until it reached this peak: "*Then the LORD saw that the wickedness of man was great in the earth, and that **every intent of the thoughts of his heart was only evil continually**" (Genesis 6:5). This was the point when God destroyed the world through a flood—the only survivors being Noah, his wife, and his sons and their wives, whom God preserved. (See Genesis 6.) If the heart of the human race was ever to be restored to Him, human beings would have to exist under vastly more humble circumstances that would cause them to reach out to their heavenly Father.

Noah was the most righteous man on the earth at the time of the flood, and that is why he and his family were spared. However, even Noah's heart was affected by the sin nature he had inherited. And, although the earth was repopulated by Noah's family, corruption infiltrated the world again, and people's hearts withdrew from God once more. This is the inevitable legacy of our corrupt nature.

Ever since humanity's initial act of disobedience, therefore, human beings have followed after the lusts of their fallen hearts, to varying degrees. We all have sinned, and we all continue to sin, in various ways. As the apostle Paul wrote, *"All have sinned and fall short of the glory of God....Through one man sin entered the world, and death through sin, and thus death spread to all men, because all sinned"* (Romans 3:23; 5:12).

An Irreversible Condition

The corruption in the heart of humanity is irreversible in the natural. No human power can alter or remove it. It is similar to rotten fruit: There is no way to reverse the process so that the fruit becomes whole again. Once a piece of fruit is spoiled, it is inedible. Moreover, it must be separated from other pieces of fruit, or it will contaminate them.

Corruption may take a while to occur, but, when it does, the process cannot be stopped. This is why none of us can produce a pure heart, in and of ourselves. As hard as we might try to embrace goodness, the iniquity we inherited through our human descent from Adam and Eve contaminates our heart from birth.

Left to ourselves, then, we are hopelessly corrupt, exhibiting various "treasures" of the evil heart that we discussed in chapter 1, such as wicked thoughts, covetousness, deceit, pride, foolishness, selfishness, adultery, and murder. Sin leads to death in many forms. Whether immediately or in future generations, iniquity will produce its corruptive effects—always downward, always getting worse. The extreme cases of degradation we observe in our society did not take place suddenly or in one generation. Human morality has continually disintegrated until it has reached the evil condition we are witnessing today.

No human power can reverse humanity's moral, ethical, or physical corruption.

The State of Our World

Throughout history, there have been periods when regions or even nations have experienced genuine revivals of the Holy Spirit and reformations that have brought people to God. During those periods, society as a whole has become godlier. However, it didn't take long before people in those regions or nations forgot about God or began to turn their backs on Him, just as the descendants of Noah did, and it was only a matter of time before the effects of heart corruption manifested.

My assessment is that we are living in an age similar to the one just prior to the great flood. As I wrote in chapter 1, the condition of our current society is that of a tendency toward resentment, rebellion, selfishness, hatred, cruelty, violence, and other manifestations of evil and iniquity. I believe that the multiplication of wickedness over the last several decades is a sign of the end times, indicating, as I mentioned earlier, the imminent culmination of human history with the coming of Christ. I could cite many current examples of wickedness, coldness of heart, and so forth, to verify this. We don't have to look far to see instances of corruption, all of which are related to the broken condition of the human heart.

The following are just a few examples of how the most vulnerable members of the human race—children—are suffering today in the midst of societies whose leaders and other citizens are corrupt of heart. These incidents reveal the depth of despair and wickedness to which humanity without Christ has sunk.

In China, on the coast of Zhejiang Province, a single woman apparently hid her pregnancy and then delivered her baby boy in a public restroom in her apartment building that contained squat toilets. The baby somehow became stuck in one of the restroom's sewage pipes—whether he slipped away from his mother by accident or she intentionally dropped him there was not clear. The woman alerted her landlord that a baby was stuck in the pipe, and firemen had to saw off a section of the tube to open up the pipe and rescue the boy, who survived. Charges against the mother were pending.[2]

---

2. www.huffingtonpost.com/2013/05/28/china-baby-saved-from-sewer-pipe_n_3344442.html.

In Texas, USA, an eleven-year-old child was "punished" by his father and stepmother for bad behavior by being locked in his bedroom for months, and he was given only bread and water to sustain him. One day, his parents found him lying on the floor, unresponsive. They washed his body and placed it in a sleeping bag, eventually abandoning it in a wooded area. The boy's grandfather called the police, explaining that it had been months since he had last seen his grandson. Authorities investigated and discovered that the boy had spent nine months isolated in his room, where he had lost weight until he was only about sixty pounds. He had apparently become so weak that it had been impossible for him to escape or cry out for help. He had eventually died of starvation.[3]

In Mexico, an eight-year-old girl was sexually abused by her father over a period of several years. While the father would rape his daughter, the mother would film and take photos of the assaults, later distributing the material through the Internet to pedophiles both within Mexico and outside of the country.[4]

Where does such neglect and outright contempt for one's fellow human beings come from? How are humans capable of evil and violence that seem to have no limits? How can a being created in God's image, who has the capacity to think and to love and to feel compassion for other people, be led by such animalistic and demonic instincts? In response to these questions, many people, perhaps in an unconscious desire to justify their own sinful behavior, ask, "If God is so good, why do terrible things happen in the world, such as injustice, cruelty, murders, wars, and natural disasters?"

The answer, as we have seen, is the inherited corrupt condition of the human heart, also known as the *"sinful nature"* (see, for example, Romans 7:5, 18, 25 NIV). It is time for all of us in the human race to assume responsibility for our own sinful actions and for the corruption humanity brought into this world, which has infected every generation of human beings to the present day.

---

3. http://www.foxnews.com/us/2012/04/01/missing-11-year-old-starved-to-death-in-locked-bedroom-dallas-police-say/.
4. http://www.lapoliciaca.com/nota-roja/violaban-y-filmaban-a-su-propia-hija/.

The Root of Sin

The root of sin is pride and selfishness, which is the opposite of the heart of God. It was pride and selfishness that caused the first humans to want to be equal with God, so that they were deceived by the devil to the point of disobeying their loving Creator. Egocentrism places ourselves first, above everyone else. The Scriptures say, *"For men will be lovers of themselves,…having a form of godliness but denying its power. And from such people turn away!"* (2 Timothy 3:2, 5). Genuine godliness—not just a *"form"* of it—can be obtained only as the supernatural power of God's grace changes our character, removing our selfishness and self-centeredness and replacing them with love, kindness, empathy, and self-sacrifice for the sake of others.

Many people attempt to change their natures through practicing various forms of religion, but the results will always be limited. Religion can only "patch up" the corruption of the heart by developing rules and laws that promote good behavior and positive principles, such as the practice of self-discipline. However, religion can never profoundly change a person's heart; it doesn't have the power to take away our fallen nature, which is perpetually self-serving.

Corruption exists in the human heart in different forms and at different levels, from generating lies to committing mass murder, but there is a way out for all of us through Jesus Christ. If we want to change the legacy of our personal history, if we want to leave our children an inheritance of blessing, if we want God to heal our nations, we must deal with the root of humanity's problems—the corruption of the heart.

Spiritual Warfare over the Hearts of Human Beings

Ever since Satan prompted the first man and woman to reject God's command, turning away from His nature, an invisible war has been taking place for possession of the hearts of all human beings. God's kingdom of light and Satan's kingdom of darkness are battling even now for our heart. Whoever holds the heart of someone also holds his potential and his resources—his entire person. We human beings must decide to whom we will surrender our heart.

You may say, "What if I decide not to give my heart to either kingdom? What if I just try to live on my own?" There is no "neutral zone" in this spiritual conflict. When we choose to live on our own, apart from God, we effectively choose to side with God's enemy, Satan. The kingdom of darkness forcefully takes over any terrain—especially the human heart—it finds vulnerable or vacant, using the most subtle weapons and tools imaginable. (See, for example, Matthew 12:43–45.)

The kingdom of darkness tried to take over the life of a man named Denis, as well as the life of his wife, Guerda, but the power of God defeated the enemy and transformed their lives. The following is their story.

When Denis was still a youth, he moved from Haiti to the United States with his mother and siblings, although they were not legal residents. For the first two months, things seemed good. But then his mother agreed to smuggle drugs into America from Haiti, and she was caught and arrested. So, Denis and his sister were sent to live with another family.

Denis's sister, who was only ten years old, was immediately exposed to a life of witchcraft and started practicing voodoo, while Denis soon embarked on a life of robbery by knifepoint and prostituting girls. Then, he opened a trap (drug) house, and word of his new "business" spread throughout the streets of Homestead, Florida, so that he was soon selling and dealing large quantities of drugs. Denis even experimented with counterfeit money for a short time. His immoral lifestyle seemed to have no limits. He started going to strip clubs and buying women for sex, throwing thousands of dollar bills up in the air, "making it rain."

One of the strippers ended up pregnant, and Denis decided to marry her in order to legalize his residency status. The woman used him for his money, cheated him, and left him high and dry without residency status and with an obligation to pay for all his divorce fees. After this, Denis's outlook on women changed. He would take women out, have sex with them, and then give them money in order to hurt them and make them feel cheap. He would throw sex parties so that his male friends could have as many women as they wanted. Denis had become the type of man everyone was afraid of—he was fearless and heartless and showed no emotion. He did not believe in rules or authority other than his own, and he was very prideful.

Then one of his friends was arrested for tax fraud and was deported to Haiti. This incident opened Denis's eyes to the fact that his own reckless lifestyle could catch up with him and end just as quickly. Denis made a decision to leave his old ways and settle down, and he got a job working for a school he had once attended. In addition, he started dating Guerda, a single mother of three who was trying to live a better life.

Guerda had been a voodoo priest, calling on a spirit that she was "married" to. She explained, "I would do readings for people; I would interpret dreams and connect with the dead. I would have parties for the spirits and provide sacrifices of dead chickens, doves, and goats. I once 'killed' another witch who crossed me, and she died in Haiti. I would also do spells to make money.

"Guys feared me and didn't understand me. I would sleep with a bunch of demons or spirits; they would never manifest in human form, but I was always aware that they were in the room with me. I would cook meals for the spirits, deliver messages to other people from them, and have dreams with them. They would tell me that they loved me, that they'd never hurt me. In one instance, a demon appeared to me in a dream and brought me to a mason log and showed me many things. He called me 'Ester, the eastern star.' He promised me fame, marriage, and money, but I had to go back to Haiti to claim my mother's 'land mantle.' He told me there would be a serpent there but not to fear. The serpent would put something in my mouth, and I would then be unstoppable. I did whatever I could to get to Haiti, but everything seemed to block my return."

Denis and Guerda continued to date and eventually moved in together. Then, a friend of Guerda's invited her to a service at King Jesus Ministry, where Guerda received Jesus Christ as her Lord and Savior. Guerda brought Denis to another King Jesus service, and he was saved and baptized within the same week.

Denis and Guerda attended a youth retreat where inner healing and deliverance were ministered, and Denis was freed from his hatred and unforgiveness toward his mother and his ex-wife. In addition, Denis and Guerda were delivered from bondage to sexual immorality—Denis from sexual addiction and Guerda from adultery. "I loved to date married men," she stated. "I was a vixen for them." Guerda was also delivered from witchcraft.

God made Denis and Guerda into new people and reconciled them to one another. To His glory, the couple got married and became leaders and mentors in a House of Peace (the church's home fellowship ministry). They are learning to become a man and woman of God. Through God's supernatural power, they are now delivering others who have been involved in witchcraft and those who have been possessed or oppressed by demons and spirits. They are also being used to liberate others who have been bound by sexual immorality. Moreover, they have experienced deliverance of the heart from the deceitful spirit of pride. Denis and Guerda turned away from the things that used to be a source of pride to them so that their hearts could be transformed by God.

The Scriptures tell us: *"Be sober, be vigilant; because your adversary the devil walks about like a roaring lion, seeking whom he may devour. Resist him, steadfast in the faith"* (1 Peter 5:8–9). *"For we do not wrestle against flesh and blood, but against principalities, against powers, against the rulers of the darkness of this age, against spiritual hosts of wickedness in the heavenly places"* (Ephesians 6:12). We must be aware of the fierce struggle for our heart taking place and make a decision to surrender our life to the Lord, who loves us and wants to give us His life. In contrast, the enemy hates us and seeks to destroy us. Jesus said, *"The thief* [Satan] *does not come except to steal, and to kill, and to destroy. I have come that they may have life, and that they may have it more abundantly"* (John 10:10).

The goal of the enemy is to take the human heart captive and to keep it captive.

What Does God See?

In chapter 1, we talked about how our heart, or spirit, is the source of our desires, motives, and intentions. Although human beings tend to focus on externals—things that can be seen with the natural eyes, such as people's physical attributes, possessions, or worldly accomplishments—God sees beyond these superficial elements to the depths of our being. When God looks at us, He sees the condition of our heart. *"But the* LORD *said to Samuel, 'Do not look at his appearance or at the height of his stature, because I have refused him. For the* LORD *does not see as man sees; for man looks at the outward appearance, but the* LORD *looks at the heart"* (1 Samuel 16:7).

What does God see in your heart? He sees the motives, intentions, and intimate thoughts that come from it, whether good or evil. Consider these questions: What is your reason for getting out of bed every morning? What moves you? Is your primary incentive personal gain, or is it a desire to honor God? Are you pursuing your own will or God's will? Do you speak and act in certain ways in order to be recognized by other people, or do you speak and act out of love and reverence for your heavenly Father? Are your actions prompted by a generous heart or a selfish one? What motivates you to take care of your family members—or to neglect them? Do you spend your money on temporal things or on eternal purposes? Why do you pray, offer praises to God, or give offerings—or not do any of these things? Is your reason for serving God that you want to expand His kingdom and bless other people, or do you merely want to receive credit for being "godly"?

These are all questions of the heart, and each of us must address them. Again, *"where your treasure is, there your heart will be also"* (Matthew 6:21). For example, if the treasure you value is position, fame, or prestige, your heart will be there also. One way to assess the condition of your heart is to see where, or in what, you are investing your money. You don't even have to examine the large amounts you spend on necessities, such as mortgage payments or rent, utilities, or transportation. Instead, look at your small but repeated expenditures for things that are not necessities, such as entertainment, fashion accessories, cigarettes, alcoholic beverages, expensive restaurants, and so forth. If you are using up large portions of your income on personal items or habits, that is where your heart is. If you are accumulating money in a selfish or greedy way, perhaps motivated by a fear of the future, that is where your heart is. God will reward us if our heart is right, and He will judge us if it is not: *"I will give to each one of you according to your works..."* (Revelation 2:23).

We need to regularly monitor our own heart, since we know that God Himself is continually searching it. As Paul wrote, *"For if we would judge ourselves, we would not be judged. But when we are judged, we are chastened by the Lord, that we may not be condemned with the world"* (1 Corinthians 11:31–32).

Rewards in this life and the next depend on the condition of the heart.

How much of your heart does God require for Him to be the only Lord of your life? Your whole heart! In what condition is your heart right now? Is it able to give Him everything? Or, is it hurt, offended, or shattered, so that it withholds from Him? Do you have difficulty truly loving or being loved? Do you find yourself incapable of trusting others and establishing healthy relationships, so that you flee from your heavenly Father's invitation to come to Him? If so, will you allow God to heal you, transform your heart, and give you a new life, so that you can draw close to Him and to other people?

Often, we attempt to hide the corruption in our heart from other people. For example, when we are in public, we may show a certain "face," which is really just a mask. In private, we know who we are in the depths of our heart, and we recognize that we are deceiving ourselves. If the motives of our heart are wrong, they will manifest in our decisions and life choices, or they will emerge when we are under pressure, regardless of the reputation we have tried to create for ourselves.

There can be no flow of life in the areas of our heart that we haven't given over to God.

The Restoration of the Heart

"The wages of sin is death…" (Romans 6:23)—the death of the spiritual heart and the death of the physical body. But that is not the whole story:

"...the gift of God is eternal life in Christ Jesus our Lord" (Romans 6:23)!
God knew that the hearts of human beings would turn from Him. But He
never stopped loving them, and He never departed from His original plan
for humanity. To restore humans to the heart with which they were created—pure and whole in His likeness—God came to earth in the person
of Jesus Christ. He came not only to teach us how to live but also to die for
our sin and rebellion—to break the hold that the corrupt sin nature had
on our heart. Long before He arrived on earth, He promised us through
one of His prophets, *"I will give you a new heart and put a new spirit within
you"* (Ezekiel 36:26).

Two things have to happen to initiate this ongoing process of heart
transformation. Everything we discuss in the subsequent chapters hinges
on the fact that the following foundational changes have taken place in
your life:

1. You have received a new heart—a spirit made alive in Christ. *"But
   God, who is rich in mercy, because of His great love with which He
   loved us, even when we were dead in trespasses, made us alive together with Christ (by grace you have been saved), and raised us up
   together, and made us sit together in the heavenly places in Christ
   Jesus"* (Ephesians 2:4–6).

2. You have received God's Holy Spirit to dwell in you. "Repent, and
   let every one of you be baptized in the name of Jesus Christ for the
   remission of sins; and you shall receive the gift of the Holy Spirit"
   (Acts 2:38).

The experience of receiving a new heart is sometimes called being
"born again." Jesus said, *"Most assuredly, I say to you, unless one is born again,
he cannot see the kingdom of God....Most assuredly, I say to you, unless one is
born of water and the Spirit, he cannot enter the kingdom of God"* (John 3:3,
5). Another term for a new heart is the *"new birth"* (1 Peter 1:3 NIV).

Jesus Christ died on the cross to restore us to our heavenly Father. This
plan was in effect from eternity. The Bible calls Jesus *"the Lamb slain from
the foundation of the world"* (Revelation 13:8). He is the One who paid for
every sin committed by the human race—all its iniquity, rebellion, and
transgressions—so that we could be free from our corrupt nature.

By His death, and by His resurrection through the power of God, Jesus enabled the human race to return to its original state of purity and wholeness of heart—the way the Father had created it in the beginning. We enter the "new birth" when we willingly receive Christ's sacrifice and His righteousness, applying them to ourselves, and accept Him as our Lord and Savior. We acknowledge that we have lived far from God—independent of Him and His purposes. We surrender our life to Him, opening up our heart so that His presence can dwell within us. Jesus said, *"If anyone loves Me, he will keep My word; and My Father will love him, and We will come to him and make Our home with him"* (John 14:23).

The above two changes make it possible for us to experience the supernatural transformation of our heart. Once we are a *"new creation,"* we can live according to the life and counsel of God's Spirit, with the ability to reject the elements of the sinful nature within us that try to win back control. We can eliminate areas of disobedience and selfishness in our life that, as James wrote, *"ought not to be so"* (James 3:10) for people who have received a new heart from God. (See Romans 8:13; Colossians 3:5.) Then, the "springs" from our heart will yield only fresh water, and not a mixture of salt water and fresh. (See James 3:9–12.)

> [Jesus said,] *"If anyone thirsts, let him come to Me and drink. He who believes in Me, as the Scripture has said, out of his heart will flow rivers of living water."* But this He spoke concerning the Spirit, whom those believing in Him would receive; for the Holy Spirit was not yet given, because Jesus was not yet glorified. (John 7:37–39)

The following is the testimony of a man who received a new heart and the gift of the indwelling Holy Spirit. Marceliano was born in Colombia and later moved to the United States. He grew up without a father, and he was full of resentment and anger.

"My father died at an early age, and my ten brothers and I were raised by our mother. Before he died, my father would frequently visit mediums who, when he got sick, did not allow him to go to the hospital because 'their god was going to heal him.' His death left such a deep void in my heart that, at the age of twelve, I began to drink. Later, I got involved in drug trafficking, including smuggling drugs hidden in people's bodies. Money became my god.

"I was accident prone. I was involved in a car accident, I jumped from a hospital building, my 'friends' tried to kill me with an overdose of liquid heroine, and I was later stabbed in the chest during a fight. Because of what was going on, my mother, in her ignorance, decided to take me to witches and sorcerers. My world consisted of alcohol, friends, and illegal dealings, but nothing filled the void within me.

"When I arrived in Miami, someone took me to a Christian church where I met the Lord. His love filled the emptiness in my heart. Furthermore, God gave me spiritual parents who lent me a hand and believed in me far beyond my terrible life. I am now free of anger, vengeance, and addictions, and I am learning to become the head of my family and to treat my wife the way the Lord intended. The illegal dealings that were once a source of pride are now shameful to me. The only good thing I kept from my past is the knowledge that God was able to forgive the worst of sinners and transform the blackest of hearts. Today I know that He has a purpose for my life and for my family."

You can receive a new heart, just as Marceliano did. If you have not yet accepted Jesus as your Lord and Savior, pray the prayer at the end of this chapter. Many people claim that they are not "sinners" in need of God's forgiveness, saying something like, "I am good, never hurt anyone, and do what is right whenever possible." Yet God requires from us a truly righteous heart—not one that is "good" according to our own definition—and we receive such a heart only by accepting the redemptive work of Christ on our behalf. We must repent (turn away from our sins), die to our old nature through Christ, and be born again, receiving the Holy Spirit. We have no goodness unless it comes from God.

A Heavenly "Audit"

Even now, God is carrying out a heavenly "audit" on human hearts. *"I know also, my God, that You test the heart and have pleasure in uprightness"* (1 Chronicles 29:17). God continually searches our heart, but I believe there are special times in which He evaluates the heart condition of His people. Right now, as I indicated in chapter 1, the main purpose of His "audit" is to prepare our heart for the great and final movement of His glory upon the earth, in which He will pour out His Spirit and bring many people into His kingdom. Out of His love for us, He is searching and testing our heart to see if it is faithful and righteous, because He wants us to participate with Him in this great outpouring and manifestation of His power.

We must realize that since our new nature still battles the influence of the sinful nature, we cannot always trust our own motivations or instincts. Moreover, we will experience increased pressure from Satan's evil spiritual forces at work during these end times. As we have seen, *"the heart is deceitful above all things, and desperately wicked; who can know it?"* (Jeremiah 17:9). I don't think this verse is implying that our heart will necessarily be deceived, but that it has the ability to deceive us. Until our heart is fully transformed, and we are living in godly humility and self-denial, we will have improper motivations and selfish intentions that deviate from the purposes of God. We cannot allow ourselves to be guided by any untransformed part of our heart!

Salvation is only the beginning of our relationship with our heavenly Father. God wants us to draw continually closer to Him and, as His children, reflect His nature. That is why He calls us to have increasingly transformed hearts that will represent His own heart.

How much of us does God have? Perhaps, He has certain parts of our life—our belongings, our service, or our tithes and offerings. Yet, until He has our entire heart, we will not fully love Him or be able to reflect His true nature. The world, the devil, and the *"lusts of the flesh"* (see, for example, 2 Peter 2:18), or the sinful nature, will continue to exert influence and power over us, pulling us in the direction of our false desires and weaknesses, and leading us into sin.

Sometimes, we give God only the things that don't matter much to us or don't interest us, or the areas that don't cost us much to give up. But when God has our whole heart, He has both us *and* all of our resources. It is then that He can trust us to be faithful stewards of His abundant wealth, for achieving His purposes on earth and for blessing His people. Again, all of us have areas of our life that we need to surrender to God. Anytime we hold back something from Him, that is a part of our heart over which we haven't allowed Him to be Lord. Instead, we make ourselves the lord over that area.

The beauty of an unselfish life is to serve God and other people without expecting anything in return.

Accountability and Rewards

God has released and will release various judgments upon the earth because of the wickedness of human beings. But He also has a judgment reserved for the works done by His children. He will judge us here on earth and in heaven. *"For we must all appear before the judgment seat of Christ, that each one may receive the things done in the body, according to what he has done, whether good or bad"* (2 Corinthians 5:10).

Romans 14:12 says that *"each of us shall give account of himself to God."* This means that we will each have an individual trial before God in which we will be held accountable to Him for what He has given us. I don't believe this judgment is for the purpose of condemning us but rather for rewarding us. The judgment seat of Christ is where believers will be judged for everything they did on earth. Each person's work will be presented on that day. The purpose of this judgment will be to prove the motives and intentions of our heart in what we have done. Paul wrote, *"Therefore judge nothing before the time, until the Lord comes, who will both bring to light the hidden things of darkness and reveal the counsels of the hearts. Then each one's praise will come from God"* (1 Corinthians 4:5).

If we have done something with the wrong motivation or attitude, our work will be burned by fire, as trash is burned. When we do something with the right motivation, we are guaranteed rewards on earth and in heaven. (See 1 Corinthians 3:11–15.) Additionally, we will be protected from the negative consequences of acting from wrong motives. Even if no one applauds us, recognizes what we do on earth, or pays us for the work we have performed, we will receive our reward from God—if the work has been done for Him. For this reason, let us remember to evaluate our motivations regularly, knowing that we should do all things out of love for God.

When someone feels forced to do something, his heart is not in it.

God's Commitment to Us

While God is always faithful and loving toward us, there is a sense in which He commits only to the portion of our heart that we have surrendered to Him. Some Christians have surrendered only 20 percent or 50 percent of their life to God, so they don't experience Him at work in the uncommitted areas. Consequently, they often have difficulties and troubles in those unsurrendered aspects of their life, and they feel frustrated and helpless in regard to them. They may start to blame God for not answering their prayers, or they may think He has forgotten about them.

If you are in such a situation, let me ask you: Will you continue to blame God for unanswered prayers in the areas of your life that you have withheld from Him? Will you persist in saying that God has forgotten about you? Or, will you take responsibility for not having fully surrendered your heart to Him—or for taking back areas of it? Are you now willing to go to God and give Him *all?* The time has come for you to decide. If your faith doesn't flow from your heart, it is merely intellectual acknowledgment or mental assent of God and His ways. Under such conditions, you cannot expect to receive results from Him.

I believe that if you will prayerfully and humbly examine your heart, you will be confronted with a spirit of independence in relation to the areas you are withholding from God. You may discover that, while you thought you were serving Him in a certain way, you were really performing a ritual that only looked like service but didn't come from a genuine motivation of your heart. If you lack the motivation of love, you will not have a genuine desire to serve God and will make little effort in that regard.

Yet, even in the midst of our selfishness and rebellion, God continues to draw us to Himself! His Holy Spirit guides us, motivates us, and convicts our heart, thus working in us *"both to will and to do for His good pleasure"* (Philippians 2:13). But God never pushes us or forces us to do anything. His manner of reaching out to us contrasts with the way in which Satan operates. His demons push us. They try to pressure us to take certain actions, or they try to snare us, in order to lead us into sin and destroy our life. The enemy desires more than anything else to usurp the dwelling place of God within us—our heart.

We have as much of God as we give to Him. Where we withhold from God, He withholds from us.

Receive a New Heart!

As we close this chapter, I want to give you the opportunity to receive a new heart and the gift of the Holy Spirit through faith in Jesus. As I wrote earlier, these changes are essential for experiencing genuine and ongoing heart transformation. If this chapter has opened your eyes to the corruption in your heart and your inability to reverse it, if you recognize that you need God to change your heart and are willing to surrender your life to Him completely, pray the following prayer. Trust that God will help you to give all the areas of your life to Him as He transforms you, for *"the one who calls you is faithful and he will do it"* (1 Thessalonians 5:24 NIV).

> Heavenly Father, I recognize that I am a sinner and that my sin separates me from You. My heart is in need of transformation, which only You can accomplish. I believe that Jesus died on the cross for me and that You raised Him from the dead. I confess with my mouth that Jesus is Lord. I repent of all my sins and break every evil covenant I have made with the world, with my sinful nature, and with the devil. Now, I make a new covenant of righteousness with Jesus. I ask Jesus to come into my heart and to change my life, filling me with the Holy Spirit. If I were to die right now, I

know I would be in Your presence when I opened my eyes in eternity. In Jesus' name, amen!

3

The Functions of the Heart

In this chapter, we will explore the various functions of the heart, as God intended them to be, so that we may cooperate with the work of the Holy Spirit to transform our inner being.

1. The Heart Regulates the Flow of Life

As we have seen, everything in our life begins in the heart: *"Keep your heart with all diligence, for out of it spring the issues of life ["for it is the well-spring of life" NIV]"* (Proverbs 4:23). *"A good man out of the good treasure of his heart brings forth good; and an evil man out of the evil treasure of his heart brings forth evil"* (Luke 6:45). The condition of our heart determines the condition of our life. Just as God designed the physical heart to pump blood to the other organs in the body, distributing minerals and nutrients, He designed the spiritual heart to "pump" life to our entire being—producing mental, emotional, and physical health.

Many people complain about their circumstances, wishing their lives were different. However, rather than grumbling about troublesome situations—whether they involve our business, marriage, social life, ministry, or other spiritual issues—we must examine our heart and start the process of change through repentance and the power of God's grace to transform us. No matter what circumstance is causing us frustration, anger, or sadness, the key to transforming our life is our heart. That is where all transformation begins.

> *The spiritual heart was designed to "pump" life to our entire being—producing mental, emotional, and physical health.*

Some people try to change their lives by sheer willpower. While the will is a participant in the process of transformation, it is not meant to function on its own. Many times, the will alone is unsuccessful in bringing about desired change, particularly when it has been allowed to grow weak. Moreover, it does not have the power to transform a person's *nature*.

Suppose an individual has done something he knows is wrong. So, he decides, as an act of his will, "I will no longer do such and such," yet he finds himself unable to change. He cannot uphold the decision of his will, because the sin he engaged in was conceived in his heart. The sin cannot be uprooted merely by his making a mental decision to reject it. Again, a work of true repentance and change must take place in our inner being—where the Holy Spirit reproves us, convicts us of sin, and prompts genuine contrition and a sincere desire to change. Unless our repentance comes from heartfelt conviction, there will be no lasting change in our behavior.

2. The Heart Is the Gatekeeper of Our Lives

The heart also functions as a gate, or door, that we open or close to external influences, all of which have the potential to affect our motivations, decisions, and actions. The devil desires to block the flow of God's life in us, redirecting us away from our Creator's original design. His goal is to destroy us or, at least, to derail God's purposes for us—whether those purposes are connected to our ministry, vocation, marriage, family life, financial prosperity, or any other aspect of our life.

Consequently, Satan attempts to manipulate our heart by planting bad thoughts in our mind and enticing our sinful nature to rise up in the form of pride, lust, rebellion, and so forth. The Bible uses other terms for the sinful nature, such as the *"flesh"* (see, for example, Romans 7:5) or the *"old* man" (see, for example, Ephesians 4:22)—the "flesh" in this sense referring not to the physical body but to our sinful desires. Whatever term we use for the sinful nature, the devil wants our heart to be contaminated by it.

Satan often attacks in several areas of our life at the same time, because he wants to wear down our patience and take away our peace, making us vulnerable to sin—sin in our heart, and then sin in our actions. So, he introduces spirits of fear, anxiety, worry, discouragement, depression, sickness, and so forth, as he seeks to corrupt our heart with doubt, unbelief, bitterness, resentment, hate, guilt, or an all-pervasive conviction of failure and hopelessness.

This is why we must make a commitment to watch closely over our heart and to monitor its health. Allow me to share a word of advice from the Bible that is useful in protecting the heart: Be careful about what, and whom, you listen to. (See, for example, Philippians 4:8; Ephesians 4:29.) Don't accept words of doubt or fear; don't receive—or join in with—other people's murmuring and complaining. As you guard the gate of your heart, grant admittance only to words that build and edify your faith, that bring you peace and joy, and that encourage truth, holiness, and a desire to seek God in a deeper way. "Listen" closely to God's Word as you read and study the Scriptures. Your heart needs to be guarded in peace.

==

Your lifestyle reflects the condition of your heart.

==

3. The Heart Facilitates Intimate Relationships

As we discussed in chapter 1, Jesus cited the following as the greatest commandment God has given human beings: *"You shall love the LORD your God with all your heart, with all your soul, and with all your mind"* (Matthew 22:37). The Lord never requires us to do anything that He hasn't enabled us to do. He may already have given us the ability to do it in the inherent makeup and gifts with which we were born; or, He may give us the resources directly through His Holy Spirit—or both. So, when we are commanded to love God with all our heart, we can know that this is something He will help us to do. We were created for intimacy with God, and we can have a deep relationship with Him through the grace and power of His Spirit.

Such a relationship with God arises from a love that is birthed in the heart and that surrenders completely to the Beloved. A similar principle applies to our relationships with other human beings. Every genuine relationship is birthed in the heart. Therefore, if a relationship that was established in love begins to die, it is because that relationship is no longer based in the heart; consequently, it grows cold and/or fades away.

God Pours Out His Love into Our Heart

When we are born again through Jesus Christ, one of the first things that is activated in our heart is a love for God; this love is evidence of the genuineness of our new birth. The Scriptures say, *"The love of God has been poured out in our hearts by the Holy Spirit who was given to us"* (Romans 5:5). After the experience of the new birth, we are often immediately able to love other people more freely, as well. We may find that certain relationships that had been lukewarm or strained are renewed, and we may suddenly discover a desire to share God's love with other people.

Any action we take for God—praying, serving others, proclaiming the gospel of Jesus Christ, giving offerings, and so forth—should flow from our love for Him. *"Whatever you do, do it heartily, as to the Lord and not to men"* (Colossians 3:23). This lifestyle of love was designed by the Creator. Again, if we discern a motivation in our heart other than love—for example, one that is merely expedient—it indicates that some area of our heart is controlled by the corrupt sinful nature and needs to be transformed into the likeness of God's own nature.

A true relationship with God arises from a love that is birthed in the heart and that surrenders completely to the Beloved.

Openness of Heart Is Essential

Openness of heart is a necessary ingredient for any close relationship—whether with God or another person. Let's consider an illustration of this principle. Suppose you have a positive working relationship with

someone at your job. You never encounter any problems with this individual. He is a hard worker, cooperates with you, has a pleasant disposition, and contributes substantially to your department. Because you enjoy
working with him, you think you'd like to develop a friendship outside the
workplace. However, you find that you cannot cross a certain point in your
relationship with him. His heart is closed to anything beyond interaction
at the job.

This scenario indicates that even when a person is intelligent and has
an open *mind* toward others, he may still have a closed *heart* toward them.
For many people, it can take a long time to feel comfortable enough with
another person to open their heart to a deeper level of intimacy—whether
in friendship, romantic love, or the spiritual relationship between brothers
or sisters in the body of Christ. These people may easily open up their mind
to others while discussing plans, goals, and procedures, and while sharing
tasks and responsibilities; but, for the most part, they will not reveal many
of the thoughts and feelings of their heart.

We will not always experience a connection of the heart with the people with whom we work or with whom we share other types of responsibility. Yet, when a person's heart is closed to us, our interactions with him can
feel impersonal, sometimes even cold. While such an association may still
allow us to function adequately in the workplace, it would be unhealthy
if it occurred in a relationship with a member of our immediate family or
a longtime friend. In these cases, the party who has closed his heart has
likely built up a defense mechanism in order to protect himself from someone or something that he fears or that has caused him to take offense—
whether that "threat" is real or imagined.

There is no relationship without an open heart.

Similar closed relationships can occur within the church. For example,
suppose a believer decides he will just attend church services but then go
home as soon as the service ends. He does not want to develop spiritually meaningful relationships with the pastor or other members of the
community of faith. Such a believer may not recognize that "[Christians],

being many, are one body in Christ, and individually members of one another" (Romans 12:5). The effect of his decision to close himself off from other believers is similar to the business relationship described above. And, there are times when such closed behavior indicates that the individual simply wants to use other people in order to get something from them, rather than offering them the love of Christ.

When a person has constructed emotional barriers that stifle the normal functions of his heart as designed by God, leading to a closed heart, this means that others—whether they are members of his family, his church, or another group—will never truly know him or be able to develop a close relationship with him.

Some church denominations teach (or imply) that to show emotion is an act of the "flesh"; others may not go that far, but they still do not encourage the members of their congregations to display their feelings openly. God gave us emotions and feelings to enable us to connect with other people and to express ourselves; therefore, they are both real and necessary. Where churches have shut down the demonstration of emotion, they have sometimes squelched a genuine move of the Holy Spirit, because what the people were feeling in their hearts, prompted by the Spirit, could not be expressed and acted upon.

Is your own heart open or closed? Are you comfortable sharing your heart with your spouse, other family members, or friends? Or, are you afraid to do so because you have been emotionally wounded by someone in the past? In coming chapters, we will discuss some of the barriers we create from emotional wounds and sinful attitudes that prevent us from opening up our heart to God and others, and keep us from being healed, thus distorting our reflection of God's heart.

God Speaks to Our Heart

In a sense, God has two "thrones": one in heaven and the other on earth. His earthly throne is found in the heart of every believer. Recall that Jesus said, *"If anyone loves Me, he will keep My word; and My Father will love him, and We will come to him and make Our home with him"* (John 14:23). In the Old Testament, the presence of God rested above the ark of the covenant, which was located in the Holy of Holies in the tabernacle or temple.

Today, we are the temple of God as we carry His presence in our heart: *"Do you not know that you are the temple of God and that the Spirit of God dwells in you?...For the temple of God is holy, which temple you are"* (1 Corinthians 3:16–17). *"But we have this treasure in earthen vessels, that the excellence of the power may be of God and not of us"* (2 Corinthians 4:7).

God speaks to us in our heart; it is the way He guides and lights the way for us. *"The spirit of a man is the lamp of the LORD, searching all the inner depths of his heart"* (Proverbs 20:27). Our heart, or spirit, is like a "satellite receptor"—it is meant to continuously receive signals from heaven. The heart also transmits "status reports" from the deepest part of our inner being back to our Creator.

Only with the Heart Can We Truly Know God

The two-way communication described above is vital for genuine relationship with God because it is the only way we can truly know Him, and it allows us to share the depths of our hearts with Him. Jesus emphasized this truth by pointing out what happens when people fail to develop this type of relationship with Him:

> Not everyone who says to Me, "Lord, Lord," shall enter the kingdom of heaven, but he who does the will of My Father in heaven. Many will say to Me in that day, "Lord, Lord, have we not prophesied in Your name, cast out demons in Your name, and done many wonders in Your name?" And then I will declare to them, **"I never knew you;** depart from Me, you who practice lawlessness!" (Matthew 7:21–23)

The Greek term translated *"knew"* in above passage can indicate "to come to know, recognize, perceive." I believe the word refers to intimacy, which is built over time. If love doesn't originate in the heart, it is not genuine. Likewise, the relationships in a person's life that endure are those that not only begin in the heart but also continue to be based there.

Jesus was saying that many people who have focused only on the works they were doing for God will be rejected by Him because they never established a heart relationship with Him, and they were not obedient to the will of God. You may ask, "How, then, were they able to prophesy and do miracles in Jesus' name?"

I have concluded that sometimes a person who lacks a genuine relationship with God will become associated with someone who does have such a relationship and who also carries an anointing to operate in the supernatural; because of his proximity to an anointed servant of God, the person can operate in miracles out of that atmosphere. This may explain the case of the people Jesus was referring to. Or, perhaps they actually exercised spiritual gifts of prophecy, healing, and miracles. Even though spiritual gifts come from God, they are not the basis of our standing and acceptance with Him. Works are never a substitute for relationship. Many people never experience the manifest presence of God in their lives because they lack intimacy with Him. If we don't want to receive the above answer from Jesus, we must make sure that we have true and intimate communion with Him based on a heart relationship.

Anything that doesn't originate in the heart is not genuine; therefore, it will not last.

We Worship from the Heart

As the facilitator of our intimate relationship with God, our heart is also the source of our worship of Him. Worship that doesn't come from our inner being is tainted. For example, suppose you enter a time of worship at your church, but, instead of focusing on God, you are absorbed by your own thoughts, desires, and needs. Such "worship" as you are able to offer in this state comes only from your soul—your heart is absent. Consequently, you do not give God the honor and devotion He deserves, you aren't able to enter into His presence, and you don't experience the flow of His life in you or see His power and kingdom manifest in your circumstances.

If this is the way you regularly "worship," then, while you might give financially to God, you should not expect to see a harvest. While you might pray to Him, you should not expect to be heard. While you might praise Him, you should not expect to feel His genuine presence. In effect, you will be wasting your time, because the life of God will not be present in your offerings, your prayers, or your praise. Accordingly, your life will not bear spiritual fruit.

What is the nature of your relationship with God? Do you know Him? Does He know you? God is ready to initiate or continue spiritual intimacy if you desire it with your whole being. Once you establish such a relationship in your heart, you will become a carrier of God's presence and power, and you will also do miracles, signs, and wonders in His name—works that have His sanction and that reap an eternal harvest.

The heart of man is the place of rest, or the Holy of Holies, of the presence of God on earth.

4. The Heart Generates Both Belief and Trust in God

The Scriptures say, *"Trust in the Lord with all your heart, and lean not on your own understanding"* (Proverbs 3:5). Trust is another spiritual element that is birthed in the heart. We must realize that faith and trust are not the same. Trust represents our "walk" with God—the manner in which we love Him, obey Him, and live for Him. The presence of trust in our heart is an indicator that we have a true relationship with Him, that we really know Him and have come to totally depend on Him. When we trust God, we rest securely in His character, integrity, and faithfulness.

Any true relationship is based on trust. A relationship with God is established by trusting Him wholeheartedly.

On the other hand, faith involves a "zone" of time in which God is ready to act in the "now." The "now" is His timing, the moment He chooses to act. Our part in faith is to receive what we "hear" in the Word of God, or directly from the Holy Spirit, and then operate according to it: *"So then faith comes by hearing, and hearing by the word of God"* (Romans 10:17). Many people are strong in faith but weak in trust. For example, they may *believe* that God will do a miracle, but if the miracle doesn't manifest quickly, they tend to give up and thereby forfeit it. They lack the trust that would have enabled them to persevere to see it manifest. This deficit of trust undermines their relationship with their heavenly Father.

Trust Is Currency

If an individual is not prepared to inspire trust within a relationship, or to trust the other party, that relationship will suffer—and sometimes die. For example, a man may love his wife, but if he is unfaithful to her, he has betrayed her trust. He may not think his love for his wife has changed, but their relationship of mutual commitment has been broken. If his wife learns of his infidelity, she might continue to love him and may even forgive him. But the question is: Will she be able to trust him once more?

A heart that has been hurt by betrayal finds it very difficult to trust again. That heart may love the other person long-distance but still find it impossible to rebuild the relationship. Trust is "currency" between people. The only hope for a marriage relationship broken by adultery is for the offending spouse to win back trust through true repentance of heart and by faithfulness demonstrated over a long period of time.

Likewise, trust is an essential part of our relationship with God and is built over time. We can count on God to be totally trustworthy toward us. Let us show Him that we can be trusted to be faithful and devoted to Him.

You are personally rich if you can trust those with whom you are in relationship and if they can trust you.

Trust Brings Perseverance

As indicated above, our trust in God not only establishes our relationship with Him but also maintains it over time. This is particularly true as we wait for the fulfillment of His promises. Consider the following questions: Is the foundation of your relationship with God one that will stay strong during the course of your life? Do you maintain your relationship with God on an everyday basis, whether you experience good times or trying ones? If you were to experience a distressing problem or enter into a difficult period that lasted a long time, would you continue to trust in Him, or would you turn to alternative sources for help? After all the ups and downs of life, will you be found still in relationship with God in the end?

Sometimes, receiving an answer to our prayers is not so much a matter of faith but rather of trusting God when the fulfillment of His promise seems to be delayed. We must realize that we won't immediately receive everything we ask for. The Scriptures tell us, *"The testing of [our] faith produces patience ["perseverance" NIV]"* (James 1:3). This statement indicates that while we are exercising our faith, a period of time may pass. That doesn't mean that we are supposed to stay sick or defeated until Christ returns. Rather, it tells us that we must persevere in order to obtain our promises and miracles from God.

What should we do when the promise doesn't manifest immediately? We should ask the Holy Spirit to give us discernment regarding which type of faith to exercise in a given situation and moment—either "now" faith that receives the manifestation immediately, or faith that perseveres until God is ready to release the miracle for us to receive. We should also wait faithfully and confidently for the manifestation of the promise. As the book of Isaiah says, *"In quietness and confidence shall be your strength"* (Isaiah 30:15). The character of our heart is established by unwavering faith, not in the emotion of a moment. If our heart trusts in God, we will remain steadfast until the manifestation of that which our faith expects to receive—and has *already* received in the spiritual realm. (See Mark 11:24.)

We must understand that the fulfillment exists "now" in the supernatural sphere until its due time comes. We cannot question God as to why He has not yet answered, because then we would be casting aspersions on His character and integrity, and that would be an insult to the Almighty. At these times, we are to trust in who God is—His character—as well as in how much He values us and desires to give us His life.

How can a weak human being, created out of the dust of the earth, have this kind of trust? I have seen believers quickly start to seek alternative sources of help when the promise doesn't arrive immediately. After giving a problem to God, they take it back and try to "fix" it through human means. Meanwhile, the answer could have been ready to manifest in their lives, but, sadly, they missed it by seeking natural solutions!

God wants us to learn to depend on Him. We don't know what may be coming in our life, but we can trust in God wholeheartedly, because His purposes and ways are infinitely greater than our own knowledge and understanding.

> *For God is not unjust to forget your work and labor of love which you have shown toward His name, in that you have ministered to the saints, and do minister. And we desire that each one of you show the same diligence to the full assurance of hope until the end, that you do not become sluggish, but imitate those who through faith and patience inherit the promises.* (Hebrews 6:10–12)

We enter into greater dimensions of faith through trust.

Trust Releases Faith

In a sense, the manifestation of what you have been waiting for—such as financial provision, marital restoration, healing, or deliverance—has always been with you, because faith *is* "now" in the eternal realm. However, as we have been discussing, sometimes the "now" has been waiting for you to trust in God. Anyone can believe in the "now" when he sees his answer manifested; but the test of trust is the condition of your heart as you wait for the fulfillment of the promise. Often, before we see the answer to a request, the enemy will try to convince us that it will never come. At those times, we must hold on to our faith and continue to believe in the Lord with all our heart, regardless of what our eyes see—or don't yet see.

Are you beginning to understand how important the role of the heart is in the realm of the supernatural? The heart is crucial to seeing the hand of God move in your life—to seeing the fulfillment of His promises and the manifestation of His miracles.

The life of the patriarch Abraham, who was a giant of faith, is a strong example of trust and its results. Abraham had to wait almost twenty-five years before God's promise of a son manifested in the "now." *"And not being weak in faith, [Abraham] did not consider his own body, already dead (since he was about a hundred years old), and the deadness of Sarah's womb"* (Romans

4:19). We could call Abraham not only the "father of faith" (see Romans 4:11–12, 16) but also the "father of trust," because he had to wait with patience and confidence, resting in the knowledge that God's promise would manifest one day. Trust allowed him to wait without losing heart—even though he sometimes had questions. (See, for example, Genesis 15:1–6.) Trust enabled him to persevere and to believe in God and His word *"against all hope"* (Romans 4:18 NIV), regardless of his circumstances.

Are you facing a situation similar to what Abraham faced? Have you been praying and believing for the fulfilment of God's promise for a long time, but your "now" has not yet come? Regardless of the problem—a bad medical diagnosis, the lack of a job, a difficult relationship—continue to trust God wholeheartedly, even if the world gives you contrary advice. If we know God and have an ongoing relationship with Him through love, prayer, and obedience to His Word, and if we remember that He will never leave us nor forsake us (see Hebrews 13:5), then we can be confident that He will answer us.

The following Scripture sums up what it means to trust in the Lord with all your heart when you are discouraged, confused, or unable to see the hand of God in your circumstances: *"Being confident of this very thing, that He who has begun a good work in you will complete it until the day of Jesus Christ"* (Philippians 1:6). Never imagine that your circumstances are so overpowering that you should stop trusting in God and give up. "[Abraham] *did not waver at the promise of God through unbelief, but was strengthened in faith, giving glory to God, and being fully convinced that what He had promised He was also able to perform"* (Romans 4:20–21).

Moreover, faith that is solidly supported by trust cannot stay silent. It has to praise God and worship Him. Abraham *"was strengthened in faith, **giving glory to God"*** (Romans 4:20). Therefore, in the midst of your circumstances, release praise and worship into the atmosphere of your home or office. Sing to God and play worship music. Express your faith and trust as you submit to the faithful God who never changes. (See, for example, Hebrews 13:8.) Your "now" is coming!

When trust is strong, faith comes into the "now."

In the Old Testament, the prophets often had to wait long periods of time to see God's promises fulfilled. In fact, many died without seeing the promises manifested. But after Christ came to earth and died on the cross, God raised Him from the dead; and when Jesus was resurrected, He brought supernatural faith with Him, and the realm of the eternal "now" extended to the realm of earth.

I pray that the following testimony from a woman named Martha, a teacher from Colombia, will strengthen your trust so that your faith can be released in the "now":

"I used to suffer from gallbladder stones, a condition that caused me great pain. Everything I ate tasted bitter. During a service, the pastor said that if anyone was sick, we should place our hand where we felt the pain, and we would receive healing. I placed my hand where the gallbladder is located and believed God. I believed that He had healed me and that, even though the pain continued, He was doing His perfect work in me. I later went to the doctor for follow-up exams. After he examined me, he said that I no longer had gallbladder stones!

"In addition, my appendix had been removed when I was fifteen years old. However, when I went to the doctor for the gallbladder problem, I had a scan of my organs, and the doctor said, 'The appendix appears normal in size. There is no inflammation.' Amazed, I exclaimed, 'Oh, Lord, how great and impressive You are!' I received a creative miracle, because I know that my appendix was removed and the operation is recorded in my medical history!

"But then I was diagnosed with a cyst in my lung that sometimes made breathing difficult. During the following nine months, the cyst grew until the doctor said it was cancerous. I immediately canceled the diagnosis. I didn't accept it, and I also received my healing! The cyst shrank in size until it disappeared."

I prophesy that those who have been trusting God to bring about change—for example, change in their marriage, their children, or their business; change in the form of deliverance, miracles, or healing—will see the manifestation in the "now"! Amen!

5. The Heart Commits to God and Other People

Much of God's activity on earth requires the commitment of the heart of human beings. Without our commitment, God will not commit to act. As we discussed earlier, it is possible for us to engage in certain works that seem like ministry but for our heart to not actually be involved in them. For example, we can serve other people, "worship" God, give offerings to the Lord, administrate, preach, or teach without a committed heart, so that we are performing a mere ritual that lacks eternal significance. If your heart is not committed to God, He may see you as untrustworthy. You need to allow the Holy Spirit to transform you, giving you the grace to genuinely commit your heart to God. And, when you commit to Him without reservation, He will pour into your heart a love for other people and a burden for their welfare that causes you to pray for them and minister to their needs.

If you do not submit, God will not commit.

A Call to Wholehearted Commitment

The following testimony may give you a clearer picture of what I have tried to communicate throughout this chapter. It is the story of Tito, a native of Colombia, who is a public accountant and export business owner:

"I came to surrender to Christ in a painful way. I was a skeptic regarding the things pertaining to God. I didn't like to tithe or to give offerings because I believed they were a form of robbing me, and I didn't want to give my money to anyone. My mind-set was contrary to God's. One day, while celebrating Mother's Day with my wife, I suffered a heart attack. An ambulance was immediately called, but they came too late—I died seconds before they arrived. However, I was resurrected by mechanical means and through the administration of drugs.

"Once I was in the hospital, the doctors decided to operate to replace an artery in my heart. I was concerned about my health, but even more about the debt I would incur due to the cost of the hospital stay. I had no way of paying for it! Yet, miraculously, I didn't have to pay for any of it. God paid it for me. I am debt free, to the glory of my Lord! God allowed this problem to take place so I would know of His existence, love, and power, and so I would change my mind toward the things of God and finally be transformed.

"After this event, I accepted Jesus into my heart. While it used to be hard for me to tithe and give offerings, this incident led me to recognize my need for God. I never would have been able to pay the debt, not even with all of my tithes and offerings! Today, I am a different man. I am committed to my heavenly Father, and I trust Him with all of my heart. I can say that I was born again—twice! I was born again into the kingdom and 'born again' after the mortal heart attack!"

Isn't it time for you, also, to commit to God with all your heart? Let's look at the following four points, which you will recognize as themes that we will return to throughout this book. Think about them carefully now and also as you read each successive chapter of *Supernatural Transformation*:

1. Evaluate Your Heart

In chapter 1, we asked the question, "What does God see in your heart?" God sees beyond the superficial elements of our life to the depths of our being. He sees our motives, intentions, and intimate thoughts, whether good or evil. And He desires to give us a heart that is healed and whole, with all the characteristics of His own nature—such as love, joy, righteousness, and wisdom.

For this to happen, we must understand the condition of our own heart in relation to God's heart. God will give us revelation of the state of our inner being as we read and study His Word and as we are sensitive to the leading of His Holy Spirit.

Many people don't take time to think about the state of their heart. Yet we must ask ourselves—and answer honestly—each aspect of this question: "Is my heart in the right place in relation to God, my family, my church, my occupation, my entertainment and recreation, and my other activities and involvements?" As we have seen, *"Where your treasure is, there your heart will be also"* (Matthew 6:21).

What is your top priority in life? Is it God and His kingdom? Or is it wealth? Success? Fame? A good physical appearance? A desire for revenge? Think about how you are spending the majority of your disposable income and the largest portion of your time, after your primary responsibilities of meeting the needs of your family and working to support yourself and your family members. Again, you can easily look at your checkbook entries and credit card statements over the past year to determine how, and on what, you are spending your money. You can also review your activities over the past several months to assess your priorities in life and the nature of your involvements in light of the character of God and the purposes of His kingdom.

2. Be True to Your Heart

What does it mean to "be true to your heart"? First, it means to be honest with yourself about what you discover to be true about the state of your heart. When you do this, it will help you to be honest before God and other people.

Have you been truthful with yourself about the things you genuinely believe in and about your real priorities? Or have you been lying to yourself about them? Perhaps you have not allowed God's Word to make the impact on your life that you would like others to believe it has. If you are aligned with God's priorities and are modeling your lifestyle after His Word, you will experience His peace and joy. If not, your conscience will bother you. You will feel convicted and unsettled. Ask yourself questions such as: "What do I truly believe regarding God, Jesus, the Holy Spirit, and God's kingdom?" "In the deepest part of my heart, do I love God and remain faithful to Him?" "Am I living according to what I say I believe?" "In what ways am I living contrary to what I claim to believe?" "Why am I not living according to my faith?" "What can I do to realign my priorities and motivations with God's will and purposes?"

3. Speak from Your Heart

Third, we must speak from our heart—not just from our head. Let us look at two points in this connection. To speak from our heart is to speak honestly, without guile or deception. For example, we must not speak lies or flattery to other people in order to get something from them. This does not mean we should be tactless in what we say to others or that we should blurt out whatever comes to our mind. Rather, it means that our words should have integrity; we should not speak something that our heart does not believe.

Next, we have noted that *"out of the abundance of the heart the mouth speaks"* (Matthew 12:34). There is a connection between the heart and the mouth. Therefore, if what you are saying is not in accord with God's Word—if you complain, gossip, curse, or speak something else that conflicts with His character—you know that there is a problem in your heart. For example, in the next chapter, we will discover how hardheartedness can block the faith that is in our heart from manifesting in our words and actions.

Yet when we surrender to God and live according to the power of His Spirit, our heart will be transformed, and our words will inevitably be transformed, as well. As we will discuss more fully in a later chapter, one of the best ways to change our heart is to memorize and meditate on God's Word until it is planted deep in our inner being.

4. Act from Your Heart

The fourth point is that we cannot just "believe" in God's Word and His principles, or even just express them—we must act on them as they become established in our heart. This will give us integrity in what we believe, what we say, and what we do. And whatever we believe, say, and do should glorify God and bless other people.

If the various actions you are taking—whether in regard to your family, your ministry, your job, or another aspect of life—aren't based on genuine heart motivations, you will lack the commitment to be faithful in persevering to complete them. Your actions won't be consistent, and you won't follow through. Consequently, your efforts will have little impact for good in your life, in the lives of others, in the life of your community, or for the advancement of God's kingdom in the world. Yet, if your actions are based on genuine heart motivations, you will, in the words of Paul, execute *"work produced by faith,…labor prompted by love, and…endurance inspired by hope in our Lord Jesus Christ"* (1 Thessalonians 1:3 NIV).

As you review and respond to these four points, commit to seek a closer relationship with God. Commit to His vision. Commit to the divine purpose for your life. Commit to your family. Commit to love your brothers and sisters in Christ. Commit to minister to others in the name of Jesus— to pray, to serve, and to evangelize. Commit to carry out the purpose of God for your life, from the depth of your heart. Do it now!

4

Heart of "Stone" or Heart of "Flesh"?

When someone is described as *hardhearted*, we usually imagine an individual who is particularly cruel—someone who treats other people harshly or who would coolly take another person's life just to get what he wanted. We don't think of the word as applying to us. Certainly, the term does fit those who act cruelly toward others. Yet the concept of a hard heart has deeper spiritual implications that are universally applicable to human beings—including believers. All of us have a heart that is "hardened" in some areas and to certain degrees, and this heart condition hinders our life. Moreover, we should be aware that any person's heart has the potential to grow increasingly hard, so that it eventually affects his entire being. We are all susceptible to such a hardening process if we do not regularly monitor our heart.

Consider the meaning of the Greek word translated *"hardness of heart"* in Mark 16:14, which reads, *"Later [Jesus] appeared to the eleven as they sat at the table; and He rebuked their unbelief and hardness of heart, because they did not believe those who had seen Him after He had risen."* This Greek term especially indicates "destitution of spiritual perception." We would not necessarily think of Jesus' disciples as having "hardness of heart," except, perhaps, for Judas Iscariot. The other disciples obviously made mistakes, lacked faith, and failed to understand Jesus' teachings at times. But hardness of heart?

Yet note again the implication of the Greek term for "hardheartedness": "*destitution* of spiritual perception." To be "destitute" is a serious condition. The word indicates a lack of spiritual discernment or sensitivity, a deficiency of understanding in relation to spiritual truth. This deficiency blocks our knowledge of the true nature of God and Jesus, limits our intimacy with God, prevents His purposes from being fulfilled in our life, and causes us to neglect or disobey His commands.

The fulfillment of the greatest commandment of all—to love God with our whole being, and to love other people as ourselves (see, for example, Mark 12:29–31)—is hindered by hardness of heart, because a lack of spiritual perception will distance our heart from God and other people. Ask yourself: "Is my heart soft and yielded to God?" "Where might my spiritual perception be blocked due to a hardness of heart?"

Love Grown Cold

I believe we are living in a season in which God is bringing "acceleration" to every area of our life, as well as a movement of miracles, signs, and wonders never before seen. By *acceleration*, I refer to a more rapid transition to greater levels of faith and a faster heart transformation that enables us to function in higher dimensions of the supernatural realm. I believe that the two movements of the glory of God—the former glory (represented by the miracles of the Old Testament) and the latter glory (represented by the miracles Jesus predicted would occur in the church)—are coming together in a dual manifestation. However, I also believe that we are living in the times Christ spoke about when He prophesied that wickedness would increase: "*And because lawlessness will abound, the love of many will grow cold*" (Matthew 24:12).

The concept of love "growing cold" refers to a hardened heart—and this is a sign of the end times. As we noted earlier, when God created human beings, He gave them a heart after His own heart; but when they disobeyed God, their heart was corrupted, and humans became filled with sins—including pride, immorality, a lust for power, and so forth—the same sins we see reflected in our society today. To a certain degree, this end-time coldness is the reason why some people are no longer sensitive to genuine love—in their heart, they lack empathy for other people's physical, emotional, or spiritual pain. They are not attuned to God, His Word, or His will.

Recovering the Heart

Yet the new birth in Christ enables us to recover—through supernatural transformation—the heart that the first human beings lost. Spiritually, God views us through the righteousness of the resurrected Jesus. However, as we have seen, the transformation of our inner being is also a progressive, daily process that includes all areas of our life.

Since we live in the midst of a fallen world, where sin operates and corruption destroys, we must watch over our heart to keep it from slowly growing cold and becoming hard from exposure to the false perspectives and negative attitudes of people around us, or as we react to the troubles and crises occurring on earth—from economic declines to natural disasters. We must allow God to soften the areas of our inner being that are still hard due to the effects of our sinful nature and the wrong attitudes we've accepted and allowed to become entrenched in our heart over the years.

God Will Circumcise Our Heart

Our heavenly Father has given us these great and life-changing promises:

And the LORD *your God will circumcise your heart and the heart of your descendants, to love the* LORD *your God with all your heart and with all your soul, that you may live.* (Deuteronomy 30:6)

I will give you a new heart and put a new spirit within you; I will take the heart of stone out of your flesh and give you a heart of flesh. (Ezekiel 36:26)

Spiritual "circumcision," whose meaning we will explore in this chapter, takes away the barriers between God and us (and between us and other people) so that we may love the Lord with our whole being. God will give us a *"heart of flesh"* in exchange for a *"heart of stone,"* and then we will *"live"*— in a true and full sense.

The Condition of a Hardened Heart

Above, we looked at the instance following Jesus' resurrection when He rebuked His disciples for their hardheartedness in disbelieving those who had seen Him alive after His death on the cross and subsequent burial. There is also a previous reference in the Scriptures to the disciples' hardness of heart. In Mark 6:52, we read, *"For they had not understood about the loaves, because their heart was hardened."*

Here is the background to that statement: Christ had just performed the great miracle of multiplying five small loaves of bread and two fish, so that there was more than enough food to feed the five-thousand-plus people who had gathered from surrounding cities, listening eagerly for a number of hours to Jesus' teachings and receiving healing. (See also Matthew 14:14.) Yet, even after the disciples had seen these demonstrations of supernatural provision by Jesus, they continued to be spiritually blind regarding who He was and how He would provide for them—as demonstrated by what occurred next.

Jesus had sent His disciples ahead of Him by boat to the other side of the Sea of Galilee, while He stayed behind so He could pray in solitude. During the night, the disciples encountered a strong wind, and they struggled as they rowed against it. Then, Jesus came to them, walking on the water. When He entered the boat with them, the wind stopped. "[The disciples] *were greatly amazed in themselves beyond measure, and marveled. For they had not understood about the loaves, because their heart was hardened"* (Mark 6:51–52). In this verse, the Greek word for *"hardened"* is apparently derived from the name of a kind of stone. The term literally means "to petrify"; figuratively, it means "to render stupid or callous," "to blind," or "to harden."

Corruptive "Leaven"

Not long after the incident on the Sea of Galilee, Jesus again miraculously multiplied food and fed four thousand people. (See Mark 8:1–9.)

Seemingly, the disciples still had not gained spiritual perception about Jesus' deity based on His massive provision for the multitudes. And Jesus soon *"charged* [the disciples], *saying, 'Take heed, beware of the leaven of the Pharisees...'"* (Mark 8:15). What was this *"leaven of the Pharisees"*?

In the physical world, *leaven* is "a substance (as yeast) used to produce fermentation in dough or a liquid." When yeast is mixed with dough, it permeates the batter. Jesus' statement would likely have reminded His listeners of the annual Jewish Feast of Unleavened Bread, which God had ordained the Israelites to celebrate, as a reminder that they should remove sin (represented by the leaven) from their lives. (See, for example, Exodus 12:17–20.)

What form of sin was Jesus referring to in regard to the Pharisees? The book of Matthew records, *"Then* [the disciples] *understood that He did not tell them to beware of the leaven of bread, but of **the doctrine** of the Pharisees and Sadducees"* (Matthew 16:12). On another occasion, Jesus told His disciples, *"Beware of the leaven of the Pharisees, which is **hypocrisy**"* (Luke 12:1). In effect, the "leaven" Jesus was referring to was the hypocrisy of the religion practiced by the Pharisees, which corrupts the integrity of the heart. For further insight into this corruptive "leaven," let us read what the apostle Paul wrote to the Corinthian believers:

> *Therefore purge out the old leaven, that you may be a new lump* ["unleavened batch" niv2011], *since you truly are unleavened. For indeed Christ, our Passover, was sacrificed for us. Therefore let us keep the feast, not with old leaven, nor with **the leaven of malice and wickedness**, but with the unleavened bread of sincerity and truth.*
>
> (1 Corinthians 5:7–8)

So, in various places in the Bible, leaven symbolizes false teachings, hypocrisy, malice, and wickedness—erroneous ideas and sinful attitudes and actions that have the potential to spread to large numbers of people, just as yeast spreads throughout a batch of dough.

Twice, the disciples had witnessed the multiplication of bread and fish by Jesus, and they had personally distributed the "miracle" food to thousands of people. However, I believe their hearts had been so hardened by "religious" and cultural perspectives and attitudes that they lacked spiritual perception of the supernatural events unfolding right in front of them. The religious leaven prevented their eyes from being open to spiritual truths about God the Father and God the Son. It is my view that a great portion of the church is in the same condition today. Any believer who doesn't continually seek the transformation of his heart, and who isn't ready to receive the new things God is doing during these last days, is at risk of falling into the same state.

> ### *The hardened heart does not see, hear, or perceive the spiritual realm or spiritual matters.*

"Stiff-necked" People

In the Old Testament, the Israelites often manifested hardened hearts, and they were referred to at various times as a *"stiff-necked people."* For example, *"The LORD said to Moses, 'I have seen this people, and indeed it is a stiff-necked people!'"* (Exodus 32:9). Perhaps God wrote the Ten Commandments on stone tablets because His people had hardened their hearts to the point that they weren't able to perceive His presence or discern His will. Furthermore, due to bad "leaven" in their lives, they failed to recognize who God really was and what He desired for them, and they turned their hearts away from obeying Him.

God has always desired to write His commandments on the hearts of His people, because it is the only way they can truly love and obey Him. Sadly, at about the same time God was writing the Ten Commandments on the stone tablets with His own finger in the presence of Moses on Mount Sinai (see Exodus 31:18), the people of Israel were rejecting God and worshipping a golden calf that they had asked Aaron, God's high priest, to create. (See Exodus 32.) In essence, they were refusing what God Himself had written, or ordained, for them. Even today, many people reject the true Word of God for a religion of their own making.

In the New Testament, when Stephen gave his address in the power of the Holy Spirit to the Jewish leaders of the Sanhedrin, he said, *"You stiffnecked and uncircumcised in heart and ears! You always resist the Holy*

Spirit; as your fathers did, so do you" (Acts 7:51). And God can say the same regarding many of the people in the church today. They have hardened their heart toward Him, demonstrating an independent spirit, rebelliousness, and disobedience to His precepts. Consequently, they have "grieved" the Holy Spirit. (See Ephesians 4:30.)

In the Western church, many people do not seek a manifestation of God's supernatural revelation or His supernatural works. Some people are indifferent toward the idea of experiencing the power of God's Spirit, while others reject the legitimacy of the idea outright. Many believers simply want to hear God's Word preached and to practice certain customs and traditions associated with going to church, so that they may remain comfortable and entertained. They don't really want the manifest presence of God in their midst, and they don't want to make the necessary personal sacrifice of dying to their sinful nature in order to grow closer to God.

Religion is ultimately birthed from hardness of heart, and it produces even more hardheartedness in people.

In many ways, this generation's faith is exercised by the mind alone. It is not exercised by the heart, which has become hardened and therefore does not produce life. A hardened heart is the reason why some people can hurt others without even realizing it; or, if they do realize it, they fail to care. How many people are hurting their loved ones, friends, and associates because their own heart has been hardened? We see parents and children, husbands and wives, pastors and church members, employers and employees, and so on, all hurting one another.

What Causes the Heart to Harden?

Hardness of heart is symptomatic of the corrupt sinful nature that human beings inherited due to the fall of humanity. Again, such hardness separates us from God and causes us to become fixed in mind-sets and attitudes that are contrary to the grace, life, and power of the Holy Spirit. The following are some ways in which hardness of heart manifests in people's lives.

1. Repeatedly Committing Sin

The writer of the book of Hebrews said, *"But exhort one another daily, while it is called 'Today,' lest any of you be hardened through the deceitfulness of sin"* (Hebrews 3:13). As I've studied the Scriptures, I've compiled and developed various definitions of sin, such as "to miss the mark," "to disobey God," "to offend the Lord," and "to violate God's law." Each time we sin, something of God in us weakens or dies. And when we commit a particular sin repeatedly, without repentance, we open the door of our heart to the enemy, allowing the devil to introduce some leaven of corruption, which causes our heart to become hardened.

Many people don't recognize when this process is occurring within them. Therefore, when they seek solutions to their problems, they deal with only the symptoms. Suppose a person is experiencing depression because he feels guilty for repeatedly committing a sin. Modern medicine's solution to this problem would generally be to prescribe an antidepressant drug. Meanwhile, in an effort to feel better, the individual might try to raise his self-esteem through mental exercises like repeating positive affirmations to himself. But if the person really wants a solution to his depression, he must deal with the root of the issue, which is found in his heart.

Sin will grieve our heart, and the resulting guilt we feel due to our wrong attitudes and actions can generate a state of "paralysis" that depresses our emotions. If an individual struggling under these conditions would ask God for forgiveness through Christ and forgive himself, and as well as forgive others who have hurt or offended him, his heart would heal, and, consequently, his depression would disappear.

Let's look at another example. Suppose a child constantly rebels against his parents because he does not receive the love and attention from them that he needs. Perhaps they are too absorbed with each other, with their careers, or with other activities. Under these circumstances, the child's rebellious behavior is not a reflection of "bad character" or a desire for independence. Its source, or root, is the pain and loss he is experiencing in his heart. The parents' reaction to his rebellion might be to punish him, to bribe him with food or gifts, and/or to send him to a psychologist for counseling. Yet to resolve this issue, the parents would need to recognize their neglect, repent of it, seek God's forgiveness, and begin to provide their child with a more supportive and loving home based on God's love. If this change does not occur, the child may become angrier and even grow bitter, hardening his heart against his parents and others—including God.

Although we are all accountable for our own sin, one contributing factor to recurring sin in people's lives is the false perspective of much of the modern church that no longer identifies sin as sin. Instead, if someone sins, he is said to have "issues," "a sickness," "a condition," or something similar. Our generation is preaching a self-help gospel from which the message of the cross and the resurrection has been removed. And yet, that message alone addresses the reality of sin, its root, and its solution. Again, if we are truly going to deal with matters of the heart, we must recognize the root of issues and not just the branches, or the symptoms. To preach without the intent of seeing people rescued from iniquity and experiencing transformation is, in essence, a deceit. It is not the gospel of Jesus Christ. We must call sin "sin."

2. Holding On to an Offense

Another cause of a hardened heart is a refusal to let go of an offense. Offenses affect millions of people who have felt affronted by a spouse or child, a teacher or classmate, a boss or coworker, a pastor or fellow church member, or someone in another realm of life. We will explore the topic of dealing with an offended heart in greater detail in the next chapter of this book.

Taking offense at other people—as well as offending them—is rather unavoidable in life. Jesus said, "*Woe to the world because of offenses! For offenses must come, but woe to that man by whom the offense comes!*" (Matthew 18:7). I haven't met anyone who has never been offended by another person or who has never offended someone else. As believers, we are called to undergo a process of spiritual and emotional development, of growing to become more like Christ. Along the way, during the maturation process, we will inevitably offend others by our mistaken attitudes, our careless words, and our hasty actions. Not only have we all been offended by others, but we are all continually being presented with opportunities to take offense, and we will all be offended for one reason or another in the future. The important thing is that we not hold on to an offense, because to do so is to encourage spiritual hardness—something we do not want to risk.

Often, after we have been offended by someone, we repeat the memory of the offense over and over in our mind. Yet an offense doesn't really reside in the mind but in the heart. The effect of holding on to an offense is as devastating as being bitten by a poisonous snake and having its venom spread throughout our body. If we refuse to let go of an offense, if we never deal with it, an area of our heart will become hardened—often in a subtle way, little by little. Then, when we least expect it, our spiritual senses will be numb; we will have lost sensitivity in the emotional and spiritual realms of our life. What's more, we may be in danger of spiritual death, for, if we want God to forgive us, we must forgive others. Jesus said, *"For if you forgive men their trespasses, your heavenly Father will also forgive you"* (Matthew 6:14).

Rather than become spiritually hardened, let us recognize that offenses can actually be useful to us, because they reveal the true condition of our heart. When we are offended, we see what is really inside us—whether anger and bitterness and contention or grace and forgiveness and peace. We have to learn to deal with offenses, not only when we experience them but also when we cause them. When we are offended by another person, we should try to understand his motivations while forgiving his faults. And, we should seek reconciliation with other people whom we are aware we have offended. If we have affronted another person, we must learn to acknowledge our error, repent, ask for the person's forgiveness, and seek to restore the relationship. This last part is necessary even if we were not in the wrong. As Paul wrote, *"Do not repay anyone evil for evil. Be careful to do what is right in the eyes of everybody. If it is possible, as far as it depends on you, live at peace with everyone"* (Romans 12:17–18 NIV).

A hardened heart will eventually result in spiritual death.

---

3. Harboring Emotional Wounds

Our emotional wounds are usually inflicted by the people whom we love the most—often, those who are closest to us and to whom we have opened up our heart. People may experience the deepest emotional injuries during childhood. Some young people are continually hurt or abused by a close relative—for example, a father, mother, uncle, or cousin—and many people are marked by such wounds for the rest of their life. Similarly, even when we are older, we may be wounded deeply by a parent, spouse, child, sibling, close friend, or authority figure, such as a pastor or boss.

Consider your own emotional wounds. Perhaps they were generated by people who failed to show you love or who neglected, rejected, abandoned, underestimated, or betrayed you; who showed you contempt or disdain; who abused you (verbally, physically, or sexually); who exploited you (for example, sexually or in the workplace); who deceived or defamed you through fraud, lies, false accusation, or slander; or who persecuted you for your faith. Whatever the origin of the wound, if you have not already been healed, you need to be healed today, because the related area of your heart has been damaged and hardened.

Hardening is an inevitable consequence when our hurt is allowed to remain. For example, we may harden our heart as a method of emotional survival when we are unable to forgive the one who has hurt us, making healing impossible. Yet, in God, we can find the grace to forgive others and to receive healing for our emotional wounds.

Solange is a businesswoman whose heart was hardened when she was a young girl after she suffered sexual abuse and experienced the resulting mental and emotional pain. She was blinded by the works of the enemy and the limitations of religion, so that she could not experience the freedom and love of God. The following is her story.

"I grew up in the United States in the Catholic faith, but I looked for Christ because I was tired of being in a vicious cycle of drug addiction and suicidal thoughts. I had been sexually molested by two uncles when I was very young, and I was raped at age fifteen. Even though I didn't tell anyone what happened to me, I still felt great shame. I hated my body and couldn't even stand to be in my own skin. That is when I started to contemplate suicide. I tried taking pills and drugs, drinking alcohol, and even starving myself. Even though I wanted to die, I was also afraid of death. But, at some point, the feeling of filthiness within me became stronger than my fear.

"I was a bitter, negative person. My heart was full of unforgiveness and hate, and I lived in judgment of everyone. I felt captive in a spiritual prison and desperately needed a way out. I had always known of the existence of a 'Jesus Christ.' I wanted to talk to Him and surrender my burden, but I didn't know how to do it. I lacked direction, and I felt lost, but I didn't know how to live any other way. I didn't know if I was coming or going. I was an emotional and mental disaster.

"When I eventually accepted Jesus as my Lord and Savior, my life began to change in ways that I had only imagined in my dreams. I went through inner healing and deliverance, and I felt whole once again. I began to accept who I was and to love myself the same way God loves me. Now I am free of shame, resentment, and hate. I thank the Lord for freeing me from so much pain!"

You don't have to spend the rest of your life in pain. If you have been hurt, now is your opportunity to begin the process of becoming whole again. Allow the Spirit of God, like holy oil, to enter your heart and heal you. I encourage you to read chapter 5, "Healing for an Offended Heart," today.

4. Disobeying the Voice of God

Our heavenly Father created human beings to be in relationship with Him. His plan was always to have clear and permanent communications with us. Even after the fall, God has continued to speak to humans through various means—sometimes directly, and at other times through His angels, His prophets, His written Word, or other avenues. His ultimate expression of Himself is the person of Jesus Christ: *"The Word became flesh and dwelt among us, and we beheld His glory, the glory as of the only begotten of the Father, full of grace and truth"* (John 1:14). *"God, who at various times and in various ways spoke in time past to the fathers by the prophets, has in these last days spoken to us by His Son..."* (Hebrews 1:1–2).

The most common question I have heard people ask is, "How can I hear the voice of God?" Many people recognize their inability to hear His voice, whereas it should be something natural for every believer, since the Scriptures say, *"The sheep follow him* [Jesus, the Good Shepherd], *for they know his voice"* (John 10:4; see also verses 11, 14). However, if our heart is hardened, it will not hear God, nor will it see or otherwise perceive Him. Often, as God was preparing to release His judgment on sinful people, He would appoint a righteous person to announce His punishment, in order to give the people an opportunity to hear God's message, repent, and be saved. Quoting from Psalm 95, the writer of Hebrews urged his readers, *"Today, if you will hear [God's] voice, do not harden your hearts as in the rebellion"* (Hebrews 3:15).

One of the most frightening results of a hardened heart is that when an individual no longer hears truth and direction from God, he begins to conform to an artificial reality. What happens next is a situation we observe in some Christians who live according to fantasy, mysticism, or religiosity. They are spiritually dry and stagnant in their relationship with God because they stopped hearing His voice and began hearing other "voices"—societal, philosophical, religious, demonic, and so forth. Let us all earnestly seek God so that we may hear His voice and *"not harden [our] hearts as in the rebellion."* In chapters 8 and 9, we will discuss what it means to have an obedient heart that is surrendered to God.

5. Unbelief

"Beware, brethren, lest there be in any of you an evil heart of unbelief in departing from the living God" (Hebrews 3:12). *"An evil heart of unbelief"* is evidenced when a person decides, of his own free will, not to believe in God and therefore not to obey Him. This decision is an open act of rebellion and defiance. In chapter 6, we will discover how to be free from an unbelieving heart. As an introduction to this topic, let's look at the testimony of a young woman named Dámari. The spirit of unbelief took hold in her through the negative influences and bad circumstances of her childhood.

"I grew up in a shattered home. My father was addicted to alcohol, drugs, and pornography; and, for as long as I can remember, he physically and verbally abused my mother. From the age of six, I would ask God to give me a sister, because my brothers never paid any attention to me. My father was obsessed with my mother, and neither of them would pay any attention to me or spend time with me. My faith diminished as my prayers went unanswered. In the midst of this great family chaos, I decided to believe that God did not exist, and I became an atheist.

"The situation at home grew worse each day. One morning, I was awakened by the sound of my mother punching defensively against a table as my father tried to strangle her. That same day, he came after my brothers and me with a knife; we ran throughout the house because he wanted to kill all of us! After this episode, he was allowed to visit with us only under supervision. But this lasted for only for a short time; he stopped coming, and we didn't know what became of him. A year later, I decided that I no longer had a father—he was dead to me.

"I grew up and started to frequent nightclubs and to use alcohol, marijuana, and cocaine. I also sold drugs. I would use drugs to fall asleep, hoping I would never wake up. By the time I turned twenty, I had already experienced what someone ten years older than I might have, and I no longer wanted to live. Life was a great disappointment to me.

"One day, I went to a church with my mother in exchange for receiving enough money to go out, but I stayed in the service. That night, I accepted the Lord into my heart—even though I wasn't really keen on the idea—and then I went to a nightclub. While I smoked and drank, I heard a voice that said, *I'm sorry, Dámari, but you repeated the prayer. You are Mine, and you no longer belong in this place.* This voice continued to speak to me, and, slowly, I followed it. I got rid of my worldly music and clothes and began to tell my friends about God and to deny them if they denied God. My mother's prayers of the past five years had been answered.

"On that day, seven years ago, I began to live. I went from being a suicidal and depressed drug addict who believed that she was an atheist to being a daughter of God. I stopped smoking, drinking, and cursing, and I began to respond to the voice of God and to have a relationship with Him. Before, I hadn't believed in the church, in pastors, or in God, but now I serve in my church and love God and my pastors. I was even able to forgive my father and restore my relationship with him. Jesus Christ saved my life and gave me the opportunity to know Him and to guide others to know Him, also."

6. Lawlessness

Another cause of hardheartedness is lawlessness. At the beginning of this chapter, we read in regard to the end times, "*Lawlessness will abound,*

[and] *the love of many will grow cold"* (Matthew 24:12). In the original Greek, the word translated *"lawlessness"* means "illegality" and indicates "violation of law," "transgression of the law," "wickedness," "iniquity," or "unrighteousness." It comes from another Greek word meaning "without law."

Increasingly, our current generation demands to live without beneficial restrictions and laws. One tragic result of this development is that those who are victims of other people's lawlessness end up hardening their own hearts. Here are some examples of scenarios that are occurring today:

+ A wife doesn't want to live within her marriage covenant, so she has an affair and divorces her husband. Her husband becomes bitter and suspicious, hardening his heart toward other people; he no longer feels he can trust anyone because the one who had been closest to him deserted him.

+ A pastor chooses to reject integrity and to steal from his church's tithes and offerings. As a result, people in his congregation or other believers who hear about the incident feel betrayed. In an attempt to protect themselves from further deception and loss, they harden their hearts toward the act of giving, choosing to withhold their finances from even legitimate kingdom purposes.

+ A woman grows up in a family that is filled with lies and abuse. Consequently, she closes her heart to love, never marrying or bringing children into the world because she doesn't want to create conditions in which her own children would potentially suffer the same experience.

+ A father continually fails to correct his son when he misbehaves, eventually making excuses for the boy as he grows older and covering up his son's lying and stealing. As a result, the child develops an attitude of entitlement and superiority. Hardening his heart, the son never learns to respect other people or to take responsibility for his actions, and he goes through life abusing and hurting others, living only for himself.

+ A government takes advantage of its citizens over a long period of time, abusing the people's rights and stealing from them. Therefore, the people's hearts grow hard; they begin to resist their government and to rebel against authority of any kind.

We can see how lawlessness leads the heart to grow cold—and a cold heart can quickly become hardened.

Signs of a Hardened Heart

There are some unmistakable signs that a heart has lost sensitivity and is now hardened. Recognizing these signs will help us to search our own heart for indications of coldness and hardness. It will also enable us to identify people around us who need healing from hardheartedness.

1. A Hardened Heart Does Not Feel God's Presence

In the Old Testament, God appeared to Jacob in a dream, telling him that He would be with him and would bless him. *"Then Jacob awoke from his sleep and said, 'Surely the LORD is in this place, and I did not know it'"* (Genesis 28:16). Jacob's reply is a reminder that we can be in a place where God's presence manifests but not perceive it. This is an indication of a hardened heart such as Jesus' disciples had when they didn't understand who Jesus was, even though He lived in their midst and demonstrated His deity to them.

I have been in church services where God's presence has manifested and most of the people there were touched (some cried, some received physical healing, some experienced spiritual transformation, and so forth), while others seemed to be cold or hard (they yawned or otherwise acted bored, as if nothing were taking place). Those whose heart is cold or hard are more aware of themselves than they are of God; they are conscious primarily of their own presence and thoughts. Yet, because of their lack of interest in spiritual matters, they miss out on the supernatural manifestation of the One who created them!

It is dangerous to be in a condition in which you are a greater reality to yourself than God is to you. The heart that doesn't sense God's presence is often hostile toward manifestations of His presence—resisting them and even rejecting them. When this happens to a once-active Christian, he begins to operate mechanically, without the involvement of God's Spirit, because religiosity has invaded his inner being. The result is that there is no real life there. For example, a person may simply quote Scripture without exercising genuine faith. He may operate through formality and human rituals that do not demonstrate God's supernatural power or have eternal value.

To transform the heart, the Word of God must be spoken from an atmosphere in which God is present.

---

2. A Hardened Heart Does Not Allow Faith to Flow

"For with the heart one believes unto righteousness, and with the mouth confession is made unto salvation.…So then faith comes by hearing, and hearing by the word of God" (Romans 10:10, 17). Faith is generated in the heart as we hear and receive God's Word. Likewise, faith develops in the heart. And, as we have seen, whatever is in the heart will come out in what we say. (See Matthew 12:34.) We rarely speak any word by accident. Our words reveal aspects of our character and the state of our inner man.

Therefore, if the confessions of your mouth don't express the faith that is in your heart, then your faith is not being allowed to flow. When this happens, a hardened heart is usually the cause. Review the areas of your life that are stagnant or corrupt and compare them to other areas of your life in which God is moving. Where faith flows, the words of your mouth will be full of God's power, but where it doesn't flow, your words will not align with His Word; they will not be a reflection of God's own faith, and therefore they will lack power.

For the most part, the culture of the Western world was built on a foundation that emphasizes and relies on human intellect and reason. That culture does not understand how genuine faith operates or manifests. It regards faith from the viewpoint of the natural world; however, faith is supernatural. As we will discuss in chapter 6, the majority of those who live in Western society are culturally programmed through the educational process to suppress faith in the heart and to operate chiefly from the framework of their intellect. Although there is a proper place for the intellect, which God gave us to use for His glory, we need to return to wholehearted faith that isn't framed by the intellect and doesn't reason according to it alone.

Faith functions in keeping with God's reasoning. As Paul wrote, "*The foolishness of God is wiser than men*" (1 Corinthians 1:25). When we allow faith to flow from our heart, we become unshakable and unstoppable in God's purposes. For when our heart is set on God, our life will be transformed, regardless of any efforts by the enemy to prevent it.

Faith is not mere optimism; rather, as the Scriptures say, it is "the substance of things hoped for, the evidence of things not seen." Therefore, our walk of faith is a supernatural one.

---

3. A Hardened Heart Moves from Commitment to "Wishful Thinking"

Another sign of a hardened heart is that a person will abandon his commitments, disconnecting himself from the projects he formerly participated in with other believers, with his family, with his colleagues, and so forth. His mind is full of desires, but they lead nowhere because hardheartedness has immobilized his will and nullified his motivation. The person loses his passion and is left only wishing for the fulfillment of things that "would be good to do" but never become a reality. He may think something like, *If God wants this to happen, He will do it,* or *If this vision is of God, it will come to pass; if not, that's all right with me.*

Many churches are filled with "wishful thinkers" whose hearts have become insensitive to faith and spiritual matters and who therefore never commit to serve others or pursue worthy projects. This is one reason why these churches do not grow or help to advance God's kingdom. The members are open to the "idea" of a vision, but their heart is divorced from the sacrifice and work needed to build it. Consequently, there is often a great gap between what they say and what they do. They may make a correct confession according to the Word of God but then neglect to act on it in faith and in the power of the Holy Spirit. It is easy to speak words that correspond with faith, but if we don't follow through with our words, we lack genuine conviction. Anything we say we believe in but don't act on exposes a lack of integrity within us—we don't really believe it in our heart. *"Faith by itself, if it does not have works, is dead"* (James 2:17).

A person's integrity is measured not by his words but by the extent to which he does what he says.

---

4. A Hardened Heart Rebels Against God

Rebellion against God is a clear sign of a hardened heart. However, it is possible for us to rebel against God without recognizing that we are doing so, because our intellect provides us with excuses to justify our rejection of certain commands or instructions He has given us. In addition, we talked earlier about how a person may manifest a spirit of indifference when he does not discern God's presence. In such cases, the person usually does not become involved in fulfilling the church's vision by serving others, spreading the gospel, or giving tithes and offerings to God. Sometimes, he simply doesn't care! Even so, he may begin to criticize the church, its vision, and its leadership. When a believer rebels against God's delegated authority, he is rebelling against God Himself.

Indifference and a critical spirit are signs of rebellion in a church.

Perhaps your pastor has recently preached a message that are you having trouble accepting. Think about that message carefully. Was it biblically based, and did it describe something that God has established for your own good? If so, why does it bother you? Some people will leave a church because the pastor preached on such topics as giving tithes and offerings, seeking holiness, making a wholehearted commitment to God, or the need for repentance of sin. The pastor didn't do anything but preach what is written in the Word of God. Consequently, the people were not really offended by the pastor but with God and His commands.

However, since these people were not able to discern the presence of God in His Word, they blamed the pastor for preaching a negative or meddlesome message. Their heart had been hardened in some area or areas, preventing them from receiving the revelation of what was being preached. As a result, their heart was not stirred, and their will remained inactive, and they were kept from humbly submitting to God's will. Because they were affronted by what the pastor said, they stopped going to the church. Such people will continue to rebel against God and His mandates in various areas of their lives unless they allow God to change their heart. The Scriptures say, "Let us...not [forsake] *the assembling of ourselves together, as is the manner of some, but exhorting one another, and so much the more as you see the Day* [of the return of Christ] *approaching*" (Hebrews 10:24–25).

If someone makes a choice not to believe in God or to obey what He has said, he puts himself into a state of open rebellion against God that is the equivalent of standing before the Almighty and calling Him a liar to His face. That may sound harsh, but how many times have we, in effect, called God a "liar" by our disobedience and rebellion? A rebellious person will defend himself, and his inability to recognize or acknowledge his bad behavior is a sign of a hardened heart that doesn't want to be forced to accept God's will and the supremacy of His wisdom—much less surrender willingly to it.

We must realize that every act of rebellion has consequences. And the Scriptures warn us that "*the destruction of transgressors and of sinners shall be together, and those who forsake the* LORD *shall be consumed*" (Isaiah 1:28).

5. A Hardened Heart Justifies Wrongdoing and Blames Others

Earlier, we discussed how the heart can grow cold after someone has been hurt or wronged, and that this coldheartedness can easily become hardheartedness. Many such people seem to have excuses for their wrong behavior. For instance, they may say something like the following:

+ "I am not a good mother because I grew up without a mother myself, and no one taught me how to be a parent. You can't expect me to do a better job as a mother."

+ "I have a blunt personality because I never received love at home while I was growing up. So, take me or leave me—this is who I am, and I'm not going to change now."

+ "I won't help out in any church program because I was hurt by someone in my previous church when I volunteered to help in a particular ministry, and I don't want to experience that again."

Some people manifest a hardened heart by having a thousand reasons for remaining mediocre and doing nothing. They refuse to seek change in their life or to commit to anything. They continually justify their reluctance to become involved, and they always place the blame for their problems or bad attitudes on others. Accordingly, their behavior does not just *damage* most of their relationships—it *destroys* them. It isolates these people from those whom they love. It stifles their opportunities to receive healing for their heart. And, it squelches their growth—spiritual, mental, and emotional. Freedom from a hardened heart requires a radical decision to allow the Spirit of God to heal and transform your inner being.

6. A Hardened Heart Resists Open Communication and Refuses Correction

Good communication is a key element in the foundation of every healthy relationship. However, some additional signs of a hardened heart are a strong resistance to two-way communication and an indifferent attitude toward the perspectives and needs of others. A person with a hardened heart will often ignore those who try to appeal to him to recognize how his attitudes or actions are hurting those who are close to him. He doesn't want to hear counsel or instruction from anyone. For example, if he belongs to a church, he usually believes he is above the spiritual authority of his pastor, his spiritual father, or other church leaders. He doesn't recognize those to whom God has delegated authority, so he refuses to hear their spiritual guidance or correction.

When the heart is hardened, it doesn't submit to authority.

7. A Hardened Heart Seeks Its Interests Alone, Becoming "Religious" and Judgmental

Another sign of a hardened heart is when a person seeks only his own interests, placing himself above God and other people. Often, merely listening to the needs of others seems tedious to him, and he considers it a waste of time to do something about those needs. For example, when a pastor no longer has a heart for serving God's people, the members of his congregation may begin to represent merely a paycheck to him, while their spiritual condition and needs are no longer a priority in his life. Then, when the members perceive his careless attitude toward them, they will become frustrated and angry. Many may begin to openly air their grievances and/or leave the church.

The Holy Spirit is absent from everything that belongs to the sinful nature.

Therefore, when a person allows his heart to lose its spiritual sensitivity, he can become egocentric, ambitious, and self-sufficient. Such a person is focused only on the externals of his life, including his reputation among other people—he is all about appearances, and he feels self-righteous about his position. He does not make pleasing God his main concern but rather develops a religious attitude that closes off his mind to the ways in which God is moving. Accordingly, he criticizes everything he does not understand or that is not done according to his preferences. If God speaks to another person rather than to him, he believes that the other person didn't really receive a word from God; he doesn't want to feel that anyone else is "better" than he is. He wants to believe he is the only one who hears God's voice and knows His Word. Consequently, he becomes a modern "Pharisee"—someone who considers himself to be an "absolute lord" of the truth. He behaves as if he is king and judge over all.

The modern "Pharisee" is a lover of self and a servant of self. He is his own cause and end result.

The above could be a description of Satan. He was created to worship God, but somewhere along the way, his heart grew cold and became hard. Satan no longer wanted to serve God but rather decided to serve himself and his own interests, and he later dragged Adam and Eve along with him in his rebellion by tempting them to sin. The Scriptures say:

> *How you are fallen from heaven, O Lucifer, son of the morning! How you are cut down to the ground, you who weakened the nations! For you have said in your heart: "I will ascend into heaven, I will exalt my throne above the stars of God; I will also sit on the mount of the congregation on the farthest sides of the north; I will ascend above the heights of the clouds, I will be like the Most High." Yet you shall be brought down to Sheol, to the lowest depths of the Pit.* (Isaiah 14:12–15)

Satan had been created perfect in every way. (See Ezekiel 28:12–17.) He was apparently the main worshipper of God and the worship leader in heaven. Yet he became so absorbed in himself that he began to rob the worship that belongs to the Lord alone. Satan allowed his God-given gifts to dazzle him and cloud his perspective. He was no longer happy with the position God had granted him, and he believed that he could and should be more than his Creator. He deceived himself, thus opening the door for his heart to become corrupt.

The manner in which Satan became corrupted shows us how a person can fall into self-deception and coldness of heart. For example, suppose an individual who has a certain degree of authority in a church or a business begins to feel he is "better" than his situation, so he indicates that he no longer wants to serve or work there. Based on his own ideas, rather than God's direction, he may say something like, "My 'season' in this ministry has ended. God has something greater for me."

The worst part of such a scenario is that, often, the type of person who makes such a statement is the one who has contributed the least to the church or business. If he is part of a church, he has usually served the people very little and given only meager amounts in support of the church's mission. But, while he has given the least, he has demanded—and perhaps taken—the most! Even so, he believes that he should be given greater status and honor, and he is filled with arrogance. Likewise, Satan believed that he no longer had to serve God and should be equal to Him. His heart had hardened, and he could no longer see beyond himself.

8. A Hardened Heart Is Emotionally Cold and Bitter Toward Others

As we discussed earlier, God gave us emotions to help us to connect with other people and to express ourselves. Our emotions also help us to recognize the pain and needs of other people and to empathize with them. The Scriptures show us that Jesus was moved by people's suffering and needs. He felt deeply for the human race.

For example, in one passage, we read, "When [Jesus] *saw the multitudes, He was moved with compassion for them, because they were weary and scattered, like sheep having no shepherd*" (Matthew 9:36). In another instance, "*Jesus wept*" (John 11:35) over the death of a friend. And, He was "*sorrowful and deeply distressed*" (Matthew 26:37) when it came time for Him to die for our sins. Much spiritual, mental, and emotional strength is required for a man to cry as did Jesus, the strongest Man who ever lived. Jesus was so moved by humanity's predicament of sin and death that He gave up His life for us. He poured out His heart with tears and anguish at Gethsemane on behalf of the salvation of humanity and in anticipation of what it would take to redeem us.

There was no selfishness or hardness in Jesus' heart. He surrendered His human will so that the divine will could be fulfilled "*on earth as it is in heaven*" (Matthew 6:10; Luke 11:2). In contrast, as we have noted, those who harden their hearts become emotionally cold, concerned only for themselves, not for the welfare of others. They may also become bitter toward other people. The Scriptures warn us, "[Look] *carefully lest anyone fall short of the grace of God; lest any root of bitterness springing up cause trouble, and by this many become defiled*" (Hebrews 12:15). A heart that cultivates bitterness, allowing it to grow, will inevitably become hard and will defile other people with whom it comes into contact.

9. A Hardened Heart Enjoys Sin

Another symptom of a hardened heart is an enjoyment of partaking in sin and in giving free rein to the "*lusts of the flesh*" (2 Peter 2:18). This occurs when people's sinful nature becomes completely enthroned in their inner being, so that it directs their life. Such people lack a proper fear of God, which would have restrained their corrupt behavior.

In contrast, when a person's heart is aligned with God's, he recognizes that sin is only a temporal pleasure that leads to destruction and eternal death, so that he doesn't want anything to do with it! To avoid a hardened heart that pursues sin, we must follow the example of Moses:

> *By faith Moses, when he became of age, refused to be called the son of Pharaoh's daughter, choosing rather to suffer affliction with the people of God than to enjoy the passing pleasures of sin, esteeming the reproach of Christ greater riches than the treasures in Egypt; for he looked to the reward.* (Hebrews 11:24–26)

10. A Hardened Heart Holds Back Tithes and Offerings from God

A hardened heart always seeks a reason not to give tithes or offerings to the Lord. To a person whose heart has grown cold, honoring God is not a priority, so he will find excuses to get out of doing so. For example, he may say that God doesn't require people's money in order to do His work, or that it is the responsibility of the government alone to help the poor and destitute, and that we should not have to give a portion of our paycheck to alleviate the needs of those less fortunate than we are. Such a mind-set is the opposite of the one belonging to Mary, a follower of Jesus, who gave the best she had to her Lord:

> *Then Mary took a pound of very costly oil of spikenard, anointed the feet of Jesus, and wiped His feet with her hair. And the house was filled with the fragrance of the oil. But one of His disciples, Judas Iscariot, Simon's son, who would betray Him, said, "Why was this fragrant oil not sold for three hundred denarii and given to the poor?"* (John 12:3–5)

Judas's heart had become corrupt to the point that he pretended to be concerned about those who were poor, when he himself was robbing the funds designated for them: "*This* [Judas] *said, not that he cared for the poor, but because he was a thief, and had the money box; and he used to take what was put in it"* (John 12:6). When Judas saw the great offering of love that Mary poured out to Jesus, his words of rebuke revealed the hardness of his heart.

11. A Hardened Heart Does Not Worship God

When a person does not desire to worship God, it is a clear sign that some hardening of heart has taken place. The person who consistently lives without the manifest presence of God usually becomes used to a religious formality that is far removed from true worship. He essentially practices the absence of the presence of the God whom he claims to serve. In fact, he often rejects the genuine presence of the Lord because it convicts him of his need to repent of his sins and his lack of love and to experience the transformation of his heart.

Dangers and Consequences of Maintaining a Hardened Heart

Now that we know the causes and signs of a hardened heart, let us turn to the serious consequences of allowing this condition to continue in our inner man indefinitely—consequences for our life and for the lives of our descendants.

1. A Fall into Calamity

"Happy is the man who is always reverent, but he who hardens his heart will fall into calamity" (Proverbs 28:14). From my ministerial experience, I can say that the person whose heart has lost its spiritual sensitivity is moving toward disaster. Disobedience and spiritual error will guide his decisions, and his end will be spiritual death, if he does not repent and turn back to God. There is no way for someone whose heart has long been hardened to please God and to walk with Him. Regardless of whether the individual appears holy, if his heart is hardened, God is not present there. All we see is a mere image—a smoke screen. It is false piety, which sooner or later falls to evil.

2. Brokenness, Sometimes Without Remedy

"He who is often rebuked, and hardens his neck, will suddenly be destroyed, and that without remedy" (Proverbs 29:1). The phrase *"hardens his neck"*

indicates a refusal to recognize a truth or to change something in yourself that is wrong; it is an insistence on maintaining a false mentality or on making your own ideas and mentality your god. In effect, it is telling God that He is wrong and that His counsel is not needed, which is nothing less than rebellion.

The consequence of the above is to be broken by God, perhaps *"without remedy."* I sincerely hope that this is not your situation and that it is not too late for you to recognize your condition before the Creator. God is a God of second chances. If you repent and recommit to Him, He can transform your heart and save you from evil, brokenness, and a lost condition.

3. The Removal of the Presence and Power of God

Even after you have hardened your heart, God's presence may remain over your life for a time. However, if the condition continues, His presence will lift, and His power will cease to operate through you. For example, Samson was a judge and warrior in Israel, but his heart was not fully aligned with the Lord's, and he repeatedly surrendered to sin. At one point, Samson went too far, failing to respect the calling God had given him, and the Scriptures say of him that *"he awoke from his sleep, and said, 'I will go out as before, at other times, and shake myself free!' But he did not know that the LORD had departed from him"* (Judges 16:20). What ultimately happened to Samson—losing the gift God had given him; being captured by his enemies; having his eyes put out; being mocked and humiliated; and, finally, when God restored his strength, destroying his enemies and himself by bringing down the Philistine temple of Dagon on them—is one of the saddest and least illustrious ends of a man chosen by God.

4. A "Seared Conscience"

The apostle Paul wrote, *"Now the Spirit expressly says that in latter times some will depart from the faith, giving heed to deceiving spirits and doctrines of demons, speaking lies in hypocrisy, having their own conscience seared with a hot iron…"* (1 Timothy 4:1–2). To have a "seared conscience" means to come into a state of indifference to sin as a result of continuous, willful transgression against God's commands. The person with a seared conscience sins without remorse because his heart has become callused. Eventually, he turns his back on the Lord Himself without any remorse.

It is essential to understand that "searing" is a process. No one who has experienced a genuine encounter with Jesus will deny Him suddenly. The process begins when a person starts committing a sin in a certain area, or when, after being hurt by someone, he continues to hold on to bitter feelings without releasing his hurt to God and forgiving the offending party.

In the beginning, the person's conscience will bother him, and he may experience conviction from the Holy Spirit that he is not in a good place. However, if he doesn't repent, then the next time he sins, he will feel less bad; the following time even less; and so forth, until his conscience stops rebuking him because it has been seared.

The searing process is similar to what occurs when a callus develops somewhere on our physical body. For example, when a person starts learning to play the guitar, the act of fingering the strings will be somewhat painful and will cause the tips of his fingers to become red. But then small calluses will form, and he will stop feeling any pain, because that part of his skin is no longer soft and sensitive but hard and insensitive.

Spiritually speaking, when a person starts to harden his heart, "calluses" will begin to develop on it. If the process is allowed to continue, the individual will come to regard sin as something normal, because he is no longer sensitive to the prompting or conviction of God; he no longer has a reverent fear of the Lord, and he has given his sinful nature free rein. The person will now justify his sin, and his seared conscience will conclude, *I have a right to do this*, or *God won't care if I do this*.

The Scriptures warn, *"For if we sin willfully after we have received the knowledge of the truth, there no longer remains a sacrifice for sins"* (Hebrews 10:26). At that point, we can say that the person has fallen into "apostasy"; he has abandoned the faith after "[having] *tasted the good word of God and the powers of the age to come...*" (Hebrews 6:5). In other words, after knowing and experiencing Christ and receiving God's supernatural works, he denies and rejects them, perhaps even mocking what he used to consider holy. He completely walks away from the Lord. In military terms, such a person would be called a deserter.

The Condition of Your Heart

After more than twenty-five years in ministry, I have seen the above consequences in the lives of church leaders and other believers who chose to maintain their hardened hearts and not allow themselves to be changed by the Lord. What is the condition of your heart today? Could it be that you no longer feel the presence of God, so that you have fallen into the mere formality of religion, and faith has stopped flowing in you? Do you observe others closely for the purpose of finding a reason to judge them? Have you gone back on your commitments to God and to His people, so that you no longer serve them? Is there rebellion in your inner man, causing you to close yourself off from others and to refuse to recognize God's delegated authority in your life? Do you find your heart centered on the desires of the sinful nature, so that you have begun to enjoy activities and practices that offend God? Do you recognize an area of your life that is not responsive to God's love, will, and authority? Do you find it hard to offer heartfelt worship and generous offerings to the Lord?

If you recognize in yourself any of the above signs of a hardened heart, I pray to God that you will decide to place yourself in His hands, that you will allow Him to operate in your heart to transform it through His Holy Spirit, so that His favor and grace can continue to flow in your life. Stop thinking about it—do it! Stop prolonging the agony that causes your spirit to be separated from God in any of the aforementioned areas. Today is the day of your transformation!

The following is the account of two sisters whose hearts became full of pride. Their condition led them to turn away from God while allowing coldness and self-interest to take over their lives. One of the sisters, Luisa, writes, "Although we were raised in a culture dominated by Catholicism, our entire family met and accepted Jesus as Lord and Savior while my sister and I were still children. We began to attend church, and we served in various ministries during our childhood and adolescent years. When we entered the university, our faith was criticized, and this criticism threatened to block us from becoming professionals, making us feel very rejected, sad, and angry. It was then that the demands of school seemed like a good excuse to separate ourselves from the church and, consequently, from God. We focused on our careers, goals, and commitments.

"After more than ten years of struggling, we graduated with honors from important universities. My sister studied literature and nursing. I studied art, literature, and philosophy. In our search for greater professional accomplishments, we moved to the United States, where we were able to fulfill our dreams. Our lives seemed to be wonderful, but the truth was that, regardless of all the good things that surrounded us, we still felt out of sorts. Without God, our lives seemed destined for ruin as we trusted more in our abilities and knowledge than on Him.

"But then a crisis entered our successful world. Not knowing what to do, we started to look for a church where we could receive spiritual covering. We knocked on many doors, but none filled our void until my sister saw a King Jesus church service on television. We attended the church and became reconciled to God and to our parents—their prayers had finally reached us. The experience was like being reborn, like breathing again after being underwater for a long time. However, as we got closer to God, adversity increased like a river until our 'castle' tumbled down. We lost many material things, but the hand of God helped to keep us strong as it polished our hearts. We died to the pride that had built our lives; we surrendered to God and learned to obey Him. Finally, He restored us. He equipped us by teaching us to fight through prayer, to live by faith, to stand on His Word, and to seek His face and wait on Him. He gave us back even more than what we had lost. Today, God is, once again, the Lord of our lives and of our time. He is our true Provider and, more than ever, the center of our existence."

The Cure for the Hardened Heart

There is a cure for the person who has a hardened heart if he will surrender to God, give up his "ego," yield his intellect and reason to God, and allow Him to transform him. If your heart has become hardened, you are not lost, because God can *make a road in the wilderness and rivers in the desert* (Isaiah 43:19). He promises, *"If My people who are called by My name will humble themselves, and pray and seek My face, and turn from their wicked ways, then I will hear from heaven, and will forgive their sin and heal their land"* (2 Chronicles 7:14). Let us explore the path that leads to the cure for the hardened heart.

"Circumcision" of the Heart

In the Old Testament, physical circumcision involved cutting off the foreskin of the male reproductive organ, symbolizing that the individual was a member of the covenant people of God. In the New Testament, after Christ shed His blood on the cross for our sins and was resurrected, circumcision became a spiritual act in the human heart—although a spiritual application was also relevant under the old covenant. For example, in Deuteronomy, we read, *"Therefore circumcise the foreskin of your heart, and be stiff-necked no longer"* (Deuteronomy 10:16).

Therefore, from the onset of the practice of circumcision, it was clear that God was primarily interested in the human heart. We must be fully aware that heart circumcision has to be maintained, because when a person stops seeking God's presence and His transformation, that individual will become stagnant and begin to backslide—he will start a reverse journey toward engaging in old habits and justifying his sin, rather than repenting of his sin and giving it up. Paul wrote, *"For he is not a Jew who is one outwardly, nor is circumcision that which is outward in the flesh; but he is a Jew who is one inwardly; and circumcision is that of the heart, in the Spirit, not in the letter; whose praise is not from men but from God"* (Romans 2:28–29). We must die to our sinful nature if we want to once again be sensitive to the voice of God and the ways in which He is working today.

> *When our heart is circumcised, we renounce our trust in fallen human nature and begin to trust totally in divine grace.*

True Repentance Provides the Only Access to Heart Circumcision

Every sin or wrong attitude that we fail to repent of contributes to the hardening of our heart. Genuine repentance is necessary in order to restore our heart from its hardened state. What is repentance? It is a complete change of heart and mind that leads to a change in behavior. Accordingly, true repentance involves a new frame of mind that reflects a change in attitude. When we realize our hardened spiritual condition before God and the rebellious nature that has led us away from Him, repentance is the decision we make to turn 180 degrees and walk in the opposite direction—toward Him. Repentance also indicates our decision not to rule ourselves any longer but to be ruled by God, according to His Word and will.

Therefore, if your heart is hard, you need to repent of sin, whether it is sin you are currently engaged in or a generational curse that was passed down through your family line—such as may be manifested in an addiction that cannot be broken or in persistent depression. Repentance will enable you to enter into God's presence again. When you turn from your sins and wrong attitudes, you allow your heart to soften toward the Lord. Without repentance, your faith will be void. For example, a thief can try to believe that God forgives the sin of stealing, but if he doesn't repent of his thieving, the faith to receive forgiveness cannot operate in him, nor will God's power be able to work in his heart to transform him.

The areas in which our heart is hardened are those in which we resist God.

Only the Holy Spirit Can Circumcise the Heart

It is vital to recognize that the only One who can circumcise your heart is God's Holy Spirit. He knows you, and He has the power and the love to circumcise you without hurting you. I pray that your eyes will be opened so you can see the true state of your heart. Although your heart may not be fully hardened, there is surely some area of your life you need to surrender to God so that you may be transformed. Don't deprive yourself of this blessing. Don't be afraid of losing something that you have, because what God wants to give you is a thousand times better!

I pray that you may experience true repentance, allowing the Holy Spirit to circumcise your heart from wrong mind-sets, wrong thoughts, and wrong habits that have created thick calluses, making you unable to feel or perceive God's presence, and making it difficult for you to establish healthy relationships with other people. I pray that the Holy Spirit will remove the "heart of stone" within you—including the wounds, pain, and feelings of rejection that have caused you to harden your heart—and will give you a "heart of flesh"—one that is new, soft, and tender; one that restores your innocence. If you will allow Him to, God will cleanse, purify, and sanctify your heart. Choose to be circumcised by the Holy Spirit, and receive an anointing from God like never before.

Realize that your heavenly Father wants to do a "heart transplant" within you right now. If you will open your heart to God, yield yourself to Him, and give Him permission to do this spiritual surgery, He will remove your heart of stone and replace it with a heart of flesh.

Reaching the fulfillment of our purpose in God involves surrendering our will to His.

Benefits of Circumcision of the Heart

The following summarizes some of the benefits of allowing the Holy Spirit to circumcise your heart. Heart circumcision…

- ✦ restores innocence to you.
- ✦ increases your sensitivity to the presence of God.
- ✦ increases your ability to receive what you need from God—and what He wants to give you.
- ✦ increases your ability to carry a greater anointing without deviating from it or contaminating it.
- ✦ maintains a continuous flow of the life of God within you.
- ✦ makes the spiritual realm more real and tangible to you.
- ✦ causes your heart to surrender quickly to God.
- ✦ causes you to no longer resist the process of transformation but rather to submit to it, knowing that it will bring you closer to your heavenly Father.

*When our heart is soft and tender, there is nothing
we won't do for God.*

Prayer for Circumcision of the Heart

If you have come to the realization that you need God to circumcise your heart and remove everything within it that is evil and hard, so that you can draw close to Him again, then please repeat this prayer out loud:

Heavenly Father, I come into Your presence praising and worshipping Your name. I present myself before You on the merits of Your Son Jesus Christ alone. I recognize that there are areas in my heart that have been hardened, but I repent wholeheartedly and ask You to forgive me. I repent of allowing past hurts and failures to usurp lordship over me; for allowing my heart to be hardened by sin, offenses, emotional wounds, disobedience, rebellion, and wickedness. Lord, forgive me for repeatedly disobeying Your voice and for not giving You Your rightful place in all areas of my life. Right now, I ask You to circumcise my heart, to remove the calluses that prevent me from feeling, perceiving, or discerning the spiritual world and the need I have of You. Please restore my innocence so that I can believe in You with the trust of a child and be sensitive to Your Holy Spirit. Father, fill me with Your power and presence, even now. Transform my heart, in the name of Jesus, amen!

Prayer for Salvation and Transformation

Perhaps you have not yet received Jesus as your Savior and Lord, but your conscience is telling you that there is a real God who wants to transform your life and is fully able to do so. I invite you to become a child of God, just as a young man named Stephen did. Stephen was raised in Rastafarianism, a religious cult. In this group, marijuana is considered to be a "holy herb" that supposedly produces physical, psychological, and therapeutic powers; it is practically a god to the Rastafarian culture. Stephen was only five years old when he began to smoke joints. He smoked marijuana as a "mediator" to the spirit world and also practiced witchcraft. Stephen grew his fingernails long and wore dreadlocks. He believed in himself and in his own power to do whatever needed to be done.

But Stephen was raised without a father, and his walk through life was a devastating cycle of deception and calamity. He learned survival skills while living on the streets. But on those streets he encountered pornography, which caused him to deviate from his natural sexual orientation. Stephen's sexual confusion caused him to become aggressive toward homosexuals, hiding the fact that he felt attracted to other men. Furthermore, he was involved in buying and selling drugs as a way to support his lifestyle. He had become addicted to drugs, and he had also developed a physical heart ailment, which made his situation even worse.

Stephen remembers the event that led him to Christ. It was an encounter with the living God that transformed his gangster character into one of a sanctified man of God who is now on the right track. Sometime earlier, when Stephen had been hospitalized for anger issues and was under the supervision of a clinical psychologist, his grandmother had given him a Bible, which he had kept but never read. Then, during a drug transaction, he walked by a table in his room and noticed the Bible. He considered its presence there to be rather strange, as he had not seen the Bible since he'd come home after his hospital stay. He recalled, "I saw the Bible and became afraid. I thought it was a hallucination, a side effect of drug use."

He left the room for a moment, and when he returned for more merchandise, he suddenly heard a voice that said, *You will not leave this place until you pick up the Bible.* The supernatural power of God prevented him from leaving the room until he physically touched the Bible. "I couldn't open the door or walk forward," he said. Stephen picked up the Bible, sat down, and began to read it. Suddenly, he was able to understand what he was reading, as if it were being spoken to him by a friend. "There was no way for me to have understood the Bible before that day; it had never made sense to me, but God made me understand it."

On another occasion, the Holy Spirit said to him, *Wash your hands, because today you begin a new season in holiness.* Stephen did this and declared that the healing blood of Jesus cleansed and liberated him from all generational curses. And, when he went back to the doctor for more follow-up tests regarding his heart condition, the results came back negative, showing no traces of the sickness from which he had suffered for years.

That is how Stephen received a new beginning in God. Today, he is on fire for the Lord as an evangelist who produces abundant fruit. Likewise, if your repentance is sincere, the Holy Spirit will circumcise your heart, and you will begin to see changes in your life that you have been unable to experience in your own strength. To repent and receive Jesus as your Lord and Savior, pray the following prayer:

> Heavenly Father, I recognize that I am a sinner and that my sin separates me from You. My heart is in need of transformation, which only You can accomplish. I believe that Jesus died on the cross for me and that You raised Him from the dead. I confess with my mouth that Jesus is Lord. I repent of all my sins and break every evil covenant I have made with the world, with my sinful nature, and with the devil. According to the power of Jesus' sacrifice for me, I break all generational curses operating in my life. Now, I make a new covenant of righteousness with Jesus. I ask Jesus to come into my heart and to change my life, filling me with the Holy Spirit. If I were to die right now, I know I would be in Your presence when I opened my eyes in eternity. In Jesus' name, amen!

5

Healing for an Offended Heart

O ver the course of my ministry, I have seen tragic consequences occur in people's lives when they have allowed offenses to become rooted in their heart. Wherever there is an offended heart, look out! As the Scriptures say, *"A brother offended is harder to win than a strong city, and contentions are like the bars of a castle"* (Proverbs 18:19).

In this book, I use the terms *offense* and *offended* in relation to the negative attitude a person adopts after being affronted by someone or something, so that he sins in attitude, word, or deed—and usually *keeps on sinning* as he develops bitterness and resentment toward the offending individual or situation. An offense goes beyond taking momentary exception to a casual comment someone makes or to the rudeness of a stranger (unless it continues to fester within you). We may be temporarily bothered by someone's remark or behavior and then immediately let it go or release it through prayer, with no lingering negative feelings. In contrast, an offense is something that remains in our heart.

As I wrote earlier, I have seen offenses divide churches, ministries, marriages, families, businesses, and organizations. I have seen people lose their spiritual and natural inheritances alike—inheritances such as miracles, healings, deliverances, and financial blessings—so that they never attain to their full purpose in God. I would suggest that the chief reason people decide to leave a church is that they were offended by someone or by some policy. If no one were ever offended, our churches and ministries would grow large and remain so; certainly, we would be more effective in expanding God's kingdom, and our testimony to the world would have a much greater impact. Jesus said, *"By this all will know that you are My disciples, if you have love for one another"* (John 13:35).

The problem of offenses is nothing new. For example, in the Bible, we find accounts of people like King Saul, who held on to an offense, causing him grave consequences, including being removed from the presence of God, forfeiting his anointing and kingship, and even losing his life. (See 1 Samuel 9–31.) The greatest tragedy of holding on to an offense—and its most frightening aspect—is that it can result in eternal separation from God if a person continues down a path of anger and revenge, allowing his bitterness either to keep him from receiving Christ in the first place or to reject his Lord.

In this chapter, we will explore what an offense is, the characteristics of an offended heart, the root of offenses, and how to deal with offenses effectively. I pray that you will be able to identify the state of your heart with respect to this subject and be set free from any destructive offenses that you may be harboring.

What Is an Offense?

Several different Greek words in the New Testament are translated as *"offense"* in the *New King James Version*. One of these Greek words is *skandalon*, from which we get the word "scandal." This term means "a stick for bait (of a trap)," or "a snare (figuratively, cause of displeasure or sin)." It indicates "occasion to fall (of stumbling)," "stumbling block," or "thing that offends." In fact, when translating *skandalon*, certain Bible versions sometimes use the word *"stumbling block"* rather than *"offense,"* such as in Matthew 16:23 (NIV, NASB).

An offense is a trap, and traps are hardly ever set by accident. When a trap is set for a person, it means that someone wants to impede that individual's progress, steal from him, or even kill him. Satan, the enemy of our soul, is behind various traps that come into our life to hinder us and to take away what God has given us; the enemy desires to rob us of our purpose, destiny, spiritual and natural inheritance, family unity, and spiritual harmony with our brothers and sisters in Christ. Contriving to thwart the advancement of God's kingdom, Satan tries to prevent the will of our heavenly Father from being established on the earth. He desires not only to deceive us but also to cause us to perish spiritually, mentally, emotionally, and physically. For this reason, Satan seeks to cause us to be offended not only by other people but also by God Himself.

In the Scriptures, we see several examples of people who were offended by God, including John the Baptist. He was imprisoned by King Herod toward the end of his ministry, during which he had served God faithfully. While John waited for some response from his cousin Jesus, he became offended when his expectation—perhaps of a supernatural rescue—was not fulfilled. His faith was in crisis, and his maturity was on trial—so much so that he began to doubt Jesus' identity as the Messiah.

John sent two of his own disciples to Jesus to ask Him, *"Are You the Coming One, or do we look for another?"* (Matthew 11:3). Christ instructed these disciples to report to John the signs that had followed Him and the miracles that had taken place by His hand, which John would recognize as being the works of the Messiah. (See Matthew 11:4–5.)

Then, Christ declared, *"Blessed is he who is not offended because of Me"* (Matthew 11:6). The word translated *"offended"* in this verse is *skandalizo*, which is the verb form of the noun *skandalon* we noted above. *Skandalizo* means "to entrap, i.e. trip up (fig. stumble or entice to sin, apostasy or displeasure)." Therefore, I believe Jesus was saying, in effect, "Tell John not to be offended with Me, because the offense might cause him to stumble in his faith or even to fall away from Me and miss out on My purpose for coming to the earth."

Many people today are offended by God because He has not yet answered their prayers; because He has not yet healed them; because they are suffering from some other adversity, and He has not yet delivered them; or for other reasons. They have come to view God as an obstacle rather than as their ultimate Source of life and power in the midst of their situation. If Jesus Himself did not avoid offending various people among whom He lived and ministered (such as John the Baptist, many Pharisees and scribes,

Judas Iscariot, and others), no one else on this earth will be able to avoid it, either. At times, when we offend someone, it is because we have made an error or have been insensitive; however, at other times, when we offend someone, it is because he expects us to do something that we cannot or should not do.

An offense is a trap of the enemy to rob us of purpose, destiny, and harmonious relationships.

Unintended Offenses

Once, when I taught at my church on the subject of offenses, I asked people whom I had offended to come to me so that we could talk through the offense and resolve it. To my surprise, I discovered that many people were offended with me! In most cases, I didn't even know that the people were offended, much less why. What shocked me most were the reasons people gave for the offenses, most of which seemed rather inconsequential. For example, someone told me, "I am offended because you walked right past me and didn't say hello." I don't remember the circumstance, but I may have been focused on a particular task or concern at the time. Someone else said, "I am offended with you because the message you preached a month ago was spoken against me." I had no idea that he had a problem related to what I had preached.

Another complained, "You didn't pray for me yourself. You had another pastor pray for me." Our church has thousands of members; it is truly impossible for me to pray for each person who asks for prayer. Because of this fact, God has equipped our church with additional pastors and workers whom we have trained in ministry and who have a heart for God, so they can help us serve His people. Those who become offended because they think they are being overlooked by me or by my wife don't understand the "blood, sweat, and tears" that we have poured into spiritually training those pastors and workers. We have invested in them with everything that God has given us, and the power of the Lord operates through them, just as it does through us.

Other people have been offended with me because I didn't personally visit them when they were in the hospital; because they were not asked to be an elder, minister, pastor, or leader; because I didn't call them to wish them a happy birthday; because I didn't give them a hug when I saw them; and for various other reasons.

What was my response when these people came to me with the above offenses? With a desire to heal their heart and to preserve our relationship of spiritual father to spiritual son or daughter, I asked them, with all sincerity, to forgive me, because it had not been my intention to offend them.

Offenses take place in the heart, not in the mind.

Various Manifestations of the Trap of Offense

There are so many reasons why people become offended. A common problem in the church is that numerous leaders are affronted by the success of others in the body of Christ. For example, they may become jealous of another pastor because his church is bigger, because he apparently has a greater anointing, or because he seems to have been blessed more abundantly by God. Unfortunately, it is common in churches for people to allow offenses to ferment within them and never be resolved. I believe this explains why many people in the body of Christ live a life of defeat and suffer various illnesses.

As with John the Baptist, people often become offended when their expectations and preconceived ideas are not met. Let's look at two scenarios from the business world. An employee is offended after being fired, so he sues the company for unfair termination or lost wages. There are times when such suits are valid because the employee has truly been mistreated. However, sometimes, the fired employee has been irresponsible or unproductive, yet he still becomes offended because he expected the company to keep him in its employ, regardless of his bad performance or lack of diligence. In his mind, he imagines he has good reasons for suing the company, but, in reality, he had not completed even the minimum amount of work necessary to fulfill his responsibilities. On the other hand, some business owners and managers believe they "possess" their employees and have a right to control them and take advantage of them. Such owners and managers will become offended if a faithful, longtime employee requests a reasonable raise or improved working conditions.

There are some people who always feel offended by others because they can't stand to see anyone else happy, blessed, prospering, or loved. They may become offended by the wealth or prosperity of others because they don't want anyone else to succeed or make more money than they do. They might become offended for the simple reason that another individual is hardworking while their own work habits are mediocre. They might be affronted by their neighbor's greater intelligence or happier family life. Such people become offended without taking into account certain considerations—the sacrifices another person may have endured; the covenants he may have made with God, which he was faithful to observe; the tithes and offerings he may have given, even during difficult times; his obedience to kingdom principles; and so forth.

In the following testimony, we can see how holding on to a painful offense debilitated the life of a woman named Jeniffer. She writes, "I got pregnant when I was eighteen years old. I had been in a relationship with my baby's father for a long time, but as soon as he learned that I was pregnant, he asked me to abort the baby. I refused, and he left me. When my mother found out through other people about my pregnancy, she suffered a lot because she was a single mother with two daughters and understood how difficult that life is. I was three months pregnant when she, too, asked me to abort the baby. My mother made an appointment at a clinic, and, the very next day, I was sitting in the clinic's waiting room.

"There were many women there, but I was the youngest. The procedure was to take approximately ten minutes or less; the women just kept going in and coming out. When it was my turn, the process was very painful! I felt as if something inside me was sucking out my uterus. That experience changed me. I directed all of the pain and bitterness in my heart toward my mother for denying me my child. I didn't express my feelings toward her, but I treated her badly. I wanted to be pregnant again. I would cry while touching my belly and behave as if I had a baby inside of me.

"I got pregnant again by another boyfriend, but I had a miscarriage. It was then that I 'lost it' and fell into a deep depression. I couldn't sleep, and I felt empty. I believed that only a baby could fill my void, and I sought refuge in fornication and pornography.

"When nothing made sense anymore, I found Christ through a coworker who invited me to a church service. When I entered the church, I felt like I had returned home. My heart was full of emotion! I went forward to the altar to receive Christ. Since then, my life has changed. Now I serve God, and I am happy. The Lord restored my relationship with my mother and erased the guilt. I understand that my babies are in heaven with my Lord."

In His love, the Lord freed Jeniffer from her offended heart, took away her guilt, enabled her to forgive, and restored her enjoyment of life. In the next section, we will explore some significant truths about offenses that will help us to learn how to deal with them effectively.

Important Truths About Offenses

1. Offenses Are Inevitable in a Fallen World

Jesus said, *"It is impossible that no offenses [skandalon] should come, but woe to him through whom they do come!"* (Luke 17:1). In this statement, Christ used a powerful word: *"impossible."* As a result of the fall of humanity and the sinful nature human beings inherited, offenses became an inevitable and grievous part of human relationships. However, when we are reconciled to God through Christ and become His children, we are called to live according to a new nature that reflects His heart. Therefore, it is essential that we learn to deal with offenses effectively. The first step is to prayerfully determine beforehand how we will behave when offenses come into our life and what the attitude of our heart will be as we deal with them. This chapter will help you to take that first step so you can become free of offenses.

2. Everyone Will Offend in Word and Deed

Because we are members of the human race, we will, at one point or another, offend others in word and deed. As the Scriptures say, *"For we all stumble ["offend" KJV] in many things. If anyone does not stumble in word, he is a perfect man, able also to bridle the whole body"* (James 3:2). In this verse, *"stumble"* or *"offend"* is translated from the Greek word *ptaio*, which literally means "to trip." Figuratively, it means to "err," "sin," "fail (of salvation)," "fall," "offend," or "stumble."

Likewise, regardless of where or with whom we live, we will inevitably become offended by another person—a spouse, child, parent, friend, boss, coworker, classmate, or someone else. However, we must realize that, in most cases, the people by whom we are offended don't even know they have affronted us. And, as we have seen, we, too, may offend someone else without even realizing it. Our cooperation with God in the supernatural transformation of our heart includes asking Him to help us to willingly let go of offenses, live free of bitterness, and resolve any discord with others as soon as possible and as far as we are able. (See, for example, Romans 12:17–18.) When we do this in sincerity of heart, we will be blessed by God and filled with His joy.

3. Offenses Are Instructive to Us

We have noted that offenses prompt reactions from us that reveal what is truly in our heart. Sometimes, we might think we have progressed far in spiritual maturity. But then we demonstrate that we have an unresolved heart issue by reacting badly—perhaps with bitterness or pride—when we are faced with an offense. Therefore, when we become offended, we should use the circumstance for good in our life by allowing it to instruct us about the true condition of our inner being and by seeking healing.

When they are affronted, some people will ignore the person who caused them to feel offended; they stop communicating with him, and they might even end the relationship. Others will lash out at the offending person, spouting insults and creating strife; in other words, they behave like a child who throws a temper tantrum when he doesn't get his own way. Still others will exaggerate the offense and—behind the person's back—will begin to seek vengeance by making accusations, involving other people in the situation in unconstructive ways, and so forth.

Sometimes, we may be surprised to see those whom we considered less mature deal better with offenses than those whom we thought were much more mature. Rather than abruptly ending the relationship, yelling at the other party, or seeking revenge, they followed the biblical pattern of talking with the person privately, seeking reconciliation, and forgiving him, especially if the offense was intentional. (See, for example, Matthew 18:15–17.) Their example is the pattern we should all follow when offended.

Let me add one other word on this subject. Suppose you become offended by a matter that is, in actuality, inconsequential—for example, someone did not greet you as you expected him to, or someone made an offhand comment that you did not like—and the other person is unaware that you were offended by it. In such cases, it is often best just to release the offense to God, ask His forgiveness for your attitude, and move forward with your life without saying anything to the individual that might prolong the matter or even make it worse.

When you are offended, discern the true state of your heart, repent of any sin, ask God's forgiveness, and be healed.

4. We Can Be Justified or Unjustified in Feeling Offended

There are many genuine offenses in this world that cause people to feel affronted—offenses that produce hurt, confusion, and despair. We all have human emotions, and when we are unjustly treated or see someone else being abused, we will naturally experience such emotions as anger, anxiety, or sorrow. Feelings of hostility or grief may rise within us, whether we want them to or not. Remember that Jesus exhibited righteous anger when He saw people acting unjustly or with hypocrisy. (See, for example, John 2:13–17.) On the other hand, as we have just discussed, there are times when we feel affronted over issues that are inconsequential or trifling.

It is not so much the initial feeling of offense that matters but what we do with that emotion. Therefore, whether our being offended is justifiable or unjustifiable in a given situation, our response should always be to choose to forgive. Otherwise, our heart will become resentful or bitter, leading to destructive attitudes and actions that we will someday regret. Jesus Christ was unfairly judged to be a blasphemer by the religious leaders of His day, and He was unjustly crucified by the Romans. However, He forgave those who killed Him. (See Luke 23:34.) He surrendered His right of offense in order to attain the higher purpose of saving human beings from their sins, including those who treated Him unjustly. Who would have more reason to be affronted by those who mistreated Him than the sinless Son of God? Yet Jesus kept His heart pure and allowed God the Father to establish justice in His own way and in His own time. In doing so, Jesus accomplished the redemption of the world.

5. Offenses Are Signs of the End Times

"And then many will be offended, will betray one another, and will hate one another….And because lawlessness will abound, the love of many will grow cold" (Matthew 24:10, 12). Previously, we discussed the fact that wickedness would increase during the end times, and that it is already increasing, causing many people to grow cold in heart. In general, people today seem much less interested in their neighbors' feelings and needs. They don't care if they hurt, offend, or mistreat others, as long as they can meet their own objectives. The worst part is that many people seem indifferent to the reality that their heart is growing increasingly cold and hard.

A major reason hearts are growing cold is that offenses are multiplying as wickedness escalates. A vicious pattern develops when there is an increase in wickedness: Offenses lead to coldness, and coldness leads to hardened hearts, and hardened hearts lead to additional offenses. It is dangerous to enter that cycle!

If we choose to remain permanently offended, we will promote the treacherous pattern described above. Instead, we must endeavor to be living examples of Christ's prophetic words in Matthew 24:13: "He who endures to the end shall be saved." A significant way we can endure to the end is by not allowing an offense to corrupt and harden our heart. Every time we are affronted by someone or something, we have an opportunity to choose between staying offended or extending forgiveness and releasing our resentment, thereby maturing spiritually and emotionally.

I know many former church leaders who were precious servants of God until they allowed a certain offense to enter their heart, and they were not mature enough to deal with the affront in a proper and constructive way. Those believers went back to the ways of the world, and, today, they are suffering the consequences: They are slaves to sin, suffering from sickness, and mourning the destruction of their family—to name just a few of their conditions. The offense they could not let go of became their stumbling block and downfall. Their heart fell into the enemy's trap of offense, becoming contaminated. Let us always keep our eyes on Christ, trusting Him in each situation and keeping our heart pure and soft by yielding to God and forgiving others.

Whenever we are affronted, we have an opportunity to choose between staying offended or extending forgiveness and maturing spiritually and emotionally.

In the following account, a man named Paul describes how he was freed from an offended heart. He writes, "I was a young man in search of the pleasures of this world, and I ended up spending a year and a half in prison. During that time, I met Jesus but did not surrender my life to Him. I also had some supernatural experiences that demonstrated the reality of the spiritual world—the reality of God as well as of demons.

"When I completed my sentence, I was released from prison, but it was difficult to find a job. Consequently, I returned to my old habits. At the time, my grandfather was very ill. We prayed for him, but he still died. I felt horrible for all the suffering that my behavior had caused him, but I continued to take drugs and to be involved with witchcraft and fortune-telling because I wanted to understand my grandfather's death. At one point, I cursed God for my life, saying, 'A God who loves would never have allowed this to happen. Why should I continue to trust Him?'

"Meanwhile, my relationship with my wife slowly deteriorated. I tried going to church again, and I found a job; however, on the same day I was hired, someone called to tell me that my mother had cancer. I traveled to see her and prayed for her. I told her that everything would be all right, but she died that same day. That was a very hard experience for me. I felt pain and anger, and I wanted to abandon everything.

"My wife and children told me about King Jesus church and asked me to attend. I was lost and had no place to go, so I agreed. I needed something that would change me forever. There, the Lord touched me. I opened my heart to Him, and He healed it. Now, I am a changed man, and I serve Him by telling people of the great things that He has done for me."

The Root of Holding On to Offenses Is Immaturity

Being easily offended and remaining offended are prime characteristics of a person who is spiritually and emotionally immature. Some people choose to live in perpetual immaturity because they will not let go of an offense. As a result, they bind themselves to that offense, and it controls their lives. We must realize—for our own sake and for the sake of others—that immature people are easily deceived and are inclined to fall prey to false doctrine. Paul wrote, *"We should no longer be children, tossed to and fro and carried about with every wind of doctrine, by the trickery of men, in the cunning craftiness of deceitful plotting"* (Ephesians 4:14).

The following characteristics are evident in those who are spiritually and emotionally immature. Immature people...

+ are easily offended by others.

+ are easily deceived by others.

+ are insecure.

+ are dominated by their emotions.

+ fail to exercise self-control.

+ become offended when they are corrected.

+ become offended when they are held accountable for their responsibilities and their wrongs.

+ are double-minded.

+ are unable to exercise effective leadership because they reproduce their immaturity in others.

In contrast, we develop maturity when we learn how to deal well with offenses, addressing them in a biblical manner. If we fail to do this, we will suffer some or all of the costs of maintaining an offended heart outlined below.

As we mature, the trap of offense loses its power over us.

Costs of Maintaining an Offended Heart

1. Offended People Will Often Withdraw from Others, Sometimes Becoming Recluses

Holding on to an offense hinders people's spiritual growth because they revert to being controlled by the sinful nature—to the way they conducted themselves before they knew Christ. They find refuge in old behaviors because they have stopped advancing in maturity and have withdrawn their heart from God and other people. They close themselves off and hide in their pain. Therefore, they no longer show much emotion or open up to other people, and they are afraid to develop new relationships. This is a dangerous place to be in because when Satan finds someone isolated from the rest of the body of Christ, he implements a plan of attack to push him into a spiritual decline that is sometimes difficult to reverse, so that it ends in spiritual death. Please, don't fall for the trap of offense!

2. Offended People Exclude Themselves from the Flow of Life

People who are withdrawn from others, as described above, experience a loss of freedom by excluding themselves from the normal flow of life and its activities—whether the life of a family, a church, a business, or another organization. If this happens to someone who is a member of a church, he may no longer feel that he is a part of the body of believers or that he shares the church's vision. He may still give tithes and/or offerings to the church, but he does not participate in its life. He may have a gift or talent that would be beneficial to share with other believers, but he does not feel at liberty to do so. He will likely experience a cooling in his relationships with others, because he doesn't support the activities they are interested in or participate in them. In addition, he may find it difficult to pray and to worship God in a corporate setting.

Consequently, the following pattern may develop in his life: He may continually refuse to be integrated into the body of believers, even when invited to do so. He may choose to sit in the farthest seat at the back of the church so that he can observe everything that goes on without being noticed by very many people, internally criticizing anything negative that occurs. He may continue to construct a thick wall between himself and others—a barrier of offenses, errors, misunderstandings, and so forth. He may still attend church for years to come out of a sense of obligation, but he will have isolated himself from the flow of God's Spirit and the joys of human fellowship.

3. Offended People Employ Defense Mechanisms

In accordance with his self-imposed isolation, an offended person will enter any new relationship with a barricade around his heart. Because he has never worked through past offenses, he places himself on constant guard to repel any attack (real or perceived) from other people against his self-esteem, personal rights, and integrity as a human being. To protect himself, he has developed defense mechanisms, such as mistrust, prejudice, negativity, and a judgmental attitude.

Those who employ emotional defense mechanisms inevitably hinder their personal relationships. For example, when a couple is preparing to marry, it is important for each one to be transparent with the other and to discuss the hurts and disappointments he or she has experienced in the past, because many people carry around burdens of pain or guilt from which they need to be healed. These issues can be addressed in premarital counseling sessions with a mature pastor or other church leader or by a Christian counselor. If the pain or guilt is not dealt with, sooner or later, it will surface in the life of that person through negative words or behavior, often directed toward the spouse. In some way or another, the spouse will inevitably be affected, and the relationship may become damaged or broken.

In another example, suppose a pastor desires to develop leaders for his church from among the members of his fellowship. That pastor will be significantly impeded from fulfilling his purpose if he has constructed a barricade around his heart as a reaction to prior offenses. Because those who have unresolved offenses often mistrust other people, the pastor may find it difficult to mentor potential leaders because of a deep-seated fear that other people will fail him or betray him. As a result, he won't be able to nurture potential leaders, delegate tasks to other people, or otherwise give others authority to act in his place.

Over the years, I have raised up many leaders, a number of whom eventually betrayed me in some way. Their behavior deeply offended me because I didn't expect that of them. However, I had to forgive them. Otherwise, I never would have been able to mentor additional leaders. Each time, God healed my heart, so that I have been able to raise up thousands of leaders from around the world to build the body of Christ and to expand the kingdom of God.

4. Offended People Conform to Their Hurt, Creating a Lifestyle of Pain

Often, an affronted person will unconsciously begin to transform the feelings of offense that caused him to become spiritually and emotionally damaged into a *lifestyle* of pain. As he constructs his wall of separation from others and equips himself with defense mechanisms, he gets used to his new isolated lifestyle. After a while, he "embodies" his feelings of offense—he becomes a "city" of pain fortified by high defensive walls, so that everything he thinks or does from that point forward is generated from that place—that identity—of pain. He refuses to trust others or to open up his heart to them. He may also decline to invest his time and money in worthy purposes because he is unwilling to risk new disappointments or hurts in relation to them. He has become conditioned to, and remade by, his negative experience, so that now he is always subject to pain, unable to attain real happiness.

A person with an offended heart may allow the emotional pain of an affront to become an excuse for refusing to function in certain areas of his life.

The story of a young woman named María who attends our church is a vivid example of how a person can build a lifestyle of pain due to offenses—but then be set free in Jesus! She writes, "I was born in Cuba. My life was in danger even before I was born because my mother wanted to abort me. Moreover, while she was still pregnant with me, she had an accident in which she fell down three flights of stairs but did not lose me. Because I survived, after I was born, she offered my life to the service of the saints in a religion called Santería.

"Years later, my father found a way to bring us to the United States to live. When I was nine years old, I was introduced to the world of the streets. I was exposed to gangs, parties, alcohol, sexual activity, drugs, robbery of homes, abuse, police persecution, and more. During my childhood, my experience at school was horrible. Other children mocked me, causing me to feel anger and hate in my heart and to want vengeance.

"When I was fourteen, my mother moved us away to take me out of that environment, not knowing that things were only going to get worse in the new place. I joined a gang, went to nightclubs, ran away from home, drank alcohol without restraint, used hard drugs, and never attended classes. I tried to commit suicide three times. I suffered two drug overdoses, was involved in major sexual activity with young men and women alike, and practiced Wicca. I thought I had the world under my feet, but the truth was that I was a slave to sin and of the one who produces it.

"By age seventeen, I had met the 'perfect' man. He told me that he was twenty-one years old and that he had fallen in love with me at first sight. His personality was captivating. He was a smooth talker, and his understanding manner made me fall in love with him, so I gave him my innocence. In time, I realized that it was all a lie—he was thirty years old and had three children. Even then, I wanted to marry him. But because our relationship was a lie, it led me to feel great hatred toward men. I felt that my life made no sense.

"However, in the midst of that dark night, I had two parents who prayed for me, for they had turned to Christ a few years earlier. One day, I attended a miracle crusade of evangelist Benny Hinn, and I said to God, 'If I am Yours, do something before I leave.' At that moment, my bones began to tremble. I started to cry uncontrollably, and, even though I didn't understand what was happening, I felt so good! The Holy Spirit had descended upon my life. Later that night, I was set free and transformed. I let go of my old lifestyle and became a new creation.

"Almost six years have passed, and I am blessed. I have identity and purpose. Above all, I am very in love with Jesus. Never in my life would I have believed that this was going to happen to me. I am living the best days of my life. If God did it for me, He can certainly do it for you."

If you, too, have conformed your life to past hurts and have created a lifestyle of pain, you can be set free though the power of God's Holy Spirit as you give up your offenses, forgive others, and receive God's forgiveness and grace through Christ.

5. Offended People Cannot Receive the Anointing of God

I have experienced the manifest presence of God and have ministered under that presence, and there have been times when I have laid hands on people and felt the anointing return to me as if it had collided against a wall. That is a sign of a heart that has been closed due to offenses and is therefore unable to receive God's anointing or experience the transformation that the anointing works in the inner being.

Likewise, I have preached messages in the power of the Holy Spirit that have transformed the lives of thousands of people in attendance, while others who were present in the same place and under the same anointing continued to have problems in their finances, family, health, or another area. I believe they experienced no change because, when the anointing fell and the Word was preached, they couldn't enter into that anointing or remain in it due to an offense (or offenses) that had contaminated their heart. Similarly, if a person holds on to an offense against a leader who is his God-given authority, he shouldn't expect to inherit the anointing of that leader someday, because no one can carry the anointing of a vessel of God that he did not honor and has perhaps even rejected.

6. Offended People Are Prevented from Reaching Their Purpose and Destiny

When a believer is offended, he does not live in the eternal "present" of God but rather dwells in the past—he remains trapped in the moment when he took offense. In this state, it is impossible for him to fulfill his God-given purpose. Let's look at the Old Testament example of Moses, who had a glorious ministry. By God's power, Moses did extraordinary miracles, including supernaturally freeing hundreds of thousands of Israelites from Egyptian slavery and leading them toward the Promised Land.

But, one day, he became offended by the people because of their unbelief. His offense was justifiable. He had every right to feel righteous anger. The Israelites were in the Wilderness of Zin (see Numbers 20:1), and the Scriptures tell us, *"Now there was no water for the congregation; so they gathered together against Moses and Aaron....Then Moses lifted his hand and struck the rock twice with his rod; and water came out abundantly, and the congregation and their animals drank"* (Numbers 20:2, 11).

The patriarch made several mistakes during this incident. First, his action was motivated by the offense. He did not obey the instructions of the Lord, who had told him to *speak* to the rock—not to strike it—so that water would flow from it. (See Numbers 20:8.) Years earlier, God had told Moses to strike a rock in order to bring forth water for the people (see Exodus 17:1–7), but that was not His instruction this time. We must always heed what God is saying to us in the present. Second, Moses erred by indicating to the people that he himself would perform the miracle: *"Hear now, you rebels! Must we bring water for you out of this rock?"* (Numbers 20:10). And third, he operated the power of God in anger rather than in righteousness and truth.

Tragically, when Moses sinned after taking offense at the people's rebellion, it cost him his entry into the Promised Land. *"Then the LORD spoke to Moses and Aaron, 'Because you did not believe Me, to hallow Me in the eyes of the children of Israel, therefore you shall not bring this assembly into the land which I have given them'"* (Numbers 20:12).

Moving to the New Testament, let us look at the case of the rich young ruler who went to Jesus because he wanted to know how to attain heaven or to find out what else he must do in order to earn it. He missed his opportunity to enter the kingdom of God and follow Jesus because of corruption in his heart that caused him, in a sense, to become offended with Jesus' reply, so that he rejected God's will for his life.

> [The rich young ruler asked Jesus,] *"Good Teacher, what shall I do that I may inherit eternal life?"…*[Jesus] *said to him, "…You know the commandments: 'Do not commit adultery,' 'Do not murder,' 'Do not steal,' 'Do not bear false witness,' 'Do not defraud,' 'Honor your father and your mother.'" And he answered and said to Him, "Teacher, all these things I have kept from my youth." Then Jesus, looking at him, loved him, and said to him, "One thing you lack: Go your way, sell whatever you have and give to the poor, and you will have treasure in heaven; and come, take up the cross, and follow Me." But he was sad at this word, and went away sorrowful, for he had great possessions.*
> (Mark 10:17–22)

That young man turned away from Jesus because the love of money had become his master—it had taken over his heart. Christ stood before the young man as *El Shaddai,* a Hebrew term that indicates "the One who is more than enough." Therefore, if the young man had given up all that he had, God would have become more than enough to him. But his wealth blinded him. The challenge from Jesus tested the condition of his heart and measured how much he was really willing to surrender to God—and what his limit was.

If the young man had given up all his wealth, Christ would have returned it to him a hundredfold. Directly after this incident, Jesus said to Peter,

> *Assuredly, I say to you, there is no one who has left house or brothers or sisters or father or mother or wife or children or lands, for My sake and the gospel's, who shall not receive a hundredfold now in this time—houses and brothers and sisters and mothers and children and lands, with persecutions—and in the age to come, eternal life.*
> (Mark 10:29–30)

If it offends you to give to God, then it should also offend you to receive from Him.

Whatever you give to God's kingdom, the Lord will return to you 100 percent. The rich young ruler believed that what he owned belonged to him, but the truth is that we human beings are just stewards of everything God gives us; we are the administrators of His goods. However, if our heart becomes corrupted by a love of money, we will not give our resources to the Lord as an act of worship. Instead, we will use our money to gratify our sinful nature. We will allow our love of money to exert power over us, and it will define our life—it will define *us*. To keep our heart from becoming corrupted in this way, we must seek God first in our life, surrendering to Him and exercising self-control over what we do with our money and the way in which we spend it, so that we can invest our finances in His kingdom and toward other positive purposes.

Some people become offended when they are asked to support various ministries of their church, to make a donation to help the poor, to fund relief efforts to assist those who are victims of a natural disaster, or to do anything else that may not be to their personal profit or give them pleasure. Yet they aren't offended when they receive a bill requiring a car payment on their luxury automobile, when they are handed their receipt after purchasing expensive clothes or fashion accessories, or when they must pay admission to a sports event or another form of entertainment.

If an individual is insulted when someone teaches from the Bible about financial stewardship, the likely reason is that the person considers his true "god" to be under attack. I have seen people leave a church service just before the offering is collected. Their behavior indicates that having money is their priority. They are not concerned with being a steward of God's resources; rather, they believe they personally own the resources God has provided for them.

If God has blessed you with financial resources, I believe that you and your family should be able to enjoy them; however, your first priority should be God and the expansion of His kingdom. (See Matthew 6:33.)

There are many people who, having received abundant financial blessing from God after they were delivered from the curse of poverty—and after they learned that the key to prosperity is to sow finances into the work of God's kingdom—stopped giving to God once their finances prospered! Why? Probably because it hadn't been difficult for them to give God a tithe of their income when it amounted to $100 a week, but it became very difficult for them when the tithe totaled thousands of dollars. The true condition of their heart was revealed when they ceased to be faithful in their tithes and offerings, and when they placed a limit on what they were willing to give God. Accordingly, those people should not be offended if God puts a limit on His provision for them. We cannot expect God to pour out abundance on us while we give Him our "leftovers."

7. Offended People May Be Removed from God's Presence

When the first human beings sinned, God was offended—in a holy sense. His righteousness was offended by their sin and betrayal. It was necessary for Him to expel them from His presence; yet, at the same time, He announced His plan of redemption for humanity through Jesus Christ. Whenever we commit sin—including the transgression of holding on to an offense—we need to be restored to a right relationship with our heavenly Father. We can be assured of that restoration as we accept Christ's sacrifice on our behalf and receive forgiveness through Him. "*If anyone sins, we have an Advocate with the Father, Jesus Christ the righteous. And He Himself is the propitiation for our sins*" (1 John 2:1–2).

We must release any offenses we are holding on to, because we cannot remain in God's presence with offenses in our heart! The reason some people do not feel the nearness of God is that they have been trying to present themselves to Him while, at the same time, they are harboring offenses. Sometimes, they aren't even aware that they are doing so. This is a primary reason why we must regularly monitor the condition of our heart according to God's Word and allow His Spirit to convict us of sin so that our heart may be transformed.

Always remember that you have full access to redemption in Jesus Christ. Do not isolate yourself from God's grace, which enables you to be forgiven by Him, to be restored to Him, and to begin anew in Him.

Additionally, because we have been forgiven and reconciled to God in Christ, we, too, can forgive others who have offended us, and we can seek reconciliation with them, because His grace works in us *"both to will and to do for His good pleasure"* (Philippians 2:13).

The Solution for Offenses

Because offenses are inevitable in our fallen world but are also opportunities for us to discern the state of our heart, the healthiest thing for us to do when we are offended is to deal with the issue immediately. Therefore, right now—before any new offense occurs—make a conscious decision that you will forgive anyone who offends you in the future, and that you will pursue reconciliation with anyone whom you offend in the future. If you neglect to do this, your relationships will be weak—and brief.

The following steps, which are based on what we have discussed in this chapter, will enable you to be liberated from the trap of offense.

1. Confess Your Offenses

"Confess your trespasses to one another, and pray for one another, that you may be healed. The effective, fervent prayer of a righteous man avails much" (James 5:16). To be free of offenses, confession is necessary—first, confession to God; and, second, confession to those whom we have offended and those who have offended us. If we are truly contrite, we should express our repentance. So, begin by confessing before God that you have held on to offenses in your heart, acknowledging that they are sins against Him and other people. Only through confession can the process of healing begin in your heart.

2. Ask God to Forgive You, and Forgive Those Who Have Offended You

It is important not only to confess our offenses but also to ask God to forgive us for them and to forgive ourselves and others for the offenses that have been committed. If we don't go beyond confessing the offenses in our heart, our "confession" may turn into a bitter complaint, serving only to verbalize our resentment but not heal it. Forgiveness is the antidote that will bring healing. So, again, we should ask God and others to forgive us for our offenses, and we should forgive everyone who has ever offended us.

We should practice forgiveness as a lifestyle.

---

3. Die to "Self" and the Sinful Nature

If we want to progress to greater dimensions of God's power and glory, we must give up our self-centeredness that demands a right to compensation and/or vengeance when a wrong has been committed against us. To be "dead to self" means that we withhold nothing from God; He is the Lord of our heart, soul, mind, strength, finances—everything! We no longer belong to ourselves but to Him.

In addition, we must die to the sinful nature by not letting it control us but rather allowing the life of Christ and God's Holy Spirit to direct our thoughts and empower our actions:

> *I have been crucified with Christ; it is no longer I who live, but Christ lives in me; and the life which I now live in the flesh I live by faith in the Son of God, who loved me and gave Himself for me....Those who are Christ's have crucified the flesh with its passions and desires. If we live in the Spirit, let us also walk in the Spirit.*
> (Galatians 2:20; 5:24–25)

When you have died to your sinful nature, you will no longer be easily offended; you will not be affronted by trivial matters. When you have died to self, you will have released your self-absorption, surrendering your life to your loving Creator and His purposes. You will know that, when a true offense occurs, God will ultimately bring about justice in the circumstance and/or use the offense for good in your life. *"And we know that all things work together for good to those who love God, to those who are the called according to His purpose"* (Romans 8:28).

4. Commit to Maturity

It is time to leave immaturity behind so that we may grow stronger, spiritually and emotionally. As we mature, those offenses that used to gnaw at our inner being will no longer find a way to stay within our heart. We will consider it irrelevant and unnecessary to spend time on such matters, not wanting to risk the health of our soul for the sake of a mere offense. We will have the love and patience to understand that those who offend us must travel the road toward maturity, just as we must.

The following is the story of Kenneth, who constructed and maintained a barrier against God for years before receiving deliverance and the healing of his heart. Kenneth writes, "In 1997, I was working in a chemical plant in New Jersey when I was in an accident that almost took my life. I was trapped inside a machine for six hours. One of my arms suffered serious damage, and a tube pierced my chest. When I was rescued, the doctors and other emergency personnel couldn't believe that I had survived.

"What is certain is that while I was inside the machine, I kept hearing a voice that said, 'Give up. God doesn't love you! You were always a nice person; there is no reason for Him to do this to you. If you surrender now, the pain will go away.' Then I heard a second voice say to me, 'If God wanted to kill you, He would have done it by now. Giving up is your decision.' It was then that I decided not to give up, but I still felt that God was unfair, and I was very angry with Him. For a long time, I chose not to speak to Him because of all the years of suffering I endured after the accident, during which I underwent thirteen surgeries and physical therapy.

"One day, my cousin invited me to King Jesus church, and I decided to receive the Lord as my Savior. In 2006, I moved to Florida to begin a new life, and there all my dreams came true. I studied for a career in criminal justice. I also met my wife, who attended King Jesus church, and I began to attend the church, too. One day, during worship at a prayer meeting in someone's house, a brother saw a wall tumbling down all around me. I had seen that wall as it was being built, many years earlier, and it kept me from communicating with the Lord—until that day. From that point on, I have been able to talk to God.

"In 2008, my wife was diagnosed with myosarcoma of the uterus. Two oncologists said the uterus had to be removed, but we believed that God had other plans, so we did not allow it. We had faith in God, and, not long afterward, my wife became pregnant and gave birth to our beautiful daughter. God healed my heart and gave me a full life."

Prayer to Forgive

An offense is a trap of the enemy designed to hurt us and to isolate us—separating our heart from God and damaging our relationships with other people. Offenses will hinder our ability to advance God's kingdom in the world and will encumber our progress in life. I invite you to be liberated from offenses as you allow God to remove the emotional torture you suffer from living in a prison of mistrust, anger, fear, and confusion. Repeat the following simple but powerful prayer. But don't pray it just once. Pray it every day, so that the truths of God's revelation concerning offenses may be established in your life.

Heavenly Father, I come into Your presence today as Your child. I acknowledge and confess that I have kept offenses and wounds in my heart. I repent of this practice, and I turn away from it. Right now, I forgive everyone who has ever offended me, and I ask You to forgive me for my offenses.

I also die to "self," including the attitude of self-absorption that seeks retribution or vengeance when I am offended. I make a conscious decision to die to my sinful nature so that the life of Christ and God's Holy Spirit may direct my thoughts and empower my actions.

I commit to move to the next level of maturity. What used to offend me will no longer offend me. I will not remain a spiritual "infant" but will grow in grace and become more like Christ. Help me to walk in love and to have a forgiving heart toward my family members, my friends, and my brothers and sisters in Christ. Remove every offense, wound, and pain from me. Make me free! I receive Your forgiveness, healing, and deliverance. In the name of Jesus, amen!

Now that you have prayed this prayer, be sure to follow it up with an act of faith that confirms your commitment. Talk to someone whom you have offended, or who offended you, and do what you can to restore the relationship through forgiveness, reconciliation, and peace.

6

Freedom from a Heart of Unbelief

God has given me the privilege and blessing of proclaiming the gospel in more than fifty countries around the world. I have preached to people of various cultures, races, languages, ages, and social strata. Over the years, I have found two things in common among these varied groups of people: (1) they all have the same human needs; and (2) the greatest obstacle to their receiving salvation, healing, miracles, or any other blessing from God is the presence of unbelief in their heart. Many people struggle to believe in God, His nature, and/or His power. Their difficulty reminds me of the man in the New Testament who sought deliverance for his son, telling the Lord Jesus, *"I believe"* (Mark 9:24) yet immediately adding, *"Help my unbelief!"* (Mark 9:24). In effect, what the man was saying was, "I believe, but I find it very hard to do!"

Struggling with Faith

Perhaps you have experienced the same struggle to believe God. For example, is it hard for you to have faith for the salvation of your family? Do you find it challenging to believe that God will provide for your material needs? Is it difficult for you to perceive God as your Healer and Deliverer—and to receive Him as such? Do you wrestle with doubts that God exists? If you answered yes to any of these questions, the reason might be that, even though you may have a general faith in Christ for salvation, some unbelief is still entrenched in your heart, and this lack of faith holds you back from living in true freedom and receiving the spiritual and physical blessings that God desires to give you.

Unbelief Is a "Departure from the Living God"

In chapter 4, we noted that unbelief is one of the causes of a hardened heart. The Scriptures say, *"Beware, brethren, lest there be in any of you an evil heart of unbelief in departing from the living God"* (Hebrews 3:12). Many people attempt to address unbelief from the standpoint of their mind alone. Yet unbelief is not so much a condition of the mind as it is a condition of the heart that influences the mind—its intellect, reason, and thoughts. Just as in the case of holding on to offenses, unbelief will cause our heart to harden, preventing us from believing what God has said and from receiving His promises and provision. And, a hardened heart subsequently produces further unbelief.

Throughout this book, we have seen that every aspect of our life originates in the heart. Whether we are praying, worshipping, fellowshipping, serving others, caring for our children, managing our home, working at our job, participating in sports or hobbies, or anything else—who we are and what we do comes from our heart. If our heart is full of unbelief, many of our endeavors will be in vain. In spiritual matters, we will be functioning according to "religion," which, as we have seen, is merely an appearance of piety that lacks true power. Works that are not birthed by faith are ultimately dead works. (See James 2:17.) When we "[depart] *from the living God"* in unbelief, our heart becomes corrupted, negatively affecting our life. Yet, the more we deal with the issues of our heart and allow God to transform us, the more evidence we will see of His healing, deliverance, prosperity, peace, and joy in our life.

Unbelief causes the heart to harden, and a hardened heart produces further unbelief.

The Origin of Unbelief

One of the Greek terms translated as *"unbelief"* in the New Testament is *apistia*. This word includes the following meanings: "faithlessness, i.e. disbelief (lack of Christian faith), or unfaithfulness (disobedience)." *Apistia* is derived from another Greek word that means "disbelieving" and indicates "without Christian faith (especially a heathen)," or an "untrustworthy person." From these definitions, we may conclude that unbelief signifies more than a mere intellectual absence of belief—it can signal a heart of unfaithfulness toward God and His Word. It can demonstrate a disloyalty in which we doubt the nature and character of our loving, powerful, and righteous God.

Doubting God Is the Root of Unbelief—and Subsequent Disobedience

Before the fall, the first human beings lived like trusting children; they accepted what God told them without question or argument. They weren't contaminated by sin, so their heart, soul, and body, while living in the natural world, functioned according to the life of the supernatural realm—above and beyond the physical realm. They didn't struggle with a mind-set of doubt leading to perpetual sickness, poverty, oppression, and so forth, as many human beings today do.

We know that the disobedience of the first man and woman occurred when they questioned the truth of God's words but believed the lies of Satan. In chapter 3, we talked about the importance of having both trust and belief in our heart toward God. Adam and Eve allowed the enemy to undermine both of these crucial heart elements, leading to their act of unfaithfulness to their Creator.

Throughout Scripture, we see that many people who were disobedient to God first exhibited unbelief, and the same situation occurs today. When our faith is active, we are faithful and obedient to God, because we trust in His plans for our good, and we know that obeying Him will bring positive results in our life. In contrast, when our faith is inactive, we can become unfaithful, hardhearted, and disobedient toward God. When our heart is hard, God cannot trust us to pursue His will and to be good stewards of what He has given us. If you identify unfaithfulness, hardheartedness, and disobedience in your heart, a spirit of unbelief may be at the root of them.

The Fallen Mind Questions God

The Scriptures say that God placed two distinct trees in the garden of Eden. "*And out of the ground the* LORD *God made every tree grow that is pleasant to the sight and good for food. The tree of life was also in the midst of the garden, and the tree of the knowledge of good and evil*" (Genesis 2:9). And Adam and Eve violated the following commandment, which God had instituted for their good: "*Of every tree of the garden you may freely eat; but of the tree of the knowledge of good and evil you shall not eat, for in the day that you eat of it you shall surely die*" (Genesis 2:16–17).

I believe that the Tree of Knowledge of Good and Evil represents natural, mental, and sensorial (relating to the five senses) knowledge—involving the intellect and reason. This level of knowledge operates purely in the physical realm, or the material world. When human beings fell by partaking of the fruit of that tree in disobedience, their spirit withered and receded, and their mind began to rely only on reason and intellect, which are not adequate for understanding or discerning the supernatural realm. They "[fell] *short of the glory of God*" (see Romans 3:23) and thereby fell short of the supernatural knowledge and eternal perspective they formerly had through their vital connection with God and close relationship with Him.

The intellect and reason are God-given gifts to human beings to enable them to function in the physical world, but, again, they are not sufficient on their own. Additionally, when the intellect and reason are detached from God by the curse of sin and are controlled by the sinful nature, they are woefully flawed. The fallen mind, devoid of supernatural knowledge and wisdom, will doubt the existence and power of God and question His purposes. The fallen mind often becomes hostile to God, or "anti-God." "*But the natural man does not receive the things of the Spirit of God, for they are foolishness to him; nor can he know them, because they are spiritually discerned*" (1 Corinthians 2:14).

In contrast, God's supernatural knowledge and wisdom operate not in the mind but in the heart—in the spirit of a person who has been made alive through Jesus Christ by the Holy Spirit. (See John 3:5.) If a believer's heart is hardened by unbelief, it demonstrates that he has, in some way, not fully turned away from the Tree of Knowledge of Good and Evil and is "feeding" on it rather than on Jesus, the *"bread of life"* (John 6:35, 48). If we find this to be our condition, we need to repent, allowing God to soften our heart and to fill us with the *"spirit of faith"* (2 Corinthians 4:13), so that we may enter into full faith and complete trust in our heavenly Father and receive all that He desires to give us.

Until a person is free of an unbelieving heart, he will not be able to understand spiritual, or supernatural, realities.

Three Types of Unbelief

As I have studied the Scriptures, I have identified three different ways in which people can manifest unbelief. Let us explore these ways, examining our own heart to see how unbelief may be influencing us.

1. Unbelief Caused by Ignorance

Ignorance is a basic level of unbelief that all human beings inherit as a result of the fall. For example, the apostle Paul persecuted Christians before he encountered Jesus on the road to Damascus and was converted. Concerning that time in his life, he wrote, *"Although I was formerly a blasphemer, a persecutor, and an insolent ["violent" NIV] man; but I obtained mercy because I did it ignorantly in unbelief"* (1 Timothy 1:13).

It is not just unbelievers but also believers who can fall into unbelief out of ignorance. I think that many of those who genuinely know Christ but work against Him and His purposes do so out of ignorance rather than wickedness. For instance, when they have not yet learned how God's Word applies to a particular realm of life, or to a specific area of their own life, many believers will make mistakes and/or fall into error. All of us have done this at one point or another. Some Christians may remain sick because they don't know that Christ has already paid for their illness on the cross (see Isaiah 53:5), or because they don't understand God's principles for receiving healing (see, for example, James 5:14–16). God forgives this type of unbelief, according to His mercy. As Paul wrote, *"I obtained mercy because I did it ignorantly in unbelief"* (1 Timothy 1:13).

2. Unbelief Caused by Rebellion in the Heart

"And to whom did [God] *swear that they would not enter His rest, but to those who did not obey? So we see that they could not enter in because of unbelief"* (Hebrews 3:18–19). Rebellion is a form of disobedience to God that is characterized by a decision not to believe in Him or trust in His Word. A rebellious person raises his fist against the Creator of the universe and says, "I don't believe in You, and I don't need You in my life. I can live independently of You. I will live my own way."

Due to their hardheartedness, rebellious people decide of their own free will not to believe God but to doubt and reject His promises and provisions, including salvation, protection, healing, and deliverance. Their hardheartedness is often a result of their having experienced rejection, betrayal, abuse, or some other difficulty or suffering at the hands of another person or persons. For example, when the Israelites were delivered by God from slavery in Egypt, they witnessed His miracles, signs, and wonders in the desert. The Lord fed them every day with supernatural bread called *"manna."* (See Exodus 16:14–15, 31.) Twice, when the people had no water, God quenched their thirst by causing water to pour from a rock. (See Exodus 17:5–6; Numbers 20:8–11.) Their clothes and sandals never wore out. (See Deuteronomy 29:5.) The Lord's presence was with them during the day in a *"pillar of cloud"* that led the way and also protected them from the heat of the sun, as well as during the night in a *"pillar of fire"* that provided light for them to travel and protected them from the nighttime cold. (See Exodus 13:21–22.) And God did many other miracles on their behalf.

Yet, even with all the demonstrations of God's provision, protection, and care, the Israelites frequently chose, in open acts of rebellion, not to believe Him. Consequently, the generation that was delivered from Egypt never entered into the Promised Land—only their descendants did, with the exception of faithful Joshua and Caleb. I believe the reason is that the hearts of the people had been hardened by the slavery they had suffered under all their lives, and they did not release that hardness of heart to the Lord so that He could heal it.

Similarly, many Christians today refuse to believe God, even though He has shown them His love and grace. The Lord has been extraordinarily good to us! He has saved us eternally through His Son Jesus Christ; and He has loved us, provided for us, protected us, and healed us. Many of us have seen Him perform remarkable works in our own life, in the lives of our family members, among the people in our church, and in our community. We have seen, heard, and experienced His supernatural power—yet we still doubt! Such unbelief in the midst of God's goodness may be a sign of a rebellious heart. As we discussed in an earlier chapter, when an individual chooses not to believe in what God has promised, he is, in essence, calling God a liar. Calling someone a liar is one of the worst of insults. How do you think God feels when we disrespect Him by refusing to believe Him?

Rebellion is a decision not to believe in God or trust in His Word.

A heart of unbelief can take over a person's life. *"For as* [a person] *thinks in his heart, so is he"* (Proverbs 23:7). An unbelieving heart paves its own way. It relies on its own judgment, while rejecting God's wisdom. Each decision we make in our own strength and ability alone is a sign of our faithlessness and our independence from God. Generally, I have found that when an individual lives independently of God, he ends in failure. If he eventually seeks God, it is when life turns against him and he reaches rock bottom, having lost everything he once valued.

When a person has a hard heart of unbelief, God will sometimes allow certain adverse situations to take place in his life—situations that go beyond his control, leaving him powerless to fix them—because that is the only way to break down his hardheartedness, prompting the individual to humble himself and to surrender to the Lord so that he may be saved and delivered.

Any lack of faith toward God produces negative consequences—sometimes terrible ones—in a person's life. Some people think they can continue to live in rebellion against God and His Word without suffering any consequences, but the Scriptures are clear that those who persist in unbelief will ultimately be punished. Living in rebellion has a price in this life and in the one to come—eternal separation from God in hell: *"But the cowardly, **unbelieving**, abominable, murderers, sexually immoral, sorcerers, idolaters, and all liars shall have their part in the lake which burns with fire and brimstone, which is the second death"* (Revelation 21:8). Carefully review the above list of those who will keep the *"unbelieving"* company in eternity. God judges unbelief as harshly as idolatry, sorcery, and murder!

If God has been speaking to you through a family member, friend, coworker, fellow student, or someone else about being reconciled to Him and receiving Christ, don't harden your heart! Surrender it to God now and renounce your unbelief, so you won't end up in that place of torment.

Born-again children of God cannot remain indifferent to unbelief in their heart, either. Nothing in our life or in our relationship with Christ will have value if we don't conduct ourselves according to faith. (See Hebrews 11:6.) Be free of unbelief! Paul wrote, *"We walk by faith, not by sight"* (2 Corinthians 5:7). Without faith, we will live only by sight, which often causes us to fear the future. So, stop questioning God, His Word, and His promises. Decide to believe Him now, and He will fulfill what He has promised.

A man named Roberto shared the following testimony about his long-term physical infirmity and what happened when he took a step of faith:

"When I was six years old, the needle of a syringe pierced my left eye, causing it to hemorrhage greatly. I was taken to the emergency room, where I was operated on immediately. To save my eyeball, doctors cut the optical vein, leaving me blind in that eye.

"I spent thirty-seven years blind in the left eye, and I had grown used to it. All I could see out of the eye was a dark shadow, so I often bumped into things when I walked. When I went to get my driver's license in order to drive an eighteen-wheeler, I was given a restricted license that permitted me to drive only during the day. This limited my opportunities at my job.

"Though I believed in the power of God, I had simply accepted my disability. But, one day, my friends invited me to a service at King Jesus church. At some point, a call for healing was made. I didn't want to go forward, but my friends insisted. Finally, I decided to go, and, once I was at the front, I closed my eyes and heard Pastor Maldonado declare, 'Blind eyes, see!' I then felt my hands go directly to my eyes, and, instantly, I felt 'fire' burning me, and I fell to the floor under the power of God. Suddenly, within me, I heard a voice that said, *You will see again*. When I got up and opened my eyes, my vision was clear and perfect. My left eye, through which I had been able to see only a dark shadow, now registered the splendor of light, people, and objects around me.

"Emotional, I shared my testimony with deep gratefulness to God. I had stopped believing that God could heal me. I had grown used to the idea of living semi-blind. Today, I feel like a new man, and I know that God is the only One who could have healed me because, according to medical science, regaining my eyesight was impossible."

Unbelief is the highest expression of disrespect and dishonor toward God, because when we refuse to believe Him, we essentially call Him a liar.

---

3. Unbelief Caused by a Wicked Spirit

The third type of unbelief is, effectively, an extension of the previous one. Some people have practiced unbelief for so long that they have opened the door for a demonic spirit of unbelief—a wicked spirit from Satan—to corrupt their heart and take control of them. When Jesus was asked by some religious leaders if He was the Messiah, He confirmed that He was the Son of God and said, *"I and my Father are one"* (John 10:30). The leaders protested, claiming that Jesus' words were blasphemy. In their stubbornness of heart, they missed the signs that Jesus was indeed the true Messiah—and that He was God in human form.

God the Father had audibly testified from heaven that Jesus was His beloved Son (see, for example, Matthew 3:16–17), but these religious leaders refused to believe it, and they became God's enemies. Similarly, today, many church leaders and other Christians don't fully acknowledge what it means for Christ to be the Messiah, and they don't believe that He still does miracles for God's people, putting them at odds with the purposes and works of God.

Unbelief plagues the human race, and Satan would like to keep it that way. When humanity disobeyed God in the garden, it was as if the spirit of unbelief eagerly purchased shares in hell's stock market. When the Messiah came to earth to redeem humanity, and the religious leaders and the people rejected Him and cried out, *"Crucify Him, crucify Him!"* (Luke 23:21; John 19:6), it was as if those shares went through the roof. However, when Jesus was gloriously raised from the dead, the value of those shares plummeted as Jesus *"led captivity captive"* (Ephesians 4:8), freeing humanity from the grip of sin and unbelief. Those who thought they had finally triumphed over Jesus were defeated, being spiritually bankrupt.

If you invest your heart in disbelieving God and His Son Jesus, you will lose your soul, because Jesus is the eternal Conqueror. Yet, if you realize that a wicked spirit of unbelief has been controlling your life, you can repent, renounce your unbelief, receive Christ as your Savior and Lord, and then bind and cast out the spirit of unbelief in the name of Jesus, so that you can be delivered. Don't risk your soul over unbelief!

We Have Been Taught Unbelief

Unbelief is a consequence of the fall that afflicts every human being. Yet we are also taught—directly and indirectly—to disbelieve God through the influence of our society, our schools, and a number of our churches.

Our Cultural Mind-set Elevates Reason Above God

Generally, the Western mind-set attempts to explain life through reason, logic, and science. In and of themselves, these faculties are inadequate to deal with the whole man, which consists of spirit, soul, and body. We are trained to doubt whatever doesn't fit neatly into the framework of the material world—and that includes God, the spiritual realm, and God's supernatural power. In some cases, false spiritual and supernatural beliefs are accepted, while the Bible and its teachings about Jesus are frequently considered suspect.

In general, modern science has detached itself from faith in God, so that it often dismisses whatever cannot be explained through facts based on natural evidence alone. It may not accept the reality of the spiritual world, so that it discards the idea of it or classifies it as myth. Accordingly, it doubts any spiritual phenomenon that cannot be understood through the intellect; or, it considers that phenomenon to be irrelevant to science, beyond the parameters of its inquiry.

Many people have made reason their god.

Furthermore, much of our modern educational system is designed to train students' intellect alone, teaching them mere facts and information, and essentially ignoring their spirit. Facts and information can be useful for living in a physical world; for example, they enable us to function effectively under the various laws and principles governing the natural realm, by which our physical planet operates. And, education itself is good—it is beneficial to learn how to analyze and to create, to acquire information and facts, to prepare for a career, and to gain skills that will enable us to prosper in life.

Yet, again, most of what is taught is meant only for the mind, not the heart, even though spiritual and emotional subjects and various creative functions cannot be addressed by the intellect and reason alone. Regardless of the subject matter and the realm to which it belongs—mental, physical, emotional, or spiritual—our educational process usually filters concepts solely through the intellect, thereby restricting the extent to which the student can apply the teaching to his life and, most important, limiting the student's understanding of that subject matter in relation to his Creator. Thus, many students live without a concept of God, so that the modern educational system has birthed "educated unbelief."

Therefore, the mind-set of our culture and our educational system has played a part in robbing us of the knowledge of God and His supernatural revelation and power. The result is that the hearts of many people have been corrupted by a lack of faith or have even become controlled by unbelief. Knowing this, those who are parents of school-age and college-age children should exercise wisdom and prepare their sons and daughters for attending school in such an environment, so their children can learn to receive what is *good* in their education and reject what is contrary to the Word of God. I want to reemphasize that I am not saying that education itself is bad. However, the spirit that operates behind most education today is, in effect, anti-God.

The modern educational system has birthed "educated unbelief."

Some Denominations, Churches, and Pastors Deny the Supernatural

In addition to being influenced by the scientific mind-set of our culture and our reason-based educational system, believers are often influenced to doubt God by the church itself—by ministers, churches, and denominations within the body of Christ. For example, a pastor may teach the doctrine of a particular denomination that attests that supernatural miracles were for the time of Jesus and His disciples alone and are not available to us today. He does not affirm Jesus' statement, *"He who believes in Me, the works that I do he will do also; and greater works than these he will do, because I go to My Father"* (John 14:12). Another pastor may teach that the miracles recorded in the Bible did not really happen but are "illustrations" of spiritual truths. The implication of these pastors' positions is that God "won't" or "can't" intervene with His grace and power in our contemporary world.

What I think is happening is that a spirit of unbelief has taken control in various churches, causing people to operate by intellectual knowledge alone, rather than by revealed, or spiritual, knowledge. To essentially state that something is impossible for our all-powerful God, especially when He has already demonstrated His ability to do it, is to contradict the nature and character of God. A large portion of the church of Jesus Christ today functions according to this mentality, justifying its lack of power by erroneous doctrine that is incapable of producing spiritual fruit that lasts. (See John 15:16 NIV.) Therefore, many pastors do not experience God's supernatural power because the unbelief in their heart prevents them—and subsequently their congregations—from doing so.

During the time Christ lived on the earth, a similar condition existed in the Pharisees who imagined they were dedicating themselves exclusively to the things of God but were merely following religious rituals. Jesus compared them to *"whitewashed tombs"* (Matthew 23:27) because there was no faith or life in their words. They taught the people unbelief because they served only the letter of God's Word but lacked the Spirit of it. (See Romans 7:6.)

Who Has the Final Word?

As a result of the prevailing cultural mind-set, the educational process, and erroneous religious belief, most people allow the fields of science and medicine, as well as other realms of human knowledge, to have the final word—and, often, the only word—in their lives. If they are sick, they merely go to the doctor. If they need money, they apply for a loan from a bank or go to a finance company to reorganize and streamline their debt. If their business is stagnant, they seek marketing, advertising, and publicity strategies; new products; modern technology; and so forth. If they have a child who is rebellious, they send him to a psychologist. If they feel depressed, they take a prescribed antidepressant.

If none of the above approaches is successful in addressing their problem, they feel there is nothing left that can be done, because they have been taught to depend solely on what reason, medicine, and science can do. The cultural mind-set and educational process have taught them what is possible and impossible—according to natural, temporal, and physical conditions. Their doctor may have told them that they have a terminal illness and that there is no cure, so they have to accept the diagnosis. Their reason then confirms that there's nothing left to be done. Or, their bank may have told them that it is going to repossess their house, and their lawyer may have explained that they have no alternative but to leave their home. Their reason may tell them they have to admit to the inevitability of the situation because they have "no way" to come up with the money. Or, perhaps their marriage has been in crisis mode for years, and they have begun to contemplate divorce. The love between husband and wife has grown cold, and neither marriage counselors nor psychologists have been able to help the couple to find a solution. Therefore, they have come to accept the idea that their marriage has ended, believing that it is "impossible" for the relationship to improve. Regardless of how much they might try, there is no way to save it.

Many people who are faced with such situations do not think of praying for healing, financial provision, or spiritual or emotional deliverance— or of asking others to pray for a miracle. But God dwells above and beyond human reason, medicine, and science! Many medical and scientific resources are excellent and enable us to enjoy good health and various advancements and conveniences. However, they can never substitute for the love and power that God our Creator wants to give us. We have to make Christ our priority and turn to Him first when we are in need. Jesus must be number one in our life, not second (or third, or fourth, or fifth…). He doesn't want to be our last and desperate option "when all else fails."

Reason and science have established limits on what is possible and what is impossible for us in this natural world.

When Jesus' mother, Mary, was told by the angel Gabriel that she would give birth to *"the Son of the Highest"* whose kingdom would never end (see Luke 1:26–33), she asked, *"How can this be…?"* (Luke 1:34). Many people today are asking the same question regarding something God has promised. If Mary—a pure young woman who loved God and found grace in His presence to bring His Son into the world—could ask *"How…?"* then we, also, will have times when we question God and His ways. Yet the point is not that Mary asked how the angel's words could come to pass. The point is, after she received the angel's explanation—which was impossible according to human reasoning—she trusted God fully and spoke from her spirit, saying, *"Behold the maidservant of the Lord! Let it be to me according to your word"* (Luke 1:38). Now is the time for you to follow Mary's example and say to God, "Let it be to me according to Your word," allowing Him to work out the miracle that you so desperately need.

The fallen human intellect doubts that physical healing or other miracles could possibly take place, leading people to ask questions such as these: "How could God do the 'impossible'?" "How could God make me well when I have an incurable disease?" "How could God restore my marriage when my husband and I no longer love each other?" "How could God cause my ex-husband to be a real father to our child when he abandoned both me and our daughter many years ago?" "How could God transform my grandchild's rebellious heart so that he will become obedient to his parents and begin to honor them?"

We try to understand how God might be able to intervene in a particular situation, and if we can't come up with a rational means by which it could be accomplished, we give way to unbelief. So, the question "How?" becomes a stronghold of unbelief in our life. God may not tell us "how" He will answer our prayer or perform the miracle we need. He simply asks us to trust that *"with God all things are possible"* (Matthew 19:26; Mark 10:27). He can provide healing, financial blessings, and renewed love—He knows "how" to do it! The only condition is *"If you can believe…"* (Mark 9:23).

Jesus is all-powerful! *"All authority has been given to* [Him] *in heaven and on earth"* (Matthew 28:18). *"*[God] *put all things under* [Jesus'] *feet, and gave Him to be head over all things to the church"* (Ephesians 1:22). We have limited God's abilities to what we can reason, forgetting that He is *El Shaddai*, "the One who is more than enough"! When we believe, we allow God to perform the miracle—when He wants to do it and how He wants to do it.

Make the decision to remove all limitations you have placed on God based on human reason.

When Emilse's son was born, he suffered a loss of oxygen to his brain, causing him to permanently lose hearing in his left ear. At the age of five, he underwent surgery for an auditory implant, yet the deafness continued. It was hard for Emilse to believe in miracles after seeing her son's condition—when not even surgery had been enough. However, during a healing crusade, I made a specific call for people who needed new ears. Emilse and her son, who was then fourteen years old, came to the front. A minister prayed for him and declared him healed. Later, in a step of faith, the young man covered up his right ear, and the minister stood behind him and clapped to see if he would respond. He did! The power of God was present to heal, and the boy's ear was opened! He had spent fourteen years without the ability to hear, but, in a matter of seconds, God did an amazing miracle by His supernatural power when medical science had no more answers.

Do You Have a Heart of Unbelief?

Can you break through the mental conditioning to which a scientific mind-set, human reason, and religious doctrine have submitted you? Of course you can! You can do so by entering, through faith, into the realm of the supernatural, believing God more than any illness, home repossession, broken relationship, or other problem you may be facing. Humanly speaking, I will not argue that some things seem impossible. But the natural world and everything in it are subject to God's sovereignty and power. And so I ask you: Which report will you choose to believe—man's report or God's?

To help you begin to break through unbelief and believe God's report, let's review the characteristics of a heart of unbelief so that you may examine your heart in relation to them.

1. A Heart of Unbelief Thinks According to the Natural Realm Alone

As we have seen, human intellect or reason supports its conclusions by facts alone, and reason has become the way through which most people today determine what they think is real and true. We have been conditioned to think in that way. Yet, in our world, facts are constantly changing, while truth is eternal—including the absolute truth that Jesus Christ and His supernatural kingdom are real. The kingdom of God is a superior reality to any human fact.

Remember that Jesus said to the man whose son was demon-possessed, *"If you can believe, all things are possible to him who believes"* (Mark 9:23). That's when this father *"cried out and said with tears, 'Lord, I believe; help my unbelief!'"* (Mark 9:24). According to our limited human knowledge and reason, there are impossibilities in this world. However, Jesus said, *"With men it is impossible, but not with God; for with God all things are possible"* (Mark 10:27).

2. A Heart of Unbelief Resists Change

As believers, we are meant to progress from one level of faith to the next, and from one dimension of glory to another; we are intended to be in a constant state of transformation into the likeness of Christ. (See, for example, 2 Corinthians 3:18; Ephesians 4:13.) Yet, a lack of faith in our heart will thwart that transformation. When various challenges come our way as opportunities to transform our heart and mind, we will reject them if we are stuck in the past due to unbelief and have become skeptics concerning our future.

Skepticism is "an attitude of doubt or a disposition to incredulity either in general or toward a particular object." Often, a person whose heart has been hardened by betrayal, abuse, or rebellion will turn skeptical, even when he sees the power of God operating in the lives of others, or even if he has experienced that power himself in the past. He finds it impossible to believe that God would do something in his favor *today*. If this is your situation, you need to resolve your unbelief and reactivate the process of transformation that leads you to Christlikeness and complete trust in God.

3. A Heart of Unbelief Blocks Miracles

When we think according to a mind-set of reason alone, and when we resist change, we will block miracles from occurring in our life. Jesus went to His hometown of Nazareth for the purpose of announcing the gospel of the kingdom and manifesting miracles and wonders, just as He had done in the other towns in which He had ministered. However, He was unable to do much there except heal a few illnesses, because His own family members, neighbors, and townspeople regarded Him with a heart of unbelief. (See Mark 6:5–6.) *"Now [Jesus] did not do many mighty works there because of their unbelief"* (Matthew 13:58).

As we have discussed, many people in the church today deny, criticize, and/or reject demonstrations of God's supernatural power, such as miracles, healings, deliverances, the spiritual gifts of the Holy Spirit, and so forth. In effect, their unbelief has become "institutionalized," so it seems illogical to them to seek supernatural manifestations from God.

If you want to receive a miracle in your life today, renounce any unbelief that is in your heart and then receive it! *"Jesus Christ is the same yesterday, today, and forever"* (Hebrews 13:8)! Jesus did miracles yesterday, He does them today, and He will continue to do them.

When doctors were unable to do anything to improve the health of Marisol, who lives in Peru, her faith moved the hand of God, and she received her miracle. Here is her testimony: "When I was twenty years old, I fell down some stairs. The same thing happened to me at age thirty-five. As a result, the fifth lumbar vertebra in my spine lost its protective cartilage—a condition that caused me great pain. I couldn't sit down or sleep sideways, and I dragged my leg when I walked. I tried several alternatives for improvement, such as massages and injections, but my condition only grew worse.

"I learned of Pastor Maldonado through his books and videos, which people had loaned to me; the content of those books and videos ministered to me greatly in deliverance. When I learned that Pastor Maldonado would be traveling to Peru, I felt that God was going to heal me through his ministry, and I wanted to go to the event. My husband, seeing how much pain I was in, didn't know how to help me to get there. My friends told me that it was better for me to go to the doctor, but I didn't want any more to do with doctors and medicine. I was determined to believe God.

"The pain was intense, but I trusted in my Lord and asked Him not to leave me in shame. He provided the money for me to attend, and I had injections for the pain that enabled me to go. During one of the ministry sessions, Pastor Maldonado said that we shouldn't expect him to touch people but that each one of us would have to take our healing directly from the Holy Spirit. I appropriated that word. I leaned against a wall, and, at that precise moment, the pain began to disappear. The pastor said that God was healing backs and that we should begin to do what we couldn't do before, as an act of faith. Again, I cried out to the Lord, and I began to move. My husband, family, and friends, who had seen the condition in which I had arrived, were amazed. My healing was noticeable! I went forward to testify, and Pastor Maldonado sealed my healing by laying his hands on my head. I fell under the fire and presence of God, and everything changed. Because of my testimony, my entire family has come to Christ. My husband now serves the Lord in the church, and our marital relationship has notably improved."

Unbelief always denies God's supernatural power.

Submit Your Unbelief to God

By now, you have identified areas of your heart in which unbelief is holding you back from receiving what God has promised. Satan doesn't want your eyes to be opened to see the reality of the infinite power of Christ; he wants to keep your heart hardened by unbelief so that you will not be able to access the supernatural. Perhaps God has called you to start a business or a ministry, to take your church to the next level of faith, or to begin to pray for the sick and otherwise move in God's supernatural power, but you continue to think, *How can this be?* The Scriptures say that an individual who is double-minded is unstable. (See James 1:5–8.) Such a person cannot receive revelation from God or become an instrument that manifests His power and presence.

You may be struggling with negative thoughts that fill your mind with reasons and arguments for why you "can't" have something that God has promised or "can't" do something that God has told you to do. Perhaps a certain sickness is hereditary in your family. Your reason is likely telling you, "Your grandfather had it, your father had it, and, according to medical science, you will have to suffer from it, too. That is just the way it goes." But, again, what does the Word of God say about that sickness? *"Surely [Jesus] has borne our griefs and carried our sorrows;…and by His stripes we are healed"* (Isaiah 53:4–5).

Or, perhaps you have been blessed with millions of dollars, and God has placed it on your heart to sow part of that money into His kingdom purposes. Your human reason may give you a series of excuses for why you shouldn't do it. Yet, so many Christian ministries need finances right now to help them extend the kingdom! So many soul-winning churches need funds to host evangelistic crusades, run orphanages, and do many other outreaches, but there is no one willing to sow the funds, because reason won't let him! People allow their reason to carry more weight than what God has placed on their heart to do, because their reason makes sense to them, while they can't comprehend God's will and ways. When "reason" makes more sense to us than God's will, our heart has been hardened by unbelief.

There is an account in the Old Testament in which the Lord asked Abraham to take his promised son, Isaac, who had been conceived and born by a miracle of God, to a mountain and sacrifice him there. (See Genesis 22:1–2.) Abraham's reason must have shouted within him, "No! You waited decades for your son, and now that you have him, you are going to kill him? That makes no sense!" Even today, this situation doesn't make sense to many people. After they read about what God asked Abraham to do, their reason protests by reacting in the following ways: Either it considers God's request to be "illogical" and "cruel," therefore rejecting that He could have made it or rejecting Him for making it, or it believes that this account is a mere fable—that it never really happened but serves as a graphic metaphor for faith.

The Faith of Abraham

Abraham had every reason to tell God that he couldn't obey Him, beginning with the fact that God Himself had promised him Isaac and had told him He would multiply his descendants! (See, for example, Genesis 17:1–21.) It didn't make sense for God to subsequently ask Abraham to sacrifice his son! However, Abraham moved forward in faith to obey God. And God prevented him from slaying his son, telling Abraham that because he had been willing to offer his son, He now knew that Abraham would withhold nothing from Him. (See Genesis 22:3–18.) The command had been a test of Abraham's faith, trust, and devotion to God.

In this circumstance, we could say that Abraham allowed his human reason to be guided by his trust in God, for the Scriptures say, *"Abraham reasoned that God could raise the dead, and figuratively speaking, he did receive*

Isaac back from death" (Hebrews 11:19 NIV). How differently Abraham's life would have turned out if he had trusted in his human reason alone! But now, his faith continues to bear fruit as a blessing to all who believe and receive the gospel of Jesus Christ. (See Galatians 3:6–9.)

Will you place your "Isaac" on the altar, so that God will know that you withhold nothing from Him? Might your "Isaac" be your business, ministry, wealth, hobby, or family? Might your "Isaac" be your intellect, your reason—or your whole heart? Will you surrender the supremacy of your reason so that your heart may be freed from the spirit of unbelief, and you may receive faith to believe that God can do the "impossible"?

Stop asking "How can this be?" Do you think it would have made sense to the intellect, reason, and priorities of fallen humanity for God to come into the world in the person of Jesus Christ? No, but He came according to His own faith, reason, and purposes. At the end of His ministry on earth, Jesus allowed people to beat and whip Him to such a degree that He was unrecognizable. He allowed them to push a crown of thorns into His scalp. And He permitted them to nail Him to a cross to die an agonizing death. Why did He do all that? It wasn't logical! But again, God didn't come to earth in the person of Jesus to die because it "made sense." He did it out of His eternal love for us.

When "reason" makes more sense to us than God's will, our heart has been hardened by unbelief.

The unredeemed, natural mind is an enemy of God (see Romans 8:7)—it questions His existence, knowledge, wisdom, and judgment; it rejects His supernatural power. *"For those who live according to the flesh set their minds on the things of the flesh, but those who live according to the Spirit, the things of the Spirit"* (Romans 8:5). To overcome the obstacle of a mind influenced or controlled by the sinful nature, we must bypass the rational mind and operate directly by the faith that has been birthed in our heart by the Holy Spirit. One way we can accomplish this circumvention is to pray in *"other tongues"* (Acts 2:4; see also 1 Corinthians 14:2, 14) by the Spirit. However, if a spirit of unbelief resides in our heart, it can block the faith that dwells there. Consequently, our heart must be *freed* from the spirit of unbelief.

Bring Down the Stronghold of "How...?"

If you want to experience the power of God in your life, you cannot enter into agreement with the sinful nature, the attitudes of the fallen world, the mind-set of our contemporary culture and educational process, the practice of "religion," or your own limited human reason. Instead, you must agree with Christ! Receive Him and what He has done for you by His death and resurrection. The Scriptures say, *"Do not be conformed to this world, but be transformed by the renewing of your mind, that you may prove what is that good and acceptable and perfect will of God"* (Romans 12:2). God's *"perfect will"* will rule in your heart and mind as you are transformed by His Word, developing a heart like His.

Faith gives us access to God's supernatural power, but that access will close if unbelief becomes entrenched in our heart.

It is time to bring down the stronghold of "How...?" that sustains unbelief in our heart; it is time to allow God to be God in our life. Something like this happened to a woman named Guadalupe. She wanted a miracle, but, when it didn't come, she decided to stop believing. Yet God, in His love, did not give up on her. The following is her story.

"I attend a church in Honduras. Approximately three years ago, cancerous tumors were detected in my thyroid gland, causing me to faint and to suffer great pain in my throat. I could barely recognize the people around me, and my eyes had to be bandaged to relieve the pain. I spent two months hospitalized. I stopped going to my church and had no plans to return to any church. I kept saying that I believed in the Lord, but I was convinced that everything would remain the same for me.

"A House of Peace group prayed for me a great deal. On one occasion, the pastor visited me. He laid his hands on mine, and I felt the presence of God—a shudder and electricity went through my body. After they prayed for me, I went back to church. They continued to pray for me, while the doctor kept saying that I needed surgery. I wanted the operation, but God had other plans. Just before the surgery, the doctor did a biopsy. He placed an instrument in my throat to detect the state of the cancer, and then he said, 'That's strange! I can't find anything!' The only thing he saw were some white lines, like scars after an operation. His conclusion was that it looked as if God had operated. I was healed from that moment! I have not experienced any of the symptoms I used to feel. I reconciled with God and believed in His power, and He delivered me of resentment and of accepting the sickness, and He healed me!'"

How to Be Free from a Heart of Unbelief

We must all be liberated from unbelief of some kind. Many of us have inherited "educated unbelief" from our culture and "religious unbelief" from our church or denomination. We need to be set free to believe God for the great things He wants to do in us and through us! Taking the following steps will enable us to attain freedom from unbelief.

1. Recognize Our State of Unbelief and Repent of It

The first step is to recognize that we have allowed an attitude, a mindset, and/or a spirit of unbelief to enter our heart. We have questioned God's character, integrity, Word, and promises. We have subjected Him to the limitations of our reason and have fallen prey to the stronghold of "How…?" After acknowledging our unbelief, we must repent of allowing it to become rooted in our heart, and we need to ask the Lord to forgive us.

2. Renounce the Spirit of Unbelief

We must remove the legal right we have unknowingly given Satan to operate a spirit of unbelief in our heart by renouncing that unbelief and commanding it in the name of Jesus to leave us. When we do this, we will recover the territory of our heart that we had surrendered to unbelief, and which the spirit of unbelief had been ruling to that point. Keep in mind that after you have renounced the spirit of unbelief, the devil will resist you and fight to regain the territory he has lost. This means that even after you repent of a lack of faith and renounce unbelief, you may suddenly find yourself struggling with various doubts and fears. Thus, it is essential to daily renounce the spirit of unbelief, as well as to take the following step.

3. Receive the "Spirit of Faith"

Ask the Holy Spirit to fill you with the *"spirit of faith"* (2 Corinthians 4:13). Remember that before the coming of the Holy Spirit at Pentecost, the disciples exhibited unbelief, for which they were chastened by Jesus. Yet after they received the baptism of the Holy Spirit, they were filled with faith and boldness. When someone is baptized by immersion, he is fully covered. Therefore, ask the Holy Spirit to give you a "baptism of faith"—a submersion in faith, enabling you to live a full life as a believer, without being hindered by doubts.

When this happens, you may no longer understand how you could have doubted! You will move in a dimension in which you will know and perceive the spiritual realm—a dimension where human reason, logic, common sense, and unbelief do not hold sway. The spiritual realm will become a greater reality in your life than the natural world.

4. Receive the Anointed Word

A further way to be liberated from a heart of unbelief is to receive anointed teaching. Recall that when Jesus preached the gospel in His hometown of Nazareth, He couldn't do many miracles there except heal a few illnesses, because the people lacked faith in Him. (See Mark 6:1–5.) The Scriptures say, *"And [Jesus] marveled because of their unbelief"* (Mark 6:6). Jesus *"marveled"* at why people would doubt God, thereby limiting His work in their lives. Ironically, by their unbelief, they had restricted miracles from coming forth from the God in whom there are no limits!

The passage continues, *"Then [Jesus] went about the villages in a circuit, teaching"* (Mark 6:6). I believe there is a direct connection between the two statements in this verse: One reason the people didn't accept the message of the gospel is that they hadn't been taught the truths of God's Word sufficiently, which would have built their faith. This lack of spiritual knowledge had preconditioned them not to believe. However, the reverse can also be true. Having adequate teaching from God's Word can precondition us to believe.

So, one way to overcome unbelief is to be taught truth from the Word of God—but not from just any teacher. As we have noted, there are unbelieving preachers who teach the Bible solely as a historical book. They approach all topics from an intellectual point of view, rather than a spiritual one. For example, it is difficult for preachers to teach on God's supernatural power when they don't truly believe in it and have not experienced it. We must therefore be taught the Scriptures by someone who has the anointing of the Spirit and is able to receive revelation knowledge for today. Aside from his own personal Bible study, a person can rise no higher than the one who teaches him. And only progressive revelation knowledge can enable people's faith to move to the next level so they can understand and receive God's purposes for them today. A preacher cannot adequately teach about what God wants to do in our life *today* when all he has is revelation of what God was doing in previous years.

We can't expect people to believe what they have not been taught. That is why, the first time I preach the gospel of the kingdom in a particular place, I teach basic themes in relation to the supernatural. The next time I go to that place, I often observe that many of the people have captured the truths I have preached and have moved forward to experience them. The original teaching broke through their unbelief, enabling them to receive God's promises by faith. So, the second time I teach the people in that place, I help them to go to the next level of faith through teachings that go deeper into God's truth.

Therefore, in addition to regularly reading the Word of God yourself, make sure you are receiving anointed preaching that will take your faith to the next level.

Unbelief makes God marvel.

5. Regularly Speak in "Other Tongues"

As I wrote earlier, another way we can bypass our human reason to reach the mind of God is to speak in *"other tongues"* by the Holy Spirit. (See Acts 2:4; 1 Corinthians 14:2, 14.) When we pray in tongues, we can activate the supernatural. The Scriptures say, "[God] *is able to do exceedingly abundantly above all that we ask or think, according to the power that works in us"* (Ephesians 3:20). Make it a practice to pray in tongues regularly so that you may break through the barrier of unbelief and receive from the spiritual realm what God wants to give you.

Prayer for Deliverance from Unbelief

God is calling us to surrender our heart to Him so that He can transform it, removing offenses and unbelief. He is preparing us for the end times, when a great harvest of souls will be reaped, and when God will transfer financial wealth from unbelievers to His children, so they may use that wealth for His glory and kingdom purposes. In order to receive that wealth and be faithful stewards of it, we must have a pure heart, one that is free of unbelief. With the *"spirit of faith,"* and *"according to the power that works in us,"* we can receive every promise God has reserved for this generation. Now is the time! Surrender to God, renounce unbelief, and allow the supernatural transformation of your heart to take place!

Dear friend, let me guide you in a very simple prayer for deliverance from the spirit of unbelief. Remember to confess it daily until every root of the spirit of unbelief in your heart has been pulled up and discarded.

Heavenly Father, thank You for opening my spiritual eyes and enabling me to see the unbelief in my heart. I praise You and bless You for teaching me how to be free of this rebellion against You and this resistance to Your will! In Christ, and with all my heart, I ask You to forgive me for having allowed my limited human reason and intellect to make me doubt You and Your promises, and for having permitted the spirit of unbelief to enter my life. Forgive me for making a "god" of my mind. Right now, I renounce the wicked spirit of unbelief, and, in the name of Jesus, I order it to leave my life.

Lord, I ask You, through Your Holy Spirit, to release the *"spirit of faith"* in me. "Baptize" me in faith to believe any portion of Your Word that I have previously found difficult to accept and receive—and to believe for even greater things! I receive Your faith right now. Help me to guard my heart and mind so that I will not allow unbelief to enter. I declare that everything that was held back in my life due to unbelief is now released. I receive my [salvation, healing, deliverance, financial provision, family restoration, or other blessing], in the name of Jesus. Amen!

7

The Obedient Heart

Everywhere I go, people ask me, "What is the key to the success of your ministry?" My answer is always the same: "Obedience to God." Although I believe that various factors contribute to the success of a ministry, a family, a business, or any other entity or project, I know that obedience to God is always the main factor. Each time God has asked me to do something, I have obeyed, regardless of the cost. And I have seen His faithfulness in the rewards and accomplishments I have witnessed as a result. Every day, thousands of lives—locally, nationally, and globally—are saved, transformed, healed, delivered, and enabled to prosper because our ministry has obeyed God's mandate to form and equip leaders as God has taught us to, according to the pattern in which He has formed and equipped us. I could share countless testimonies of the times when God has honored our obedience.

That is why I believe this book would be incomplete without a chapter on the obedient heart. Every heart transformed by the supernatural power of God manifests obedience as one of its key characteristics. Obedience is not easy. In fact, making the choice to obey is one of the greatest difficulties believers encounter when they begin to draw close to God in a desire to submit their whole life to Him. This is because we humans are rebellious, independent, and egocentric by nature—by the sinful nature, that is. In this chapter, we will examine some of the themes from previous chapters in more depth, in order to better understand the rebellion against God that frequently erupts in our heart and that is manifested in our decisions and behavior. We will also discover how to establish a lifestyle of obedience to God.

Obedience Flows from a Love for God

Jesus said, *"If you love Me, keep My commandments"* (John 14:15). When we love God, we desire to obey Him. In fact, we express genuine love for Him by obeying His Word. Any love that would keep us from following His commandments is false love.

In the following testimony, we see a clear example of obedience to God inspired by a deep love for Him. It was loving devotion to God that led Alejandro of Costa Rica to leave his profession as a medical doctor and surgeon to follow the call of God on his life to be a pastor. He writes, "A family member who was a pastor felt the need to come to Costa Rica and preach the Word to my family. My mother, sister, and aunts received the Lord Jesus through her. My sister later asked me, 'Alejandro, do you want to receive Jesus into your heart?' My answer was, 'Yes, what should I do?' That was my conversion experience; there was a desire for God within me that went beyond the capacity of my reason, because my analytical and intellectual mind had often been an obstacle in me. I believe there was a void within me of which I was unaware, which led me to accept Christ above my reason.

"Although I fondly remember my time at the university, I also remember having a deep need to serve God. Every year, I wondered when that moment would come. For nine years, I served at the church—learning, growing, evangelizing, and preparing to make the decision to dedicate my life fully to God's service. I knew it would not be an easy decision because of my family history; the most ridiculous thing I could do was to leave my profession to become a pastor! But God confirmed the decision in my heart, and I decided to face my family. My mother, sister, and aunts supported my decision because they were already Christians, and my father also supported me, but the rest of the family opposed such 'craziness.' I have served my Jesus with all of my heart to this day, and I will continue to do it!"

Love is the motivation behind true obedience. Any love that doesn't result in obedience to God is false love.

God will not necessarily ask you to give up your profession in order to follow His will for your life. In Alejandro's case, God had called him to change vocations and become a pastor, and he willingly obeyed because God had placed that desire in his heart, which was open to the Lord. The point is this: Whatever your situation in life, your profession, or your future plans, are you following what you know God is calling you to do, and are you doing it from a heart of love for Him?

Obedience Also Flows from Faith in God

The Greek word most commonly translated as *"obedience"* or *"obedient"* in the New Testament is *hupakoe*. It means "attentive hearkening" and implies "compliance or submission." Like the obedience of Abraham that we examined in chapter 6, true obedience is based on both a love for God and a faith in Him that is *"fully convinced that what [God has] promised He [is] also able to perform"* (Romans 4:21). When an individual is fully obedient to God, it means he has gone beyond the point of no return in fully trusting his heavenly Father. When we doubt our ability to obey, it is usually because we are not really convinced of God's love, authority, and/or power to fulfill His promises. Someone with an obedient heart listens carefully to God's Word, accepts God's authority, and submits to God's will by choice, with the full conviction that He will do everything He has promised.

Obedience to God is birthed in the heart, not in the mind.

What Is Disobedience?

If we are to obey our loving heavenly Father, we should understand what it means to disobey Him, or to rebel against Him. Disobedience is a heart attitude that won't allow anything or anyone—particularly God—to persuade us to see an issue or situation for what it really is and to respond to it appropriately. Disobedience manifests when we refuse to believe that God's will is best for us. Our sinful nature is inherently rebellious and always resists the truth. Judas Iscariot is a perfect example of someone who permitted the rebellious sinful nature to control him, so that he ended up betraying Christ. Afterward, he wasn't persuaded by the biblical truth that if we repent of our sin, God is faithful to forgive us. Instead, he continued along the path of corruption leading to his death. Some people choose to remain in disobedience for so long that it becomes very difficult for them to accept God's forgiveness and to turn away from their sinful behavior.

Disobedience is a heart attitude that won't allow anything or anyone to persuade us to see an issue or situation for what it really is and to respond to it appropriately.

The Battle Within

Jesus came to earth proclaiming the kingdom of God and its power to liberate us from sin and from the kingdom of darkness. A battle commences each time God's kingdom arrives to destroy the kingdom of darkness in the "territory" of a person's heart. Furthermore, once God's kingdom is established in an individual's life, a new conflict breaks out between his born-again heart, or spirit, and the sinful nature. Formerly, the person may not have experienced much conflict in regard to his attitudes and conduct toward God, depending on how sensitive his conscience was. But now that his spirit has been renewed, he struggles against his sinful nature, which he won't be entirely free of until he goes to be with the Lord or until Christ returns. People often wonder, "Why do I always struggle to obey God?" It is because of this ongoing battle within us, as well as Satan's continual attacks on us as he attempts to win back the "territory" that he has lost.

The apostle Paul wrote, "*For what I am doing, I do not understand. For what I will to do, that I do not practice; but what I hate, that I do. If, then, I do what I will not to do, I agree with the law that it is good. But now, it is no longer I who do it, but sin that dwells in me*" (Romans 7:15–17). In these words, you can almost feel the internal conflict Paul described. If you desire to obey God, but something seems to "push" you to disobey Him, it is because the sinful nature is rebelling, trying to assert control in your life.

Put Off the "Old Man"

"*Put off, concerning your former conduct, the old man* ["old self" NIV, NASB] *which grows corrupt according to the deceitful lusts*" (Ephesians 4:22). Paul wrote the above instruction in a letter to believers in Ephesus who were truly born again and full of the Holy Spirit but apparently lacked revelation of the sinful nature battling within them. Previously, we noted two synonyms for the sinful nature that are used in the New Testament— the "*flesh*" (see, for example, Romans 7:5) and the term employed in the above verse, the "*old man*," or "*old self*." Some additional synonyms are "*carnal mind*" (Romans 8:7 NKJV, KJV), "*lust*" (James 1:14 KJV), "*body of sin*" (Romans 6:6 NKJV, KJV, NIV, NASB), and "*body of the sins of the flesh*" (Colossians 2:11 NKJV, KJV). Additionally, some theologians and other believers call the sinful nature the "Adamic nature."

Let's briefly review how the sinful nature came into being. God had clearly instructed Adam and Eve, "*But of the tree of the knowledge of good and evil you shall not eat, for in the day that you eat of it you shall surely die*" (Genesis 2:17). Satan denied God's words, saying, "*You will **not** surely die*" (Genesis 3:4). When the first human beings believed the enemy's deception and disobeyed God, the sinful nature was born. Adam and Eve placed themselves under Satan's authority rather than God's. Consequently, human beings became corrupt physically, emotionally, and spiritually, and this corrupt nature has been passed down to all people, from generation to generation, to the present day. The Scriptures say, "*All we like sheep have gone astray; we have turned, every one, to his own way*" (Isaiah 53:6).

Yet, even when human beings first disobeyed and went their own way, God made them a promise that He would redeem them through a coming Messiah. By this redemption, the heart of humanity would be transformed so that it could become a *"new man"* (Ephesians 4:24) in God's likeness again. God said to Satan, *"I will put enmity between you and the woman, and between your seed and her Seed* [Jesus the Messiah]; *He shall bruise your head, and you shall bruise His heel"* (Genesis 3:15).

We know that Satan, or the devil, rebelled against God first. Rebellion is his nature, and the *"old man"* is his *"seed,"* or "child." Rebellion is nothing more than disobedience, which occurs when a person decides to separate himself from God in order to pursue his own will, to satisfy himself, and to govern himself—to act independently of the heavenly Father. This decision inevitably results in an alignment with another *"father,"* the devil, who does not obey the truth and is the "father" of lies. Jesus told some leaders who considered themselves religious, *"You are of your father the devil, and the desires of your father you want to do. He was a murderer from the beginning, and does not stand in the truth, because there is no truth in him. When he speaks a lie, he speaks from his own resources, for he is a liar and the father of it"* (John 8:44).

Every born-again believer must be careful not to be deceived by Satan into committing disobedience. *"Be sober, be vigilant; because your adversary the devil walks about like a roaring lion, seeking whom he may devour. Resist him, steadfast in the faith"* (1 Peter 5:8–9). We must all be alert to Satan's schemes. Obedience to God is not just a matter of believing in Jesus or of having good conduct. Our heart needs to be continuously transformed if we are to remain obedient to God. Let us explore the process by which Adam and Eve disobeyed God, so that we can recognize the devil's schemes in our own life.

The only power the enemy has is that which we give him when we are not under God's authority.

The Original Process by Which the Human Heart Became Disobedient

1. Adam and Eve Were Attracted to Satan's Lies Through Their Physical Senses and by Their Desire for Wisdom and Power Independent of God

The serpent tempted the first human beings through the physical senses. The Tree of Knowledge of Good and Evil appeared to Adam and Eve to be *"good for food,…pleasant to the eyes"* (Genesis 3:6). Satan also made it sound attractive to become as wise as God (see Genesis 3:5–6), which may have seemed to Adam and Eve like a pathway to greater spiritual enlightenment. As a result, they were presented with a temptation they found very difficult to resist. Just like Adam and Eve, we struggle with temptations based on our physical senses and ambitions that push us to disobey God.

2. Adam and Eve's Misplaced/Wrong Desires Led to Their Being Enticed to Sin

The Scriptures say, *"Each one is tempted when he is drawn away by his own desires and enticed. Then, when desire has conceived, it gives birth to sin"* (James 1:14–15). Rebellious desires are perversions of God's will. Adam and Eve ate from the Tree of Knowledge of Good and Evil, even though God had warned them not to. Perhaps they believed it would be all right to do it "just once." However, that one act generated lust in their nature. Sin came to stay, giving birth to additional sin and establishing a perpetual pattern of disobedience. Human beings were unable to get rid of sin or the curse it released. Satan's goal was not just to make human beings sin once but for them to *practice sin continuously in a sinful state.* In this way, he could gain entrance into their lives to control and oppress them.

If you are a believer, I warn you: You cannot play with sin. You must repent of all sin and turn your back on it, because it is a mortal trap. It is an endless downward spiral; once it begins, it continues to produce evil unless it is renounced, forgiven through Jesus Christ, and forsaken.

3. Adam and Eve's Sin Produced Death for Them—and for All Humanity

"*Sin, when it is full-grown, brings forth death*" (James 1:15). The entrance of sin into the world produced spiritual death in humanity—separation from God—as well as physical death. Satan's purpose in tempting us to sin is to separate us—permanently, if possible—from our heavenly Father.

When we understand the above truths, we recognize the fact that each time we act according to the sinful nature, we essentially repeat the process by which the first humans fell. That is why the apostle Paul urged us, "*Put off, concerning your former conduct, the old man* ["old self" NIV, NASB] *which grows corrupt according to the deceitful lusts*" (Ephesians 4:22). We must decide daily to "*put off...the old man*"—to reject sin and to obey God—so that we may escape death and receive His abundant life.

The corruption of the "*old man*" can lead an individual to think that death is his only option, and that he should end his own life. During a spiritual retreat at King Jesus Ministry, five women were delivered from the spirit of suicide. One of them, named Flor, had felt very depressed and empty because her daughter had died two year earlier. Flor had decided to end her own life, so she took more than a hundred sleeping pills, but her suicide attempt failed. Two weeks later, she again planned to kill herself, but someone invited her to the retreat. While she was there, she experienced the presence of God and received the love of the Father, so that she no longer had a desire to die. She was set free from the spirits of grief and suicide.

Another woman, Catalina, had started to take drugs and to drink alcohol at the age of thirteen because she felt rejected by her mother and because she felt deeply the absence of her father from their home. By age eighteen, she didn't want to live anymore, but she attended the retreat. There, the fatherhood of God embraced her and made her feel worthy and loved. She realized that God was her Father and that she had a purpose, and she left her addictions and suicidal thoughts behind. Today, she is a new person!

Milena was a young married woman with precious children, but she wanted to commit suicide because she felt very guilty and unworthy. She was quick to become angry, and she was extremely aggressive with her husband and children. Milena felt so guilty over her behavior that she just wanted to disappear from this world, so she wrote out her last will and testament, intending to end her life. However, to God's glory, Milena decided to attend the retreat, and it was there that she was set free from the spirits of manipulation, guilt, and suicide. Now, she is learning to be a good wife and mother.

Cesia and Sarah are sisters who were abandoned by their mother when they were very young. Their father was an alcoholic, a drug addict, a drug dealer, and a murderer. He never took care of them or their younger brother, so the girls practically raised themselves, as well as their brother. When the girls were sixteen and twelve years old, respectively, they, too, began to use drugs and to drink alcohol. Shortly thereafter, they were introduced to the lesbian lifestyle.

When Cesia and Sarah's father died, they moved with their brother to the United States to live with their mother, who worked in a bar and was also an alcoholic. When their mother realized that her daughters were drinking, she put them to work in the bar and joined in their drinking. However, the mother was an illegal alien, and she was soon deported by the authorities. So, the sisters and brother became homeless again. The girls had become violent and would hurt each other. They soon reached their limit, and the only thing they wanted to do was die. In fact, the older sister had already tried to take her life and had been hospitalized for a month. Then, someone invited them to the deliverance retreat, where they received the Lord and were set free from the spirits of suicide, abandonment, lesbianism, rejection, bitterness, anger, unforgiveness, and addiction. They are now starting a new life. They know what the lifestyle of the world is all about, and they never want to return to it.

The Sinful Nature Is Continually Corrupt

The sinful nature is in a constant state of decay, and it prompts people to commit one corrupt act after another. Even though the corruption is not always evident, it is always present; and, in the long run, its destructive effects will manifest. For example, today, you might see a young man or woman who is physically attractive, educated, and wealthy and who seems to "rule the world." However, if that person follows the desires of the sinful nature, then, sometime later, you will see that the good looks and strength will have decreased, and the body will have begun to look worn out, due to physical, intellectual, and spiritual decadence, as well as the general effects of the fall.

In communities and nations across the globe, there is a constant pattern of social decay due to the corrupt sinful nature. Governments and other institutions can do little to prevent human corruption from infecting society through such evils as lies, deceit, fraud, violence, and other abuses, especially since most of the leaders who run the institutions also have a corrupt heart that asserts control over them. Satan can easily provoke rebellion in many people because, unless their heart has been transformed, they are by nature "*sons of disobedience*":

> *You He made alive, who were dead in trespasses and sins, in which you once walked according to the course of this world, according to the prince of the power of the air, the spirit who now works in the sons of disobedience, among whom also we all once conducted ourselves in the lusts of our flesh, fulfilling the desires of the flesh and of the mind, and were by nature children of wrath, just as the others.*
>
> (Ephesians 2:1–3)

There is a "rebel" in every human being that produces deceitful desires and evil thoughts that lead him to disobey God. Nothing can stop corruption or decadence in the human race except the power of Jesus Christ!

The sinful nature is rebellious, leading to spiritual, moral, and physical corruption.

The Characteristics of Jesus' Obedience

Jesus Christ is the supreme example of full obedience to God the Father. His life of obedience was marked by two characteristics:

1. The Surrender, or "Denial," of His Divine Attributes

Jesus was 100 percent God and 100 percent Man. He had a sinless nature, and He never committed any sin, so He did not have to deny the "old man" or a rebellious will. However, He did have to surrender, or "deny," His divine glory and power when He came to live on this earth as a Man. "[Jesus], *being in the form of God, did not consider it robbery to be equal with God, but made Himself of no reputation, taking the form of a bondservant, and coming in the likeness of men*" (Philippians 2:6). Similarly, our obedience to God may include not only the crucifixion of "self" but also the denial of some of our human "privileges" and "rights" for the greater good God calls us to.

If Jesus set aside His divine attributes when He came to earth, how did He perform His miracles, such as healing, delivering people from demon-possession, multiplying bread and fish, and walking on water? He did so entirely as a Man, using the same resources that are available to any born-again believer today—by the exercise of faith, under submission to God the Father, and with the anointing of the Holy Spirit. If He had done any of His miracles as God, they would have been "illegal," since Jesus came as our Representative to live a life of full obedience to God as a human being and to die on the cross as our sinless Substitute.

Note that when Satan tempted Jesus in the wilderness, he attacked Jesus' divine identity, saying, "*If You are the Son of God....*" Yet Jesus did not defend His deity to the devil or banish the enemy with His divine power. Instead, He answered each of Satan's temptations with Scripture, as we are also able to do today under the Spirit's guidance. (See, for example, Luke 4:1–12.)

When Jesus was arrested in the garden of Gethsemane, and Peter tried to defend Him with a sword, Jesus told him, "*Do you think that I cannot now pray to My Father, and He will provide Me with more than twelve legions of angels? How then could the Scriptures be fulfilled, that it must happen thus?*" (Matthew 26:53–54). As God, and as the Father's beloved Son, Jesus could have been rescued from His persecutors by an army of angels. Yet He chose to remain obedient to the Father's will and to die on the cross for our sake.

When Jesus was dying on that cross, He was mocked by passersby who said, *"If You are the Son of God, come down from the cross"* (Matthew 27:40). Again, He did not attempt to prove His deity to anyone. He continued to set aside His inherent, rightful divinity in order to obey the Father and to fulfill the purpose for which He had come to earth.

As fallen—but redeemed—human beings, we must die to "self" and deny the inclinations of the sinful nature, such as selfish ambition and impure thoughts. Which do you think would be easier—Jesus giving up His divine attributes to depend totally on God the Father and the Holy Spirit to live as a Man on the earth, or our dying to "self" and denying the sinful nature? I believe it is easier for us to deny ourselves because, on the cross, Jesus provided us with the grace and the power that enable us to do so. Jesus has already conquered sin and death for us. What He did for us was not easy—it was excruciatingly hard and painful. If Jesus gave up everything for us, we should give up all for Him.

2. Continued Submission to God's Authority

While Jesus was on earth, He continually relinquished His will to God's will. As we have just discussed, Christ had a holy nature, not the Adamic, sinful nature. However, as a human being, He did have free will, which God has granted to all humans. Every day, Jesus denied His own will—His ability to do whatever He wanted—in order to obey the Father's will; He lived in constant submission to God's authority. Jesus said, *"I can of Myself do nothing. As I hear, I judge; and My judgment is righteous, because I do not seek My own will but the will of the Father who sent Me"* (John 5:30). The book of Hebrews tells us, *"Though [Jesus] was a Son, yet He learned obedience by the things which He suffered"* (Hebrews 5:8).

Although Jesus surrendered His will to God daily, His greatest test came when He had to submit to the cruel mockery and torture of death on the cross. Surrendering to this ordeal was a struggle for Him. However, after much prayer, He was able to say with conviction, *"Father, if it is Your will, take this cup away from Me; **nevertheless not My will, but Yours, be done**"* (Luke 22:42).

Gethsemane was where Christ fought as a Man to obey the Father. It is likely that every evil principality and stronghold expected to see Jesus fail.

The devil and his demons had not been able to make Jesus fall by tempting Him with fame, wealth, immorality, pride, or riches to deny the will of God. But this time He faced physical and spiritual torture and agonizing death. Gethsemane was Christ's personal "Armageddon"—His last battle. The conflict that took place in His heart was so intense that *"His sweat became like great drops of blood falling down to the ground"* (Luke 22:44). Medically speaking, His capillaries burst. His heart was broken that night.

Yet Jesus was a Man who lived under God's authority. We don't know how long He prayed, but when His prayers were complete, He was surrendered and ready to do God's will, to finish the work for which He had come to earth. *"And being found in appearance as a man, He humbled Himself and became obedient to the point of death, even the death of the cross"* (Philippians 2:8).

You are committed to obey God to the extent that you are submitted to Him.

Do you feel as if you are facing your own Gethsemane? Learning obedience is a process. It was the same for Jesus, even though He was sinless. We are not born obedient, and obedience is not a gift that can be imparted to us. As we go through this process of learning obedience, we will make mistakes, and we may have times when we disobey, because our will is difficult to break. However, that fact should not discourage us. Even though learning to obey takes time, obedience is not impossible, because the grace of the Holy Spirit will enable us to obey. Each time we surrender our own will to carry out the will of God, we are led to greater levels of obedience, which, in turn, give us access to greater spiritual rewards.

When we are at the beginning of this process, God will ask us to obey Him in small and perhaps seemingly insignificant matters. If we are faithful, He will give us increasingly challenging matters in which to submit to Him. I believe that's how it was with Jesus. He learned obedience from the simplest of things to the hardest—which was to surrender Himself to God the Father as the sacrificial Lamb. It is interesting to note that Christ "died" to His will many times before His physical death on the cross. He obeyed the Father in every stage of His life and endured the suffering that all human beings experience on earth. (See, for example, Hebrews 2:18.) He did this in order to learn obedience and to fully identify with the human race. Jesus had to go through the process of learning obedience in which He continually *chose* to submit to the Father's plan. That is why Christ can say to us, *"If anyone desires to come after Me, let him deny himself, and take up his cross, and follow Me"* (Matthew 16:24).

When Jesus died after surrendering His own will to the Father's will, the veil of the temple was torn in two, signifying the restoration of the relationship between God and man. Then, God resurrected Jesus! Christ understood the principle that resurrection—literal and figurative—is the result of death to "self" and obedience to God. He had previously said to Pilate, *"My Father loves Me, because I lay down My life that I may take it again. No one takes it from Me, but I lay it down of Myself. I have power to lay it down, and I have power to take it again. This command I have received from My Father"* (John 10:17–18). The Son of God was obedient unto death on the cross because, again, He had placed Himself under God's authority. And His obedience made Him fitting for resurrection.

None of us can crucify the sinful nature until we surrender our will to God. Ask the Holy Spirit to give you His supernatural grace, so you can learn to daily surrender your will to the Father's, just as Christ did.

God the Father raised Jesus from dead because He died under God's authority.

Obedience to God's Authority

We must make a choice to obey God and His delegated authorities. If we aren't in submission to the godly authority God has placed over our life, we are in a state of rebellion. We obey our leaders in the church, for the Word says, *"Obey those who rule over you, and be submissive, for they watch out for your souls, as those who must give account. Let them do so with joy and not with grief, for that would be unprofitable for you"* (Hebrews 13:17). We obey the delegated authorities at our places of work, because the Scriptures say, *"Be obedient to those who are your masters according to the flesh, with fear and trembling, in sincerity of heart, as to Christ"* (Ephesians 6:5). We obey the authorities in our homes, because we are commanded, *"'Honor your father and mother,' which is the first commandment with promise"* (Ephesians 6:2). We obey the laws and leaders of our governments, for God's Word says, *"Let every soul be subject to the governing authorities. For there is no authority except from God, and the authorities that exist are appointed by God"* (Romans 13:1). When we obey the earthly authorities delegated by God, we obey Him, and when we disobey them, we disobey God.

Obedience to God includes voluntary submission to His delegated authorities.

The "How," "When," and "Where" of Obedience

As we noted earlier, obedience is linked to faith. It is not a feeling or an emotion but the result of an internal conviction that originates in the heart. *"Faith is the substance of things hoped for, the evidence of things not seen"* (Hebrews 11:1). To walk by faith is to have a strong conviction about the reality of the sovereign God and His invisible spiritual realm. When we obey God, our conviction is manifested in the natural realm as He works in our life in supernatural ways.

To have a heart of true and total obedience means to do what God commands—how, when, and where He says to. Such an obedient heart reflects great faith. Sometimes, we may agree with God about the things He commands but still fail to obey Him in the "how" and "when" of them, so that we end up obeying Him only partially in regard to the "where." This is what happened to King Saul when he did not wait for Samuel to come and offer a sacrifice to the Lord but offered it himself, which he was not authorized to do. (See 1 Samuel 13:1–13.) Another time, Saul obeyed the "where" and "when" but not the "how." God had told him to destroy the Amalekites and all their goods, including the animals. Although Saul *"attacked the Amalekites"* and put the people to death (see 1 Samuel 15:7–8), he and his army *"spared Agag* [the king] *and the best of the sheep, the oxen, the fatlings, the lambs, and all that was good, and were unwilling to utterly destroy them"* (1 Samuel 15:9). Because Saul's heart was disobedient to God, the Lord rejected him as king. (See 1 Samuel 13:14; 15:10–11, 22–23.)

The prophet Samuel told Saul, *"Behold, to obey is better than sacrifice"* (1 Samuel 15:22). We need to take these words to heart, because a similar scenario occurs in the church today. Some people obey God and His delegated authorities only partially, and this has given the enemy a right to attack them. The Bible clearly says, *"Do not give the devil a foothold"* (Ephesians 4:27 NIV). We know that Christ conquered Satan at the cross and stripped the enemy of his power and authority; the devil has been defeated, dethroned, and disarmed. If they know this, why are so many believers defeated, sick, poor, depressed, and anxious? Sometimes, the cause is disobedience—full or partial—which has given the enemy an entry, or *"foothold,"* into their lives.

Partial obedience is equivalent to disobedience.

Because Christ defeated Satan, giving us the victory over him, the only way the enemy can have a legal right to exercise power over us is through our disobedience. If this situation applies to you, today is the day to take away his rights and to reclaim your victory in Christ! Repent, ask God to forgive you, close every door of disobedience, and rebuke the enemy from attacking your health, your home, your finances, or any other area of your life. Paul wrote to the Romans, *"For your obedience has become known to all. Therefore I am glad on your behalf; but I want you to be wise in what is good, and simple concerning evil. And the God of peace will crush Satan under your feet shortly"* (Romans 16:19–20).

Our disobedience to God empowers Satan, while our obedience disarms him.

Taylor is a college student who returned to God after experiencing the consequences of falling into a life of rebellion and disobedience. He writes, "I was raised in the church, but I slowly turned my back on God as I grew older. I experienced depression and anger, even though I never mentioned it to anyone. One night, after returning to my room at the university, I contemplated taking my own life. I was about to do it when 'something' led me to reach out to a Christian friend. I went to her room, where she prayed for me and invited me to a meeting at the campus. This was not the first time she had invited me. Previously, I had always given her an excuse not to go, but this time I went.

"In the meeting, I was prayed over and ministered to. Then I was invited to an inner healing and deliverance service at the church. I was skeptical because I had never seen anything like it, and I wasn't sure that it would really work. However, when I began to understand what it was all about, I cried uncontrollably, and I surrendered my heart to the Lord. At that moment, eighteen years of burdens and oppression lifted off my shoulders. When the pastor gave the altar call, I ran to it. I felt that God had been calling me for years to return to Him, but I had ignored Him all of that time.

"After giving my life to Christ, I felt free and filled with a peace I had not experienced before. I used to lead a life of immorality, depression, anger, bitterness, and fear, but I was set free from all that by the power of God. He began to transform me in order to make me the person He had planned for me to be. Now I allow God to do things His way through me and to use me to bring others closer to Him."

Barriers to Obedience

All of us have various spiritual, mental, and emotional barriers that keep us from giving total obedience to God. We overcome these hindrances as we go through the process of learning full obedience. The most important aspect of this process is to continue surrendering to God and depending on His grace to accomplish the transformation of our heart. Let's examine several of the barriers to obedience, at the same time assessing our own heart in relation to them.

1. *Comfort and Convenience*

Thousands of believers have allowed comfort and convenience to become their "god," keeping them from obeying the Lord and making personal sacrifices on His behalf. If they were to lose their comforts and conveniences, many people would quickly demonstrate how weak their love, patience, kindness, perseverance, and surrender to God really are. In most cases, the financial and material blessings they enjoy originally came to them as blessings from God, but they hold on to them tightly and don't use them for the purpose of blessing others in addition to benefitting themselves. Or, they are focused on the pleasure they derive from these gifts rather than focusing on the Giver Himself.

I know of families whom God has instructed to attend our church, but they won't come because they consider the church too far away from where they live. They prefer to attend a church that is closer because it is more comfortable and convenient for them to do so—even at the price of spiritual stagnancy and disobedience.

Are you willing to obey God even if it means giving up some comfort and convenience?

2. *"Profitability"*

In regard to doing God's will, some believers ask, "What's in it for me?" They may know that God wants them to do something in particular, but since it would not be financially profitable, they are unwilling to obey. It is sad to find Christians who choose not to obey God unless they receive some material reward for their efforts. Some people obey only when they are offered a better position, more money, or something else they believe is to their advantage.

As I travel around the world to preach the gospel of the kingdom, there are some places where I am given financial support for coming and ministering to the people. There are other places where I am not given anything for ministering; the people either can't give or won't give, so our ministry has to cover the expenses of the mission. Yet my criterion for deciding whether to go to a country to manifest the supernatural power of God is not based on the promise of an offering or of reimbursement for travel expenses. My criterion is God's will. If He wants me to go, nothing can stop me, because I have learned to obey Him, regardless of whether it is financially profitable or not.

Are you willing to obey God even when it doesn't seem "profitable" to do so?

3. Human Reason and Understanding

We discussed the barrier of human reason in some depth in the previous chapter. When God asks people to do a certain task or to surrender something to Him, but the purpose for doing it goes beyond their human reason and understanding, some are not willing to obey. This is a key point because many things that God asks us to do will not make sense to our human reason! If we don't learn to overcome this limitation, we won't move very far along in our walk of obedience.

The most powerful miracles God has done through me have taken place after I have acted in faith to do something for Him that went beyond the limits of my reason. I didn't understand this principle until I made the decision to step out and obey God even when I didn't understand why He wanted me to do something or how He would do it. Then, as I saw Him work, I grew in faith. One of the greatest manifestations of this principle I have ever witnessed was the manner in which our church building, which holds six thousand people, came into being. We purchased the land and built the church in just two years—without loans or debt. The whole endeavor required giant steps of faith to obey what God had spoken to us, both directly and through His prophets. And He was faithful in every stage of the building process.

Are you willing to obey God even when it doesn't make sense to your human reason?

With each act of obedience, the heart expands;
with each act of disobedience, the heart shrinks.

4. Sacrifice

The idea of sacrifice doesn't sit well with many people today because our generation wants everything free, quick, and easy—with instant gratification. People want success without diligence, prosperity without sowing financial "seed" into God's kingdom, health without faith, and deliverance without a denial of self. In many churches, the biblical message of sacrifice is often replaced with an extreme view of the free grace of God. This view promotes the idea that we do not have to exercise personal responsibility or take up our cross daily to follow Jesus.

We should make sacrifices based on our love for God and our desire to advance His kingdom. As we saw in the case of Saul, any sacrifice we offer is worthless if God did not tell us to do it. (See 1 Samuel 15:22.) Believers are God's priests. (See Revelation 1:6; 5:10.) As such, we are called to offer *"spiritual sacrifices"* (1 Peter 2:5), such as prayer, tithes and offerings, and the presentation of our physical body as a *"living sacrifice"* (Romans 12:1) to God. The only way our sacrifices will be pleasing to God is if we do them with a heart of obedience, by faith, and according to revelation of His will—either through His Word or directly by His Spirit.

Are you willing to sacrifice your personal time and resources to serve Christ? Are you willing to walk the extra mile to restore your marriage? Are you willing to offer God your business, profession, gifts, talents, and vision in order to do what He wants you to do?

Obedience as a Lifestyle

Perhaps you continually struggle to obey God, so that you ask yourself the various questions we have just discussed—and maybe some additional ones—when you are trying to decide whether to obey God's will. For instance, you may ask, "Is there something in it for me?" "Will it bring me pleasure?" "Does it offer me security?" "Is it convenient for me?" "Will it make me comfortable? "Will I have to sacrifice anything?" "Will people laugh at me?" "Do I have to do it right now?" If you often ask yourself questions like these when you are called to obey God, then obedience is not yet a lifestyle for you.

When obedience is your lifestyle, it means that you have purposefully made a commitment to obey God, regardless of the outcome. And, when you commit to do God's will, He commits to give you whatever you need— and often more—to fulfill what He's called you to do. Therefore, you need to make an overarching decision of obedience in which you affirm to God, "I will obey You, regardless of the place, the time, the circumstances, or the difficulties I might face."

God doesn't commit until we submit.

When you have made such a commitment, you will no longer allow comfort, convenience, profitability, human reason, or personal sacrifice to prevent you from obeying God. Once you know His will on a certain matter, you obey—and that's that! You have accepted the fact that Christ is your Lord and that He governs and controls your life; therefore, you surrender in faith to His will for you.

Do you trust the God whom you serve to guide you and keep you? Do you trust that He will direct you to make the right decision in every situation because He desires to give you what is best for your life in accordance with His glory?

A lifestyle of obedience comes from making an overarching decision to obey God, no matter what, and to leave the results up to Him.

How to Establish a Walk of Obedience

Learning to obey God is a process in which we continually step out in faith to do what God has said, while denying the sinful nature and its destructive desires. To progress to higher and higher levels on the path of obedience, we must purposely (1) *"put off...the old man"* (Ephesians 4:22), or the sinful nature, and (2) *"put on the new man"* (Ephesians 4:24), or the new nature of Christlikeness.

1. "Put Off...the Old Man"

"Put off, concerning your former conduct, the old man which grows corrupt according to the deceitful lusts" (Ephesians 4:22). As we discussed previously, society tries in various ways to control corrupt human behavior. Let us examine the main ways by which our culture attempts to do this, so that we will not rely on human methods to accomplish God's work in us.

The "Old Man" Cannot Be Defeated by Human Psychology or Counseling

Many psychologists, psychiatrists, counselors, medical doctors, teachers, and even preachers try to "cure" the sinful nature using human methods and techniques. Yet, their results are limited and temporal because they usually deal with only the symptoms rather than with the root of the problem, which is sin. Many of their treatments attempt to build up a person's ego, thus making "self" the center of the counselee's existence. From this approach come the terms *self-realization* and *self-help*. At first glance, these concepts might seem good; however, in practice, they often encourage human beings to seek within themselves for a solution to sin. Since they are directed at "self," these treatments allow the rebellious nature to continue to reign within an individual.

The "Old Man" Cannot Be Defeated by Laws and Cultural Standards

Many governments and law enforcement agencies attempt to curb people's negative behavior by threatening various fines, punishments, and/or other consequences for those who do not keep society's laws or cultural standards. Yet laws and standards can prove ineffective. For example, not even the threat of the death penalty prevents some people from killing or raping other people or committing other horrible crimes. While laws and cultural norms are helpful for maintaining general order in society, ultimately, they cannot offer a permanent solution for the rebellious heart or change the sinful nature.

The "Old Man" Cannot Be Defeated by Religion

The practice of religion focuses primarily on people's external behavior, often giving the follower an appearance of holiness that neither touches nor modifies his corrupt heart. Without the transformation that comes from the living Christ, the inner man continues to be a corrupt tree that produces bad fruit: *"Every good tree bears good fruit, but a bad tree bears bad fruit. A good tree cannot bear bad fruit, nor can a bad tree bear good fruit. Every tree that does not bear good fruit is cut down and thrown into the fire"* (Matthew 7:17–19). Religion, like laws, may help to keep human behavior in check temporarily, but it cannot change the sinful nature or transform a disobedient heart. Eventually, the "old man" will follow a path of corruption until it perishes.

The "Old Man" Can Be Defeated Only by Being Put to Death

The remedy for the sinful nature cannot be found in psychotherapy, laws, religion, or education. But neither can it be found in merely citing Scripture, singing worship songs, taking classes on morality, or listening to motivational preaching. The remedy is to *execute* the "old man" through a work of spiritual crucifixion. The cross is the only solution for dealing with the sinful nature! As Paul wrote, *"I have been crucified with Christ; it is no longer I who live, but Christ lives in me; and the life which I now live in the flesh I live by faith in the Son of God, who loved me and gave Himself for me"* (Galatians 2:20).

The crucifixion of the sinful nature is a continuous, daily process of submitting to God and denying "self." *"Put to death, therefore, whatever belongs to your earthly nature: sexual immorality, impurity, lust, evil desires and greed, which is idolatry"* (Colossians 3:5 NIV). It is our responsibility to *choose* to crucify the sinful nature—and God will give us the supernatural grace to do it.

"Putting off the old man" and "putting on the new man" are two sides of the same coin of God's plan for the transformation of our heart. The old nature must be crucified. Meanwhile, the manifestation of the new nature must increase in proportion to the crucifixion of the old nature. The "new man" within us is the nature of Christ Himself. And, as John the Baptist said, "[Jesus] *must increase, but I must decrease"* (John 3:30).

The manifestation of the new nature must increase in proportion to the crucifixion of the old nature.

Every day, we must deny the demands of the old nature that rebels against God, in order to give place to the new nature that obeys the will of God. We know that the old nature will continue to act as if it has the right to control us, because it is addicted to doing, thinking, and acting in wrong ways; it is filled with deceitful desires and pride. But, by the Spirit of God, if we crucify the old nature, it will die. That is the only way to establish a lifestyle of obedience to God. The choice is ours! If we live according to the old nature, the fruit we bear will be sin, sickness, lack, death, and endless corruption. But if we live according to the new nature, the fruit we bear will be a manifestation of true life—a life of faith, love, obedience, health, deliverance, power, and peace. We will have the blessing of knowing that God's kingdom is being established on earth and that Christ is being glorified—through us!

"For if we have been united together in the likeness of [Jesus'] death, certainly we also shall be in the likeness of His resurrection, knowing this, that our old man was crucified with Him, that the body of sin might be done away with, that we should no longer be slaves of sin" (Romans 6:5–6). The phrase *"knowing this"* indicates a fact that has already taken place. Unless we acknowledge the reality that our old nature was crucified with Jesus, we will continue to disobey God.

We must apply Christ's completed work of crucifixion in order to defeat the rebellious sinful nature that continually tries to reassert itself in us. Here is the key: We have to receive Christ's work personally. Many people don't understand this principle. For most believers, the crucifixion of their old nature exists in the theoretical realm alone; they do not consider it a reality they can experience here and now. That is why, even though the sinful nature was put to death on the cross with Christ, they continue to be slaves to it—succumbing to corrupt thoughts, such as bitterness and hate; and deceitful desires, such as sexual immorality and greed. It is also why, even though Christ died for their infirmities and their poverty, they continue to be sick, depressed, and in financial need. Their lives are dominated by rebellion, stubbornness, pride, arrogance, and fear.

The good news is that the transformation of our heart is truly possible, because Christ has set us free from the corrupt sinful nature! The apostle Paul said, "*O wretched man that I am! Who will deliver me from this body of death? I thank God; through Jesus Christ our Lord! So then, with the mind I myself serve the law of God, but with the flesh the law of sin*" (Romans 7:24–25). There is a difference between receiving forgiveness for our sin and putting to death the rebellious sinful nature. When I was a new believer, I would commit certain sins that I knew I would commit again even after confessing them. As a result, I used to wonder whether it was worth confessing them. I was trapped in a pattern of sin, and I felt like a hypocrite and a disobedient Christian. What I had was a form of religion.

It wasn't until I received the revelation of the cross, until I received the gospel of the kingdom with power, that I was set free from recurrent sin. The gospel of the kingdom resolves the problem of the corrupt heart; it reveals the only solution for the problem of sin—the crucifixion and death of the old nature. God's plan of redemption involves not just forgiveness for past sins but also victory over a rebellious heart that pushes us to commit acts of disobedience. We must fully understand that when Christ died on the cross, He executed and removed the old nature—once and for all!

Christ executed the old nature on the cross so that we could receive a new nature in Him.

---

2. "Put On the New Man"

"*Put on the new man which was created according to God, in true righteousness and holiness*" (Ephesians 4:24). This mystery of "putting on the new man" must be understood and carried out through revelation by the Holy Spirit. It cannot be analyzed in the mind, because the intellect cannot possibly comprehend it. It has to do with a freewill act that consciously applies the life of the resurrected Christ to us. On the cross, our old nature died. Through the resurrection, we receive a new nature. We must confirm this reality each day, putting on the "*new man*" by asking the Holy Spirit to activate the life of Christ in us. Jesus has already done the work for us. He defeated sin and death, and He rose victoriously as the new Man. The rest—applying that work—is up to us! Ask the Holy Spirit to open your spiritual eyes so that you can receive a clear revelation of what it means to "put on the new man."

Characteristics of the "New Man"

- *The "new man" comes from the new birth.* When we accept the gospel of the kingdom, repent, and experience the new birth through the Holy Spirit, we receive a new nature.

- *The "new man" was produced by God.* A human being cannot produce a new nature by his own strength; neither can laws, religion, good works, or anything else that originates in human methods. The new nature is produced in us solely by God.

- *The "new man" was created in God's likeness—in righteousness and holiness.* It was God's purpose through Christ that a new human race would be born, in which His nature would be restored according to His original plan. (See, for example, Romans 8:29.)

- *The "new man" has an incorruptible nature.* The nature of the new man cannot be corrupted, because it was born of the seed of God, through His everlasting Word: *"Having been born again, not of corruptible seed but incorruptible, through the word of God which lives and abides forever"* (1 Peter 1:23). The seed of which we were born again is incorruptible; therefore, our new nature is incorruptible. Only God could have accomplished this in us. I am not saying that a born-again Christian will never sin. What I am saying is that we have a divine nature that has the capacity not to sin—a nature that was produced in us by Jesus, the Word of God, accomplished through the supernatural exchange of righteousness for sin that Christ effected on the cross and by His resurrection life.

3. Apply God's Supernatural Grace

The old nature expresses itself through rebellion; the new nature expresses itself through obedience. The decision to deny and crucify our old nature is our own. No one can do it for us. However, once we decide to die to "self," the Holy Spirit will empower us with His supernatural grace to carry out the "execution." Again, we cannot transform ourselves in our own strength; when we try to do so, the fruit we produce is dead works. But when we are transformed according to God's grace and strength, we produce the fruit of the Spirit in abundance.

God's supernatural grace enables us to do what we can't do in our own strength.

4. Restore God's Original Intent

The two primary reasons God created human beings are as follows:

+ To reproduce in us the image and likeness of God: "*God said, 'Let Us make man in Our image, according to Our likeness'*" (Genesis 1:26).

+ To give us dominion, power, and authority over the created world: "*God blessed them, and God said to them, 'Be fruitful and multiply; fill the earth and subdue it'*" (Genesis 1:28).

When God restored humanity, He gave us the new nature for those same reasons. Understanding these two purposes is essential to walking in obedience to God. If we know that we were created for these reasons, and if we pursue them in the Spirit, we will automatically live in a way that is pleasing to God.

"*The first man Adam became a living being.' The last Adam became a life-giving spirit*" (1 Corinthians 15:45). Jesus Christ came as the "*last Adam*" to end the legacy of sin and corruption in the human race due to the first Adam's disobedience, so that we could carry out our two original purposes. We believers have the responsibility of reflecting the image of God on earth and of exercising dominion and lordship over the natural world and over the kingdom of darkness. "*For whom* [God] *foreknew, He also predestined to be conformed to the image of His Son, that He might be the firstborn among many brethren*" (Romans 8:29). Do you want to be one of those "*brethren*" who are formed in the image of God's Son? Will you make a commitment today to reject the sinful nature and to obey God's will?

The following testimony is about a husband and wife who decided to die to the old nature that was corrupting them. Jessica and her husband had practiced witchcraft for ten years. Jessica testifies that while her husband was in prison, he met Christians who preached Jesus to him and made him "crazy." But, one day, he came across my book *How to Walk in the Supernatural Power of God* and was so impacted by reading it that he gave his life to Christ. Then, he called his wife and told her that she needed to find King Jesus Ministry and begin to attend church there.

Jessica said that due to their practice of witchcraft, she would hear voices and footsteps in her home that frightened her and didn't let her sleep in peace. Since she was already attending King Jesus church, a team from the church went to her apartment one day to pray and spiritually cleanse the atmosphere there. Later, the team testified that demons manifested in that place in such a strong way that even the necklaces used in the practice of witchcraft moved on their own. They removed over sixty industrial-sized garbage bags full of objects the couple had used in Santería—books, music, images, outfits, necklaces, drums, dolls, altars, and much more—with a value of approximately $120,000. God's power entered that apartment, and, ever since, there have been no more voices or footsteps. Jessica is happy with the peace in her home today. And, as a result of that deliverance and transformation, her mother-in-law and sister-in-law have also given their lives to Jesus.

Dear friend, it is time for you to make a decision. Have you been persuaded by God's promises for you? Are you convinced that He will do what He has said? If your own life is manifesting the works of the sinful nature more than the works of the Spirit, then what Jesus accomplished on the cross has been mainly theoretical to you, and you haven't allowed God's power to transform your life. You need to apply the work of Christ, crucifying the old nature, so that you can live according to your new nature. God is waiting for you to make the decision to obey Him before you experience the consequences of your disobedience. Now is the time for you to straighten your path so that you may reflect the image of your loving Creator and start to exercise dominion and lordship over the earth, according to the authority of Jesus and in the power of the Holy Spirit. If you want to exchange your disobedient heart for an obedient one, pray the following prayer of commitment to God's will—and begin to be transformed!

Prayer of Obedience

Heavenly Father, thank You for Your Son Jesus Christ, who crucified the old nature on the cross so that I could receive a new nature through Him. I ask You to forgive me for living to please the desires of my sinful nature and for not denying them in order to pursue Your purposes. Today, of my own free will, I choose to "put off the old man" and to "put on the new man" in order to live a lifestyle of obedience to You. I desire to obey You always, regardless of whether it is "convenient," "reasonable," or "profitable" for me. Since I know that I cannot do this in my own strength, I appeal to You to accomplish it in me through the supernatural power of the Holy Spirit. Grant me the grace to yield my will to Yours and to exchange my priorities for Yours in regard to every goal and decision I make. I declare that, from this day forward, I will obey Your will and pursue Your purposes. In Jesus' name, amen!

8

The Heart Surrendered to God

Surrender. Submission. Yielding. Sacrifice. Holiness. Today, inside the church as well as outside it, these concepts are unpopular or incomprehensible to most people. Additionally, many who do understand these ideas are afraid of them because they involve the denial of self. The greatest struggle people have with God is accepting and obeying His command to die to "self" and to surrender to Him wholeheartedly.

As we previously discussed, modern psychology and psychiatry have tried for years to provide a cure for people's mental and emotional problems through treatments that empower their ego. These treatments do not take into consideration the human need for total surrender to the Creator or the healing people can receive when they yield to Him. Similarly, in the church, some people have adopted an extreme view of God's grace that produces egocentric and selfish believers who seek instant gratification. Many of these believers do not appreciate the nature of Jesus' sacrifice for them or the lifestyle of surrender to God that He set as a pattern for us. They don't believe they need to give up anything to God; they think they should just receive from Him without fulfilling any responsibility on their part.

God Requires Continuous Surrender

The only way to experience ongoing transformation of the heart and to receive God's blessings is through daily surrender to Him. Jesus said:

Unless a grain of wheat falls into the ground and dies, it remains alone; but if it dies, it produces much grain. He who loves his life will lose it, and he who hates his life in this world will keep it for eternal life. If anyone serves Me, let him follow Me; and where I am, there My servant will be also. If anyone serves Me, him My Father will honor.

(John 12:24–26)

God requires total and continuous surrender on our part. Yet He does not ask us to do anything that He is not willing to do Himself and that He has not already done. From eternity, the God of the universe has surrendered Himself on our behalf. The Father surrendered His Son to be the Savior of the world. The Son yielded His will to the Father throughout His life on earth, culminating at Gethsemane and the cross. And the Holy Spirit yields Himself to the Son. Jesus said, *"When He, the Spirit of truth, has come, He will guide you into all truth; for **He will not speak on His own authority, but whatever He hears He will speak.…He will glorify Me,** for He will take of what is Mine and declare it to you"* (John 16:13–14). And we are to follow God's example. *"Be imitators of God as dear children. And walk in love, as Christ also has loved us and given Himself for us, an offering and a sacrifice to God for a sweet-smelling aroma"* (Ephesians 5:1–2).

The act of surrender, or the giving up of oneself or something that is a part of oneself, is a concept found in the heart of God. The "law of surrender" applies to God, as well to humans, because to sacrifice oneself for the sake of others is an intrinsic part of His nature. I believe that of all God's characteristics, attitudes, and actions, this aspect of surrender reflects the deepest part of Him. Christ was never higher than when He surrendered Himself to become the lowest for us. *"[Christ] made Himself of no reputation, taking the form of a bondservant, and coming in the likeness of men"* (Philippians 2:7). Since surrender and sacrifice are aspects of God's nature, and we know that Jesus surrendered Himself fully to the Father, especially in sacrificing Himself for our sake, why do we look for excuses and justifications—including theological ones—not to surrender ourselves to God? Surrender brings us into harmony with Him and with the nature of His kingdom.

*God does not ask us to do anything that He is not willing to do
Himself and that He has not already done.*

The Surrendered Heart Reminds God of His Son's Sacrifice

Just as our redemption came through Christ's surrender to God's will on the cross, most of what God gives us comes through a "death," or surrender, to Him. I believe that when God sees a person whose heart is truly yielded to Him, He sees Jesus' crucifixion anew; and wherever there is such a crucifixion, God imparts a resurrection! Surrender is the path that Christ walked, and He has paved the way for us to follow Him on that path, which will lead us to supreme exaltation in Him. "[Jesus] *humbled Himself and became obedient to the point of death, even the death of the cross. Therefore God also has highly exalted Him…*" (Philippians 2:8–9). The way "up" to God always starts by going "down" in surrender and humility before Him.

Many people believe in God, go to church, and worship Him, but they don't commit to Him beyond attending Sunday morning services. They don't want to follow the path of surrender that Christ paved for them because it involves giving up "self," subjugating the ego, making spiritual sacrifices to God, and undergoing the transformation of the heart. People don't want to give up their sinful practices or indulgent lifestyle, and they don't want to share in the sufferings of Christ, something that the apostle Paul sought as a vital aspect of his relationship with Jesus. (See Philippians 3:10 NIV.)

Their attitude separates them from the Father's heart because God sees Christ in us not necessarily in the miracles He performs through our lives or in the good deeds we do but in each act of surrender in which we fully submit to Him and His will. Let us remember Jesus' warning: "*Many will say to Me in that day, 'Lord, Lord, have we not prophesied in Your name, cast out demons in Your name, and done many wonders in Your name?' And then I will declare to them, 'I never knew you; depart from Me, you who practice lawlessness!'"* (Matthew 7:22–23).

Willing Surrender Versus Unwilling Surrender

There are those who "commit" to God but never truly surrender to Him. Surrendering goes much deeper than even commitment, because it compels a person to address the deepest part of his rebellion against God. There is a great difference between willing surrender and unwilling surrender. For example, a soldier may commit to military service because his country is at war and his government has instituted a draft, and there is no other option for him than to serve, because he does not want to go to prison. However, his heart may not be in alignment with the reasons why his country is at war or with his own participation in that war. The entire time he serves, the soldier may be internally rebelling against his obligation. If he could walk away from the commitment, he would not hesitate to do so. Likewise, a person may commit to God in order to avoid punishment in hell but never truly surrender his heart out of deep love for God and a devotion to His purposes.

A person will not rise any higher than his level of surrender.

The Surrendered Heart Yields Its Rights

One dictionary definition of *surrender* is "to yield to the power, control, or possession of another upon compulsion or demand." That definition corresponds to the illustration of the drafted soldier we discussed above. Another definition of *surrender* is "to give up completely or agree to forgo especially in favor of another." This definition seems to correspond more closely to our act of surrender to God. Surrender involves giving up the demands of the "self" and the sinful nature in favor of what God wants for us, and giving up our own rights and desires in favor of what would be best for those whom we are called to serve in His name.

I often like to define surrender in this way: "to deny 'self' by choice and conviction," and "to give up one's rights to God." A person whose heart is yielded to God has given up his doubt, unbelief, personal ego, and reliance on his own strength; he has given total control of his life to God. He has moved beyond the natural realm in order to live in the supernatural. He has died to his fears and insecurities so that he may *"live by faith in the Son of God"* (Galatians 2:20) and be *"transformed...from glory to glory"* (2 Corinthians 3:18).

Surrendering our heart to God is one of the greatest acts of faith, because when we think that we have the "right" to hold on to something, it is very difficult for us to understand why we must relinquish it. Surrender has to do with completely trusting the assurances of God's Word that yielding to our heavenly Father will bring forth real, significant, and eternal blessings for us. Faith required for this type of surrender is rooted in a love for God and in an acceptance of the fact that He has promised we will receive back much more than we yield to Him. (See, for example, Matthew 6:33; Mark 10:29–30; Luke 6:38.)

When we surrender our rights and needs to God, we will receive back much more than we yield to Him.

In our society, we hear much about "rights" yet little about responsibility and maturity. The fact is that we cannot expect to have rights without fulfilling our responsibilities; and we cannot assume responsibilities unless our character is mature. If you fulfill your responsibilities in your relationship with God, and if you yield your rights in order to do His will, you will be able to claim the rights that Christ won for you by His surrender and obedience on the cross of Calvary, where He redeemed humanity from the curse of rebellion. Among those rights—of which we are heirs (see Romans 8:17)—are salvation, healing, deliverance, prosperity, peace, and joy. Remember that we don't have these rights by deserving them. We have them only because they are given to us through Christ.

A person whose heart is surrendered to God has moved beyond the natural realm in order to live in the supernatural.

The Surrendered Heart Activates the "Law of Exchange"

In the spiritual world, the "law of exchange" means the following: The measure in which you die to "self" is the measure in which God's life will increase and manifest in you; the measure in which you give of yourself to God, yielding to Him through His grace, is the measure in which He will give of Himself to you, with all His blessings. God will receive you if you have surrendered to Him, so that you can receive Him through the life and power that He "yields" to you.

We know that human beings have legitimate inherent rights and needs, such as the right to life and to having their bodily needs met—food, shelter, sleep, and so forth. However, when a person surrenders to God and his life is centered on Christ, as well as on the needs of other people, even these rights and needs take second place. As John the Baptist said, "[Jesus] *must increase, but I must decrease*" (John 3:30).

Much of modern Christianity teaches that we will receive God's blessings "free of charge"—meaning, without any responsibility on our part. This is a false mentality. Nothing is free! Salvation is free for us solely because Christ paid the price for sin—a price that was impossible for any human being to pay. But salvation and every other aspect of a life of faith require our surrender to God. Some people in the church want all of God's blessings without having to obey Him, submit to Him, pray to Him, give tithes or offerings to Him, or seek His face. They want to "use" God for their purposes, as if He were in their employ, or as if He owed them something! They maintain this attitude due to their erroneous ideas about God's grace.

Read what the apostle Paul wrote about his walk with God: *"By the grace of God I am what I am, and His grace toward me was not in vain; but I labored more abundantly than they all, yet not I, but the grace of God which was with me*" (1 Corinthians 15:10). Everything we receive from God is according to His supernatural grace. However, that doesn't mean there is nothing for us to do; without our surrender and personal participation in God's purposes, the giving of that grace would be in vain.

In the "law of exchange," the measure in which we give of ourselves to God is the measure in which He gives of Himself to us.

The Surrendered Heart Is a Sign of Spiritual Maturity

God's principles of blessing will therefore be effective in our life as we surrender to Him our heart, our will, and our rights. Many people want to automatically "fix" everything that's wrong in their life by using biblical principles as if they were magic formulas. But God's power doesn't work that way. Consequently, there are a number of people in the body of Christ today who are frustrated because they think they are applying biblical principles of prosperity, health, and other areas, but they never see any results because they have not fully surrendered to God. Many of these people live with the immature attitude of a spoiled child who refuses to assume responsibility for his actions but expects gifts and privileges anyway.

If implementing biblical principles were as simple as applying a formula, there would be no difference between God's principles and the principles of magic, witchcraft, and other practices that are anti-Christ and anti-surrender of the "self." True Christianity is about a relationship with our heavenly Father that leads us to reflect His very nature and life. It is not about speaking "magic words" through which we can achieve our own purposes, regardless of how good those purposes might seem.

The Surrendered Heart Freely Obeys and Yields by Choice

When we fully surrender "self," our ongoing submission to God will not seem offensive to us, because we will be acting from our own free will.

It won't matter what we are called to do or what sacrifice is involved—we will obey. We will serve God joyfully out of love and deep conviction, without complaint.

The following is the testimony of a man named Frederic, who describes the blessings he received by surrendering his heart to God. He writes, "When I was a child, my father was a pastor. My entire family was involved in the church, and I evangelized with my mother. However, what I remember most was the way my father would beat my sisters, my mother, and me. He was an ex-member of the French Special Forces, with whom he had served for many years in Indochina, and he had returned home with post-traumatic stress disorder.

"He used to tell me, 'Men don't cry,' then beat me as if he were beating a soldier, saying that if I cried, he would kill me. After the beatings, he would not allow my mother to take me to the hospital or to tell anyone in the church about it, threatening to kill her if she did. He would often drag her before me and beat her while yelling, 'What will you do, Son? Can you fight me and defend your mother?' He also taught me martial training in which the objective of each movement was to break a bone of, and/or to kill, one's opponent. By the time I was ten years old, I had suffered many fractures—of the teeth, nose, hip, ribs, wrists, ankles, fingers, and toes—as well as countless head injuries. In addition, my father raped and abused me until I turned seventeen, when he realized that I was no longer a child, and I almost killed him with his own technique.

"After that event, I was so afraid of what he would do that I left home and never returned or spoke to him again. I sought refuge with family members who had formed a criminal organization. They took me in and used the hate that I carried in my heart, and my fighting abilities, to do their dirty work. When I turned twenty-one, I discovered that the man who had raised me was not my biological father; he was my stepfather. He and my mother had brought me up because of a promise they had made to my real father, who had felt guilty for abandoning me. I never met my real father because he was killed only a few years before I discovered the truth. My world crumpled beneath me. I was so angry that I even tried to commit suicide by taking pills.

"I had money and fame, and I traveled from country to country consuming drugs and alcohol. Every relationship I was in failed. One day, my mother called to tell me that my stepfather had committed suicide. That made me even angrier, because I had waited many years for him to ask me to forgive him, and now that would never happen.

"In time, I met a Christian girl. We fell in love and moved in together. A little while after that, I lost my job and, with it, every opportunity to participate in the dirty work I had been doing. My ties with organized crime ended, but I didn't care about anything, as long as I had the love of my woman. But then she told me that God had ordered her to leave me because we were going down different paths and she loved God more than she loved anyone else.

"One night, realizing that she was not about to change her mind, I cursed her, the church, and Apostle Maldonado. I declared that if God wanted war, I would go against Him and His church. But suddenly, and against my will, I fell to my knees and spent the entire night crying. In my mind, I heard a voice that said, *Surrender!* Later, I had a dream in which I was in a room without doors, fighting against a very strong Man. He fought me as if He knew every one of my moves, anticipating all of my attacks. He hurt me so much that the pain woke me. Then I heard a voice say, *Surrender now, and allow your heart to open up, so you can return to Me.*

"The next day, I shared the dream with my girlfriend, and she invited me to church. During the ministry part of the service, tears began to flow from me. I felt very ashamed for crying in front of all those people, because I remembered my stepfather's words that 'men don't cry.' But I quickly stopped fighting it and said out loud, 'I surrender!' At that moment, I felt my heart come back to life, and I experienced an inner peace I didn't recognize. I felt God's love, and my soul was full of joy.

"Since that day, my life has been totally transformed. I apologized to the apostle, and he said to me, 'You are my son, and I love you.' Those words repaired the negative image I had of fathers, broke the curse of rejection, and even led me to forgive my father and stepfather. For more than thirty years, my heart had been as dead as a rock, but when I surrendered it to God, He gave me a new heart and filled it with His love."

For the person who is fully surrendered to God, obedience and submission are not a "sacrifice" but a pleasure.

Attitudes That Can Hinder Surrender

Contrary to what many people think, surrender to God brings peace, joy, and purpose into our life. Accordingly, negative attitudes toward surrender and affirming attitudes toward "self" will block our surrender to Him. In the last chapter, we discussed how we cannot follow Christ and do His will if we have a rebellious, disobedient heart that seeks to please the sinful nature, or the "old man." And, we saw that the only way to *"put off... the old man"* (Ephesians 4:22) and to *"put on the new man"* (Ephesians 4:24) is by crucifying the sinful nature. In contrast, much of modern psychology and psychiatry generally focuses on "improving" the self—not dying to it. These branches of human knowledge don't start or end with God. They begin and end with "self," or the human ego. They are based on the idea that man is his own ultimate source, and they place science in the position of supreme truth. However, humans were not created to be "gods" or to make the intellect their god.

These approaches are unable to deal effectively with the problem of a person's iniquity and heart corruption, and they cannot transform a heart. Let's further explore these themes by looking at three popular concepts of "self-realization" that can hinder our full surrender to God.

On the surface, the following concepts don't appear to be negative ideas. Yet, we will see that when they are taken to their logical conclusions, they oppose God's will because they empower the fallen ego and lead people to focus on self. Ultimately, therefore, they are substitutions for surrendering to God. In contrast, Christ commands us to "crucify" the "self" and the sinful nature, so that we will be able to genuinely love God and other people and serve others in His name.

1. "Know Yourself"

The first concept is "know yourself." We often hear this idea in the media and from psychologists and counselors. Discovering who we truly are is, of course, a good thing; however, the idea here is generally to evaluate ourselves solely in relation to ourselves and other human beings. If we do this, we will always have a limited view of ourselves, and we will miss the essence of who we are. We must see ourselves in the light of our Creator and the way in which He has made us and desires for us to live. To know ourselves in merely a human sense gives us a temporal, earthly, fallen perspective of who we were meant to be. Moreover, it does not tell us all that we can *become* in Christ!

We are eternal beings. And, when we are born of God, we become His children and begin the process of being conformed to the image of His Son Jesus. We are transformed into the likeness of the One who is the most beautiful, holy, pure Person who ever lived. When we look at ourselves in Him, we know who we really are—and what God's transformation process is making us into. Any other image than that is a distortion of true humanity as God intended it to be.

2. "Accept Yourself Just as You Are"

This idea encourages people to accept everything about themselves— good and bad—without feeling a need to change, so that they adopt the perspective that says, "This is just who I am." But how can we accept the sinful nature, which is addicted to fleshly desires, lies, unforgiveness, anger, bitterness, strife, and many other evils? How can we accept "self" when it is full of conflicts, contradictions, guilt, fear, and egocentrism? To accept ourselves in such a state is unthinkable! If you were somehow to stand outside of yourself and then ask yourself if you could accept living under the conditions I just described, your answer would certainly be an emphatic no. Yet this is what people are being encouraged to do. The saddest part of this situation is that when they try to do this, many people find that they are unacceptable to themselves. Life becomes unbearable to them.

At first, we might think that a diet of "self" and ego tastes sweet and satisfying; but when we begin to digest our selfishness, our "stomach," or inner life, becomes bitter! This is because we were created to surrender to

God and to give of ourselves for the sake of others. We were not made to merely indulge our own desires and preferences.

Why do we become angry with other people? Often, it is because they have interfered with what our "self" wanted. Why do we lie? Because our "self" wants to maintain its position, security, and reputation, no matter what. Why do we participate in sexually immoral acts? Because we seek to please the appetites of the corrupt "self." Why do we experience envy? Because someone else has received what our "self" wanted. The aforementioned negative attitudes and sins are merely the fruit of a "self" that refuses to surrender its control to God. Lack of surrender is the root of many sins; the sins themselves are external symptoms of the internal heart condition. When we deal only with the symptoms, we show that we are ignorant about the true culprit behind them.

Is it ever valid to "accept yourself"? Yes, when you have been born again and your heart is being transformed continually by the presence and power of God. For example, when someone surrenders his heart to Christ for the first time and receives salvation with the forgiveness of sins, he may say that he feels a peace he has never experienced before. There is peace within him because his spirit has been renewed in the image and likeness of Christ, and the process of dying to his sinful nature has begun. Only when we are being *transformed...from glory to glory*" (2 Corinthians 3:18) can we be at peace with God and with ourselves.

In contrast, to tell people to accept their old egocentric, selfish nature is to ask them to deny the work of the cross and the grace of transformation that are available through God's Holy Spirit. What would be the need for Jesus' death and resurrection if we could solve all our problems by just accepting ourselves—sin and all—rather than by experiencing the new birth and the tran

3. "Express Yourself"

The third concept, "express yourself," also places the ego at the center of life. Such an approach often feeds the sickness it is trying to cure, because many of the problems that human beings face are a consequence of expressing their own selfishness and egocentrism to others. The "self" imposes its needs (whether valid or invalid) on others, asserts its point of view, and demands various rights and benefits.

Moreover, when the views and needs of a person's ego run counter to the sovereign will of the Creator, that individual will reveal his rebellion as he expresses himself. *"For out of the abundance of the heart his mouth speaks"* (Luke 6:45). We live in a society that generally accepts such practices as abortion, homosexuality, and cohabitation as rights related to "freedom of expression" and "diversity." Yet, if someone expresses an opinion against these practices, he is often regarded by others as discriminatory. Because many people have enthroned the ego in their heart, they are not willing to tolerate anyone who points out that their behavior is against the will of God. They resist being led toward repentance and surrender to the Father. In fact, in many nations, it seems that the fallen human ego has obtained so much clout that laws have been instituted to defend it.

Surrender Leads to Deliverance

The major flaw in the foundation of the above three concepts is their claim that the answer to people's problems—such as depression, emotional wounds, broken relationships, and generational curses—is found within the "self." But the true solution to these issues is the transformation of the heart, which comes by surrendering ourselves fully to God.

The crucified self is a blessing. It is a means of deliverance that allows the "new man"—the redeemed and sanctified self—to fulfill the charge of Isaiah 60:1: *"Arise, shine; for your light has come! And the glory of the LORD is risen upon you."*

When we continually surrender to God, He continually works in us and through us.

Clayton is a Haitian student who was trapped in drugs, delinquency, and sexual immorality until he surrendered to an invitation to return to faith in God. The following is his testimony: "I come from a dysfunctional home, so I was raised by my grandmother until I was ten. She took me to church and taught me the fear of the Lord. However, when my parents brought me to live with them, my life completely changed for the worse. My father was a drug dealer, and I adopted his lifestyle. I had weapons, girlfriends, money, and fame as a motorcyclist—and my life was headed directly to perdition. I grew up with such a perverted mentality that I even led my friends to practice bestiality. The desire to have intimacy with horses consumed me, even when I was with my girlfriend.

"On a certain occasion, some drug dealers placed a price on my life and on my cousin's life. We were really afraid. We were under so much stress that we would smoke a quarter pound of marijuana every night. I didn't want to know who was going to kill me, so I would make every effort not to be aware of anything so I could stop thinking about it. I remember saying, 'Christ or death!' I used many different drugs, abused alcohol, and viewed pornography. I lacked purpose, and I didn't have a way out. I was a waste of oxygen.

"When I turned eighteen, I didn't want to live anymore, so I decided I would take my own life. One day, I came across a girl I knew who stopped and said, 'Come with me. Let's go to church.' She had given me the same invitation many times, and I had always arrogantly refused. I don't know why, but, that time, I stood up and followed her. And, that day, I exited my dark world and entered the light of God. As I crossed each street on the way to the church, I felt as if the weight of the world was being removed from my shoulders and was falling to the ground. I have never looked back."

Denying oneself in obedience to God is a sign of surrender to Him.

Christ said, "*If anyone desires to come after Me, let him deny himself, and take up his cross, and follow Me. For whoever desires to save his life will lose it, but whoever loses his life for My sake will find it*" (Matthew 16:24–25). Is this command hard to accomplish? It is—if we try to do it in our own strength, rather than allowing God's supernatural grace to work in our heart so that we may fulfill it. Jesus' admonition demands total surrender, requiring everything of us, but it is for our own well-being.

The issue is not really *whether* we will surrender ourselves but *to whom* we will surrender. The sinful nature demands our full surrender, too. It requires more than just our time, loyalty, trust, resources, or service; it demands that we surrender to it—spirit, soul, and body—in order to serve selfishness and egocentrism on a path in which we will be consumed by sin until we are ultimately destroyed.

The sinful nature demands that we surrender to it—spirit, soul, and body—in order to serve selfishness and egocentrism, which will ultimately destroy us.

We will never enter into the fullness of God's presence, with His anointing and power, unless our "self" surrenders. We will never experience higher dimensions of God's glory until our ego dies. How much of God's presence and glory do you want? The degree to which you are willing to die to "self" depends on the strength of your desire for more of God. The person who is truly dead to his ego doesn't have self-centered desires, and he doesn't fight with others over egocentric matters. Instead, while death to "self" is taking place in him, new dimensions of God's glory are continually being revealed to him.

Blessings and Benefits of Surrendering Our Heart to God

Let us now review the major blessings and benefits of surrendering our heart to God.

1. The Heart Increasingly Becomes a Holy Dwelling Place for God's Presence

Surrendering our heart to God allows the Holy Spirit to work His transformation in us. When we yield to God, we are changed into genuine people. Our heart becomes transparent, and we stop hiding from Him, which Adam and Eve did when they sinned and forfeited their communion with their Creator. (See Genesis 3:8.) The more we surrender to God and die to "self," the more God will fill us with His presence, so that we become a holy dwelling place for Him. (See, for example, Ephesians 2:19–22.)

2. We Are Able to Know the Lord Better and to Manifest His Nature

Paul wrote, *"Yet indeed I also count all things loss for the excellence of the knowledge of Christ Jesus…; that I may know Him and the power of His resurrection, and the fellowship of His sufferings, being conformed to His death"* (Philippians 3:8–10). There is no way to know God intimately—no way to know His true person and nature—without surrendering our egocentric heart, which is full of selfishness and pride. Additionally, we will not be able to manifest God's likeness—thereby experiencing and manifesting our own true nature—if we do not relinquish our self-centeredness.

Surrendering to God does not involve practicing religious rituals, physically punishing ourselves for sin, or trying to crucify the sinful nature in our own strength. It has to do with yielding our will and placing "self"— with all of its demands and rebellion—on the cross. We can live for God only by His supernatural grace, but we can't fully do that until we "die" by grace, so that the life of Christ can rise in us as the "new man," redeemed from sin and death.

The area in which you are struggling is the area that you have not surrendered to God. Surrender now!

---

3. We Receive a Greater Measure of God's Power

"That I may know Him and the power of His resurrection" (Philippians 3:10). Christ's resurrection, with all its power, occurred after He surrendered Himself to God, taking our sinful nature on Himself on the cross so that we could be liberated from sin and death. Similarly, a person who lives in full surrender to God, continually denying the "self," will always carry within him a great measure of supernatural power. Most men and women who have walked in God's power have learned to surrender to Him; they have understood that without spiritual sacrifice and *"the fellowship of*

[Christ's] *sufferings*" (Philippians 3:10), there can be no power. This principle was signified in Jesus' baptism in the Jordan River.

> *Then Jesus came from Galilee to John at the Jordan to be baptized by him. And John tried to prevent Him, saying, "I need to be baptized by You, and are You coming to me?" But Jesus answered and said to him, "Permit it to be so now, for thus it is fitting for us to fulfill all righteousness." Then he allowed Him. When He had been baptized, Jesus came up immediately from the water; and behold, the heavens were opened to Him, and **He saw the Spirit of God descending like a dove and alighting upon Him.*** (Matthew 3:13–16)

In the New Testament, the Greek word translated *"Jordan"* comes from a Hebrew word meaning "a descender." I believe baptism in the Jordan River symbolized surrender to God, which is the entrance to the supernatural, including the working of miracles. Remember, the way "up" to God always starts by going "down" in surrender and humility before Him. Jesus was empowered by the Spirit after His baptism in the Jordan River. (See Luke 4:1.) The Scriptures say, *"God anointed Jesus of Nazareth with the Holy Spirit and with power, who went about doing good and healing all who were oppressed by the devil, for God was with Him"* (Acts 10:38).

A number of biblical events are connected with the Jordan River. For example, in the Old Testament, the prophet Elisha instructed Naaman of Syria to dip seven times in the Jordan to be healed of his leprosy. At first, Naaman was offended and suggested that he might bathe in superior rivers located in his own nation. Those other rivers represent human ability rather than God's supernatural power. When Naaman was persuaded by his servants to follow Elisha's instructions, he was completely healed. (See 2 Kings 5:1–14.) It was not the water of the Jordan itself but Naaman's obedience to God's command that brought about his miraculous healing.

When you surrender voluntarily to God, He will not deny you His power; it is guaranteed!

Many Israelites chose to be baptized by John in the Jordan as a sign of their repentance. (See, for example, Matthew 3:1–2, 5–6.) Each new generation of people must come to their own "baptism in the Jordan"—their own "descent" from pride and self-sufficiency through surrender to God and yielding to His will. Many people in today's generation want a shortcut to God's power without having to surrender their will to Him or having to die to "self." Yet, to be empowered by God, we must be willing to yield to Him. The reason Christ was anointed with the Holy Spirit *"without limit"* (John 3:34 NIV) is that He continually surrendered to His Father.

We all need a Jordan experience, a place of surrender, before we can receive a fresh anointing from God. Such power is poured into an individual who is God's "vessel," someone who has found his identity in Christ, so that he is enabled to manifest the activity of the supernatural. Every time I surrender a specific area of my life to God, I see His divine anointing move into that area, and I experience an increase of His supernatural power. This is a great benefit of surrender. As we yield to God, we are enabled to heal, to deliver, and to believe God for other miracles.

What are some areas in your life in which you need empowerment? Are you willing to surrender your will to God in regard to your relationships, your finances, your ministry, or any other area about which God is speaking to you, in order to be empowered as Jesus was?

The place/area of your life in which you yield your will to God is the place/area in which you will be empowered.

The following testimony, by a man named David, demonstrates the power of surrender. He writes, "My arrival at King Jesus Ministry can be explained only as a supernatural intervention of the living God. I started as the pastor of a religious organization that did not believe in signs, wonders, and miracles from God. However, my insatiable hunger for God caused me to question that doctrine. Slowly, a series of events led me to the revelation that there was much more for me than what I had previously known. Several years later, while I was praying, God spoke one word to me—a word that changed my world by uprooting me and leading me to a place I had never imagined going. That word was *Miami*.

"Encouraged by my wife, I explored the possibilities, and, a short time later, we made the decision to resign from the church where we had thought we would spend the rest of our lives, and move to a city where we didn't know anyone. We arrived in sunny South Florida with 'dreams and visions.' Our plan was to start our own church, but God's plan was very different.

"One Father's Day, while I was praying and fasting and seeking God's will for our future, His audible voice came to me with a specific order: 'Go to King Jesus Ministry.' We entered the church anonymous and unnoticed but greatly enthusiastic. I was so touched during the service that, for the first time in a church environment, tears flowed down my cheeks. At a later service, Apostle Maldonado spoke to my wife and me. He asked us to set our dreams aside and receive training in order to be sent out by King Jesus church to minister, and we agreed.

"We had to surrender to God, allowing our old foundation to be transformed. We let go of one mantle and received a new one. We had a humble beginning, like that of a new believer. The hardest decision to make was to give up my credentials as a pastor from our previous organization, not knowing if I would ever have that title again. God spoke to us about surrender, so we followed His instructions, gave up control, and committed to walk by faith in His will for our lives, disregarding the titles and the status we'd formerly had, with the understanding that God had a mission for us.

"In time, Apostle Maldonado ordained us because the Lord had put it in his heart to do so. Ever since then, I have enjoyed the privilege of traveling to the nations with him as part of his team. We received everything we wanted for our ministry and for our family because of our surrender. As we've lived a life of surrender, God has opened many doors for us, and we are active in the vision of the ministry. Now I understand what it means to walk in the supernatural power of God, to cast out demons, to set the oppressed free, and to heal the sick. My wife and I are very happy to be at King Jesus church. We hunger to move in God's love in order to manifest

His power and to continue to do the work of His ministry, so that our lives can bring other people closer to Him."

Surrender involves letting God be God in and through us. When you surrender to Him continually, you can give to others out of what He has given to you. It should be the passion of every believer to manifest God's presence wherever he goes and to be used by Him to heal the sick, win souls for Christ, and set free the oppressed.

The level of anointing that operates in your life is proportionate to your level of surrender.

A measure of God's anointing is held back from us when we have not fully surrendered our heart to Him. God has provided divine anointing not only for healing, deliverance, and other miracles but also for business, the arts, communications, sports, and other fields. These anointings are waiting for God's people to fully yield their lives to their Creator. We receive everything from God by His grace, but that grace is activated through the surrender of our heart.

When Shane from Puerto Rico decided to surrender to God and commit to Him once and for all, his life was transformed. He writes, "During my childhood, I continually looked for love but was unable to find it. I never met my biological father, and my mother was in prison until I turned five. My brother, sister, and I lived with our grandmother, and when my mother was released from prison, she came to live with us, but she was battling a drug addiction that kept her away from me time and time again. She spent nights as a prostitute, smoked crack, used cocaine and heroin, and was constantly in and out of jail.

"When I turned seven, my mother called a taxi so she could go and buy drugs, but when the taxi arrived and she got into it, I jumped onto the hood of the car and begged her not to go, because I knew she would not return for months. The Department of Children and Families opened an investigation into our family and decided to take away my mother's custody of my siblings and me. From the ages of ten to fourteen, I lived separated from my siblings and grandmother. When I was fourteen, one of my cousins adopted me; but when I was seventeen, for lack of money, he threw me out into the streets.

"I lived in the streets, left school, and started using drugs. I would sleep in my sister's car. I remember saying to the Lord, 'Father, I need help because I don't know in what direction my life is heading.' For two years, I lived a lifestyle of immorality, alcohol, and drugs. Every morning, the Spirit of God would tell me to change my life; otherwise, the only thing I had waiting for me was death and destruction.

"The homeowner where I then lived was a Christian, and one day she said to me, 'I don't know what you are doing with your life, but you have to change; otherwise, you will not live with me for much longer.' At that moment, Jesus spoke to me and said, *Let go of all your fears. I am with you.* I opened up the Bible and read a Scripture about God guiding the children of Israel through the desert, and essentially saying to them, 'Remember when you didn't have shoes for your feet or clothes on your back or food to eat? I was there. I took care of you and prepared the way.' The Spirit of God fell upon me, and I began to cry in His presence. The next day, I went to King Jesus International Ministry, where I surrendered my life to God. Since that day, He has filled me with His love, joy, and peace and has transformed me. I have known the love of the Father through everything that I have learned in this ministry. I earned my high school diploma, obtained a full-time job, and am currently attending college. God restored my life, and I live to preach the gospel of Christ and to share His love with the world."

Consequences of Refusing to Surrender to God

There are many blessings related to surrendering to God. But there are also consequences for those who refuse to surrender to Him. Let us review several of them.

1. *The person who refuses to surrender to God never advances in the process of heart transformation—or he stalls somewhere in the midst of that process.* He becomes conformed to "self," so he does not grow and mature in Christ and, consequently, reflects a distorted image

of God. If he is a believer, he may even begin to walk away from the Lord.

2. *The person who refuses to surrender to God suffers an inability to believe in His promises and to access His supernatural power.* In practical terms, the individual's only reality will be the natural realm, and he will always feel dissatisfied because he will live outside the spiritual atmosphere in which he could receive and experience the life and blessings of God.

3. *The person who refuses to surrender to God cannot carry out his true purpose in life.* He is unable to hear what the Lord is saying to him, and he is distracted by interests that are not aligned with God's will for him.

4. *The person who refuses to surrender to God often experiences friction in his relationships.* Because he has not died to "self" and subdued the sinful nature, he continues to feed his selfishness and stubbornness. Consequently, his family ties, friendships, and other associations may become severely strained. His may even experience the breakup of his family.

Surrender is one of the means by which we have access to, and can appropriate, the power of God.

God will sometimes use adverse circumstances in people's lives to cause them to seek Him and to surrender to His will, so that they may receive His blessings. For instance, though He never causes sickness, He may use sickness to draw someone's attention to Him. This is what happened to a woman named Vanessa. When she was seven years old, she began to suffer from uterine bleeding. By the time she was fifteen, she had already undergone several surgeries. When she was twenty-one, the doctors diagnosed her with uterine cancer. She had quarterly medical examinations and eventually underwent a hysterectomy. But then she began to suffer frequent dizziness, and she was later diagnosed as having multiple sclerosis.

Then she met one of the leaders of our church, who invited her to our New Year's Eve service. That day, I preached about our supernatural God who can heal any sickness and change any adverse circumstance. Vanessa returned home angry. She was furious with God because she didn't consider herself a sinner, and she had prayed and sought God for healing; yet, instead of improving, her body kept getting weaker and weaker.

Then she cried out to God with a surrendered heart, asking Him to show her that He is real. She made a covenant with Him, saying, "If You heal me, my children and I will always serve You." The following Monday, she went to a doctor's appointment to have a test related to the multiple sclerosis. The technicians kept repeating the test, and she was there for four hours. She was told that the machine was broken, because they couldn't find anything wrong with her; yet even when they used another machine, the results were the same. Vanessa went home upset with the doctors, but when she went for an appointment with her oncologist, something similar happened. The doctor took biopsies, and four doctors reviewed the results of the tests. Finally, her doctor said, "Vanessa, I don't see anything." When she was back at home, alone in her bedroom, she started to cry. She was broken and grateful, recognizing that the supernatural power of God had healed all of her sicknesses.

Christ is Lord of your life only in those areas that you have surrendered to Him.

Qualities of the Surrendered Heart

When an individual has a surrendered heart, he manifests the following qualities:

+ *The person with a surrendered heart is quick to respond to God and to answer Him.* He does not doubt God or stubbornly resist Him, because his internal struggle with "self" has diminished, and his obedience is usually immediate.

+ *The person with a surrendered heart always says yes to what God asks.* This response leads him to be in God's perfect will and to receive all His blessings without restriction.

+ *The person with a surrendered heart yields to change.* He has a willing spirit that allows the Holy Spirit to continuously transform his heart, leading him to reflect Christ's nature and to help establish God's kingdom on the earth.

+ *The person with a surrendered heart worships God as an act of submission and love, not out of a sense of obligation.* He knows the reality of David's prayer, *"In your presence is fullness of joy; at Your right hand are pleasures forevermore"* (Psalm 16:11).

Prayer of Surrender to God

Surrendering to God is a personal decision that must be made feely and continuously in every area of our life—daily, weekly, monthly, and yearly. It is a choice that no one else can make for us—not our spouse, children, siblings, church leaders, or friends. Therefore, the best thing I can do now to encourage you to yield to God is to offer you a prayer that, of your own free will, you can pray in surrender to Him. Use the following prayer as a pattern for your daily surrender. Yield your whole life, including your spouse, children, friendships, career, finances, health, thoughts, dreams, and emotions. Do it right now, and continue to do it every day. Surrender is not always easy, especially at first, because as soon as you choose to die to "self" and the sinful nature, the "old man" will rebel and want to retake the throne of your heart. Thus, in order to surrender, you need to rely on God's supernatural grace, which goes beyond your own strength! He will give you His grace as you trust in Him.

Father, in the name of Jesus, I open my heart to You. I want more of Your presence, anointing, and power. Right now, I surrender my will to You and crucify the "self." I declare that I am dead to "self" and the sinful nature so that I can do Your will. I surrender to obey Your Word and to follow the direction of Your Spirit. I am being transformed into the image of Christ, who is the perfect Man. I pledge to be under spiritual authority and not to rebel against You or Your delegated authorities. In the name of Jesus, I submit everything I have and everything I am to You, asking You to be Lord and Master of all. I yield my life to You and choose to let You be in full control. Amen!

Prayer for Salvation and Transformation

If you have never before opened your heart to Jesus, allowing Him to enter and to be your Lord and Savior, and allowing God to fill you with His Spirit, I want to give you another opportunity to do so right now. You will not be able to fully surrender your heart to God or have access to His blessings and promises until His Spirit is dwelling in you. God will give you the supernatural grace to do, according to His will, what you cannot do in your own strength. Repeat the following prayer and yield your heart to the Lord today.

Heavenly Father, I recognize that I am a sinner and that my sin separates me from You. My heart is in need of transformation, which only You can accomplish. I believe that Jesus died on the cross for me and that You raised Him from the dead. I confess with my mouth that Jesus is Lord. I repent of all my sins and break every evil covenant I have made with the world, with my sinful nature, and with the devil. According to the power of Jesus' sacrifice for me, I break all generational curses operating in my life. Now, I make a new covenant of righteousness with Jesus. I ask Jesus to come into my heart and to change my life, filling me with the Holy Spirit. If I were to die right now, I know I would be in Your presence when I opened my eyes in eternity. In Jesus' name, amen!

9

The Broken Heart

In the last two chapters, we've discussed the obedient heart and the surrendered heart. Yet what happens when we persist in going against God's will, refusing to surrender to His plan for our life or a specific area of it? Continuing to rebel against God has a high price—the price of spiritual brokenness. In some cases, for those who harden their heart and maintain their resistance to Him, the price is spiritual ruin.

Many people know they are rebelling against God as they live an immoral lifestyle, ignore God's call on their life, refuse to submit to a specific command He has given, or disobey Him in some other way. They function according to their own terms and standards, resisting the purposes of their Creator.

Often, while people are in this state of resistance, they believe they can escape God's chastisement and correction. Yet God disciplines and corrects those whom He loves. (See, for example, Proverbs 3:12.) It is much better for us to willingly submit to our heavenly Father than to have to experience brokenness—either by way of the destructive circumstances we've created for ourselves or by a direct intervention of our merciful God, who sometimes has to "break" His disobedient children for their own good. The Lord always has our best interests in mind in His dealings with us. As the writer of Hebrews said, *"We have all had human fathers who disciplined us and we respected them for it. How much more should we submit to the Father of our spirits and live!"* (Hebrews 12:9 NIV).

Transformation Through Brokenness

There may also be times when we experience a period of brokenness not because we are in active rebellion against God but because we are battling a difficult situation in life, such as an illness, a deep sense of hopelessness, or the distressing behavior of a wayward child. Other times, we may go through brokenness because God desires to instruct us about an aspect of His nature and ways. The hardest periods of my life have been the times when God has "broken" me. While I am in the midst of the process, I don't always understand why it needs to happen; however, I understand and appreciate it once it is over. *"No chastening seems to be joyful for the present, but painful; nevertheless, afterward it yields the peaceable fruit of righteousness to those who have been trained by it"* (Hebrews 12:11).

After we have been broken, our priorities change, and what matters most to us is God. Each time I have undergone brokenness and submitted to my heavenly Father, I have received greater spiritual freedom and blessing. My heart has been transformed: My passion to please God and to do His will has increased. I have experienced deeper inner peace and a greater sense of fulfillment. I have become more sensitive and humble, and I have become more willing to recognize my dependency on God. I am more teachable and forgiving. I also produce more fruit in my personal and ministerial life. But, above all, I experience a greater hunger and thirst for God, leading me to higher levels of surrender and a closer relationship with Him.

"Unconditional Surrender"

We all have areas in our life over which we know we haven't given God full control. Yet, instead of yielding those areas to our Creator and Lord, we often argue with Him about them! At times, we justify our sins, thinking that because we have been trying to overcome a certain weakness for a long time, without apparent results, there is nothing more that we can do about it. We become spiritually stagnant in that area and no longer give it to God or seek transformation. When this is the case, we reveal that a degree of complacency, independence, selfishness, unbelief, and/or rebellion is still operating in us.

The Lord doesn't want us to remain in a condition that keeps our heart and mind from being united with His, preventing us from doing His will and experiencing all the blessings He desires for us. And brokenness of heart is often the means God has to use to deal with our stubbornness, pride, and other obstacles that are in the way of our total obedience to, and trust in, Him. Brokenness is a painful condition in which we realize there is nothing within us that can help or save our situation—and sometimes even our life. Our only help is to submit to the love and lordship of Christ. In that place, our heart no longer tries to argue, reason, or excuse itself before God. We have arrived at the point where we are willing to yield to Him and to obey Him without reservation. We come before God under terms of "unconditional surrender."

The Gift of Brokenness

Regardless of the reason for our brokenness or what form it takes in our life, we can know this: As painful as it is, brokenness is a gift, because it allows us an opportunity to return to God and/or to know Him in a deeper way. The illustration of the loving and generous father in the parable of the prodigal son is a picture of our heavenly Father's attitude toward us when we go through brokenness. Just as in the parable, the Lord welcomes us back with open arms when we step back onto the path that leads home to Him. (See Luke 15:11–24, 32.)

The heart of our heavenly Father longs for His children to turn from their rebellion and to draw near to Him. His heart is reflected in Jesus' lament over Jerusalem—over the hardened and indifferent hearts of the people: *"O Jerusalem, Jerusalem, the one who kills the prophets and stones those who are sent to her! How often I wanted to gather your children together, as a hen gathers her chicks under her wings, but you were not willing!"* (Matthew 23:37). When our heart is hardened or indifferent, God will allow us to experience brokenness for the purpose of renewing us, so that the transformation of our heart into the image of Christ may continue.

Every human being who surrenders to God during the process of brokenness has a breaking point—a point at which he recognizes the inadequacy of his own strength and resources and finally yields his heart to the God of unlimited strength and resources. In today's vernacular, reaching the "breaking point" is sometimes referred to as "touching rock bottom" or "eating dust." Some people reach that point faster than others. Certain people yield only after enduring adversity or suffering the consequences of their rebellion for a long period of time.

A man named Frank experienced a brokenness that led him to rethink his decision to walk away from God. He writes, "I grew up in Cuba experiencing lack in basic areas of my physical life, such as food and health. From the age of two, I suffered from chronic asthma attacks. Many times, I would arrive at the hospital on the edge of death. I was also emotionally deprived. My relationship with my parents was hell. They fought with each other every day, and the yelling and violence were unbearable. When I was eleven years old, my parents divorced. My father left the country with the intention of bringing us out someday. His departure caused me great pain.

"One night, I went with my mother to a church, and together we accepted Jesus as our Savior. Immediately, we began to enjoy a personal relationship with Him and to serve Him. But, at age fifteen, I walked away from Jesus completely. I lost my relationship with God, and sin took over my life. By the time I was seventeen, my life was in chaos. I was rebellious and prideful and refused to listen to reason. I felt alone, rejected, helpless, and miserable, and I reached the point where I considered taking my own life. I tried to fill the void in my heart with sex and popularity, but nothing worked. However, my mother was praying for me.

"At the peak of my desperation, I began to seek God's face, and I made a firm commitment to serve Him, regardless of the price. Little by little, God began to set me free, and I started to feel His presence once more. Later, my father was able to bring us out of Cuba, and we came to the United States. Here, God gave me a wonderful church with the best spiritual parents. He healed me of asthma and restored my relationship with my father. I also met the most beautiful woman I had ever seen, and God joined us in marriage with the purpose of serving Him together.

"Two years later, she became pregnant. Our joy was immeasurable! When she was three months along, we went for a routine appointment at the obstetrician's office, where we expected to hear our baby's heartbeat for the first time, but everything suddenly changed. The doctor told us that the baby was dead. After the initial shock, we returned to our car and began to pray. While we prayed, the Father's embrace comforted and healed our hearts. Later, God gave us two precious children who fill our hearts."

We must remember that God doesn't cause sickness or death. However, He can use the brokenness that difficult situations produce to draw us closer to Him. And, if we have rebelled against God, He can enable our hardened heart to once again become sensitive to Him and to surrender to His purposes.

Brokenness means going to God under terms of "unconditional surrender."

The Broken Heart Versus the Wounded Heart

To understand brokenness, it is essential to know the difference between a heart that has been "broken" and a heart that is emotionally wounded. Many people tend to think they are the same thing, but these conditions are opposites in regard to the heart's openness to God, willingness to be taught by Him, and ability to receive healing.

A person with a broken heart humbles himself, surrenders to God, and gives up his will in order to do God's will. His focus is no longer on his own problems and needs but on God alone as his Source and Sustainer. In contrast, a person with a wounded heart is usually centered on himself rather than on God. The troubles he has experienced may have been self-inflicted, or they may have been imposed on him by others. Regardless of how his difficulties occurred, the character of his heart has been infected with self-pity and bitterness. His heart has open sores that continue to bleed and to cause pain.

It is said that the most dangerous animal is a wounded animal, because it is always on the defensive. It rejects being helped, and no one can approach it without being injured. When people have been wounded, they are often unable to trust others, and they try to protect themselves from everything and everyone whom they perceive might hurt them. Consequently, they have few, if any, close relationships.

In the realm of the church, I believe that the most "dangerous" people are wounded pastors and other leaders, because they often preach, teach, and minister out of their emotional pain rather than from knowledge and revelation of what Christ wants to say to His church. A wounded leader is unable to be a clear channel through which God's anointing can flow. Additionally, I believe that those who are emotionally wounded can attract demons that desire to control and even dwell in their heart. If you are a pastor, a teacher, an evangelist, or another type of church leader, and you find yourself hurting other people spiritually, mentally, or emotionally, it is probably because you have been emotionally and/or spiritually wounded and have never resolved the pain in your heart. While we all have to deal with various emotional and spiritual issues, I don't believe God wants a leader to be ministering to others if he is in a state of woundedness. He wants leaders to serve His people in a state of spiritual health, with *"the fruit of the Spirit"*—*"love, joy, peace, patience, kindness, goodness, faithfulness, gentleness and self-control"* (Galatians 5:22–23 NIV).

Consequently, wounded people should not be placed in positions of leadership or active service until they have been healed of their pain, because little good will come out of their ministry otherwise. For example, I have seen pastors use the pulpit to verbally attack other people, divulge an individual's private business, seek revenge, or defend their personal situations—all in God's name. The pulpit is too holy to be used to attack and slander other people or to defend oneself. Pastors who are acting in this manner must repent and seek emotional healing. Their hearts must be transformed before they can continue ministering to God's people.

Moreover, wounded leaders usually produce other wounded leaders, because we often pass along our attitudes to those whom we mentor. Sadly, there are currently many believers in churches who are experiencing spiritual and emotional pain and bitterness of heart because they have been led by wounded leaders who have—intentionally or unintentionally—mistreated and/or hurt them. These believers have not been properly formed, trained, or equipped in Christlikeness. And many of them may remain wounded unless someone is available to lead them to restoration.

A wounded leader often hurts those whom he is leading.

God seeks those whose hearts are broken so that He can manifest to them His love, His glory, His power, and His kingdom. Although He desires to heal the person who has a wounded heart before he continues hurting himself and others, He knows that the person with a broken heart is ready to be helped because he has reached the end of the line in terms of his own strength and ability. And God is ready and willing to provide that help: *"The Lord is near to those who have a broken heart, and saves such as have a contrite spirit"* (Psalm 34:18).

God seeks those whose hearts have been broken
and are ready to be healed.

The following testimony, from a man named Faiber, illustrates how God can use our deep brokenness to draw us to Him, so that we may be healed of our woundedness. "My mother was a young lady with no one to defend her," says Faiber, who was born as the result of a rape. Faiber grew up lonely, without love or a father figure. People called him "Faiber the bastard," and he would beg his mother to find a husband so that he could have a father to love. When he was seven, his mother got married, and Faiber thought that his dream had come true. However, he hadn't counted on the violence, drunkenness, and prostitution this man would bring into their lives.

When Faiber finished school, he decided to leave home, but he didn't get very far, because the bad habits he picked up took over his life. Faiber lived on the streets for six months. In addition to abusing drugs and alcohol, he became involved with married women—one after another, until he lost track. The beatings he received at the hands of their husbands often landed him in jail or the hospital.

One night, a ministry took him in. For a week, this ministry fed and cared for him. At the end of the week, he was presented with two options: either return to the streets or go on a spiritual retreat. Although he didn't want anything to do with God, he decided to make a covenant with Him; otherwise, he knew that his next—and last—step was suicide.

Faiber began a new life in Christ, and everything changed. He embarked on a career and got married. In time, he came to King Jesus Ministry, where God restored his marriage. The Lord provided better jobs for Faiber and his wife, as well as a new home. Today, they work hard to facilitate the supernatural restoration of marriages and families that are in need of God's healing power. Faiber had to touch bottom before he surrendered his heart to God and allowed Him to transform his life—healing him, restoring him, giving him a family, and providing him with a sense of purpose.

Let Go, so that You May Receive

Perhaps God is dealing with you right now, prompting you to surrender to Him. Is it because you are running away from His call on your life? Is it in regard to your irresponsible spending habits? Is it your refusal to submit to His delegated authorities? Is it your lack of commitment to His kingdom purposes? Or could it be your anger, laziness, or fear? The Father searches our heart; He knows the areas of our life where we are rebelling against Him or where we are unaligned with His will. He reminds us of those areas so that we will yield to Him, and He can transform our heart. If we don't surrender, we may find ourselves undergoing the process of brokenness.

The sinful nature pushes us to live a self-centered life, independent of God, in which we seek absolute control—trusting in our own intelligence, education, social status, strengths, gifts, abilities, and so forth. Our "self" rejects the idea of surrendering our life wholeheartedly to the lordship of Christ. The "old man" tries to satisfy its corrupt desires rather than die to its destructive impulses.

Yet you don't need to hold on to anything that God wants to remove from your life, because He will never give you anything evil in exchange for it. He desires to bless you. Again, He doesn't inflict sickness, poverty, or oppression on us. He is the Father of all good things: *"Every good gift and every perfect gift is from above, and comes down from the Father of lights, with whom there is no variation or shadow of turning"* (James 1:17). Yet, as we have seen, God does allow us to face difficult circumstances in order to bring to our attention various obstacles that prevent us from loving Him and giving Him control over our life. You will never lose out if you yield everything to the Lord. Rather, you will win God Himself—with all His attributes and blessings!

The hardest people to break are the stubborn and the prideful.

Avenues of Brokenness

When God breaks us, He often focuses on one area at a time that is unaligned with His nature and purposes. Generally speaking, He will bring to our attention something that has usurped first place in our heart over Him or that is otherwise hindering us from doing His will. It might be a negative attitude, a destructive habit, an ungodly pursuit, or an unhealthy relationship—something or someone that is harmful to us but that we won't let go of. Let us look at three avenues through which the process of brokenness can occur.

1. The Painful Consequences of Sin

God never causes us to sin, and He doesn't want us to sin against Him. Yet when we choose to disobey Him, we create situations and reap consequences that—sooner or later—cause us to become spiritually, emotionally, mentally, and/or physically broken. In this scenario, our brokenness is produced by our own willful disobedience. There are always consequences for disobedience—especially sustained rebellion. Due to the fallout from our sin, we come to a "breaking point" in our life. When we reach this point and make a genuine decision to repent and to return to God, He extends His love and forgiveness to us and restores our relationship with Him. It is important to cooperate with the Lord when we undergo the process of brokenness. David wrote, *"The sacrifices of God are a broken spirit, a broken and a contrite heart; these, O God, You will not despise"* (Psalm 51:17).

2. A Crisis We Are Unable to Resolve

On occasion, God will allow situations to come into our life that are outside our capacity to resolve, so that He can meet us at our breaking point with His salvation, mercy, and grace. We may experience a financial emergency, a family crisis, the loss of something valuable to us, or another predicament. After we exhaust all our resources—our knowledge, wisdom, strength, talents, and other abilities—without finding an acceptable solution, we finally have to conclude that the situation is beyond us. At such a time, we have an opportunity to submit to God, acknowledge our weakness and need, and allow Him to work out the situation as He sees fit.

3. God's Direct Dealing with Our Heart

Sometimes, God deals directly with our heart through His Holy Spirit, bringing conviction and causing us to search ourselves to see how we have strayed from Him. At such times, He leads us to repentance and submission to His will. His ultimate goal is for us to trust in Him alone, not in any earthly power, strength, or resources. We can describe this avenue of brokenness as a sovereign act of God that leads us to recognize His lordship, power, and majesty. An excellent example of this form of brokenness is the biblical account of Jacob wrestling all night with a *"Man"* who, at daybreak, touched the socket of Jacob's hip, causing him to limp. The *"Man"* with whom Jacob was wrestling was God Himself. (See Genesis 32:24–32.) Because of Jacob's stubbornness, the Lord had to break him.

God uses different ways to break us for the purpose of transforming our heart. In the following testimony, a man named Emerson had to reach the point of brokenness before he finally surrendered control of his life to God. He writes, "To put it simply, while my wife had been living as a faithful Christian, my job had become my god; it was my life. Then, we both lost our jobs and found ourselves in serious financial trouble. We lost our home and our car, and we didn't have enough money even to buy food.

"My wife and I attended church at King Jesus Ministry. Yet I was depressed, afraid, and angry, not knowing what to do, because we still couldn't find work. One day, I heard a sermon about the mercy of Jesus and realized that during this entire time, the only thing I had really needed was Christ in my life. Another time, I was resting after having straightened the chairs in the church when Pastor Maldonado came to me and asked me how I was doing. I said I was 'fine,' but he insisted on knowing how I was really doing. I started to cry and told him everything that was happening. He ministered to me for forty-five minutes; that time was very valuable to me.

"Later, the church's Department of Human Resources contacted me. Three months after that, I was offered a job downtown. However, on the day I was supposed to start, I received a phone call from the new company saying that they couldn't hire me. My burden was so great that I couldn't carry it on my own. I decided to give it to Jesus, so that He could work it out according to His will. One hour later, I received a call from the church asking if I was interested in working for their IT Department on a contract basis. My wife also started to work part-time in the school that is sponsored by the ministry.

"Six months later, I began working full-time as a network administrator at the ministry, and my wife was hired full-time as a teacher. The supernatural provision came. In addition, God miraculously provided several months' worth of payments that I had owed on my car loan. The bank told me that I was up-to-date on my payments, although I knew I had not made a payment for four months. Now, God is working to help us to modify our mortgage.

"Our lives have completely changed. I used to be upset all the time, unhappy, arrogant, and antisocial. I thought I knew it all, and I neglected my family, so that my marriage was going downhill. I wasn't spending time with my son, and I had no friends. Furthermore, I was being a poor steward of the things God had given to me. I didn't have a future or a relationship with Jesus, and I was on a path straight to hell. Now, I have a beautiful relationship with Jesus, with my wife, and with my son. My financial situation has been restored—thanks to divine intervention and not to my natural abilities. Brokenness led me to understand that without Jesus, I can do nothing."

When a person is broken by God, his life is in transition
to positive change.

Resisting God: The Case Study of Jonah

The story of the prophet Jonah is a good illustration of the way God may work when someone resists His will and then manifests stubbornness even during the process of being broken. Jonah eventually obeyed God, but he still had heart issues that needed to be addressed. God had told Jonah to do something very important, but he had his own opinion about the situation. He therefore ignored God's command and "ran away," trying to hide from the Creator of the world. Here is his story:

> Now the word of the LORD came to Jonah the son of Amittai, saying, "Arise, go to Nineveh, that great city, and cry out against it; for their wickedness has come up before Me." But Jonah arose to flee to Tarshish from the presence of the LORD. He went down to Joppa, and found a ship going to Tarshish; so he paid the fare, and went down into it, to go with them to Tarshish from the presence of the LORD.
> (Jonah 1:1–3)

Jonah was angry with the people of Nineveh because they were fierce warriors who had attacked the Israelites. Consequently, Jonah wanted to see them punished and destroyed. In contrast, God in His mercy (see Jonah 4:2, 11) had commanded Jonah to go and warn the Ninevites that He would soon punish them for their wickedness, in order to give them an opportunity to repent and be delivered. However, Jonah's resentment and hate were apparently greater than his love, so that he quickly decided to disobey the Lord's instructions.

Has God ever asked you to do something for another person with whom you didn't get along? What did you do? Did you choose to disobey God? Sometimes anger, resentment, and hate will carry more weight in our heart than the fear of the Lord.

Let us examine, step-by-step, how the Lord brought Jonah's heart to brokenness, and what He told Jonah after the prophet stubbornly held on to his resentful attitude even then.

1. God Sent a Storm

"*The* LORD *sent out a great wind on the sea, and there was a mighty tempest on the sea, so that the ship was about to be broken up*" (Jonah 1:4). Because of Jonah's rebellion, it was necessary for God to use the process of brokenness to turn him around. Even in the midst of a terrible storm in which his life was in jeopardy, Jonah apparently wasn't moved to repent and obey God. He preferred to die at sea rather than preach to his enemies about turning from their wicked ways.

Jonah didn't realize that God was dealing with *his* heart—not just the hearts of the Ninevites. The Lord wanted to transform the prophet's heart to be like His own heart, and to teach him to "let God be God." Similar situations occur today. Many people don't recognize that God is dealing with them to love others in the midst of a circumstance in which they feel they have been unjustly treated, because they think they are in the right and the other people are in the wrong and therefore deserve to be punished by God.

The account in the book of Jonah continues, "*Then the mariners were afraid; and every man cried out to his god....But Jonah had gone down into the lowest parts of the ship, had lain down, and was fast asleep*" (Jonah 1:5). The crew of the ship eventually discovered that Jonah was the cause of the storm. Jonah told them that if they threw him overboard, the storm would cease. The sailors didn't want to kill Jonah, but, after trying to row against the storm unsuccessfully, they finally threw him overboard, asking God to forgive them. Instantly, the storm disappeared. (See Jonah 1:6–16.)

Have you ever found yourself in the midst of a storm caused by someone who was trying to run away from God? Is your own rebellion against

God creating a storm for the people close to you, so that you are putting them at risk spiritually, emotionally, mentally, physically, or financially? Could this be the cause of your marital problems? Could this be the reason your business is on the brink of capsizing? Could this be the explanation for why your ministry or church is unable to stay afloat? When we run away from God and what He has asked us to do, we often cause our own brokenness, affecting not only ourselves but also other people in our life.

2. God Prepared a Large Fish

"*Now the* Lord *had prepared a great fish to swallow Jonah. And Jonah was in the belly of the fish three days and three nights*" (Jonah 1:17). What was God's purpose for having a large fish swallow Jonah? He had arranged for Jonah's temporary confinement there in order to break the prophet's rebellious will. Jonah spent three full days and nights inside that fish, contemplating his condition and reconsidering his attitude. The fact that Jonah didn't die inside the fish shows that God was in complete control of the situation. He wanted to bring Jonah to brokenness in order to transform his heart—not kill him. He wanted the prophet to repent and fulfill His will by preaching in Nineveh.

The Scriptures say that, after three days, "*Jonah prayed to the* Lord *his God from the fish's belly*" (Jonah 2:1). He made a covenant with the Lord, saying, "*I will sacrifice to You with the voice of thanksgiving; I will pay what I have vowed*" (Jonah 2:9). Note that Jonah surrendered to God when he believed the end of his life was near; only then did he make a covenant with the Lord. Have you known people who have turned to God only when they came to the very end of the line? Are you in that situation right now?

Imagine Jonah inside the belly of that fish, with its gastric juices and odor! How sad it is that only then did the prophet come to the point where he decided to obey God. Even so, Jonah's heart still needed additional softening in relation to Nineveh. Perhaps Jonah repented to the extent that he wanted his relationship with God restored—but not fully enough to appreciate God's mercy toward Israel's enemies.

Jonah obeyed the Lord's command and proclaimed God's impending judgment throughout the city of Nineveh. What happened next? The whole city repented, and God spared them. (See Jonah 3:5–10.) "*Then God*

saw their works, that they turned from their evil way; and God relented from
the disaster that He had said He would bring upon them, and He did not do
it" (Jonah 3:10). Jonah was angry with this outcome, telling God that the
reason he hadn't wanted to preach to the Ninevites in the first place was
that he knew the Lord would have mercy on them! *"For I know that You are*
a gracious and merciful God, slow to anger and abundant in lovingkindness,
One who relents from doing harm" (Jonah 4:2). Following this, Jonah went
outside the city of Nineveh and sat down, apparently to see if God might
still destroy it. It was a hot day, and Jonah made himself a makeshift shelter
from the sun. (See Jonah 4:5.)

3. God Prepared a Worm

The Lord continued to deal with the state of Jonah's heart by using an
object lesson:

> And the LORD God prepared a plant and made it come up over Jonah,
> that it might be shade for his head to deliver him from his misery. So
> Jonah was very grateful for the plant. But as morning dawned the next
> day God prepared a worm, and it so damaged the plant that it with-
> ered.   (Jonah 4:6–7)

The plant had given Jonah shade, and he was irritated that the worm
had destroyed it. (See Jonah 4:8–9.) Furthermore, in his anger over his as-
signment to Nineveh, Jonah couldn't see the fact that the Ninevites were as
much God's creation as the Israelites were. He was more concerned about
one plant being ruined than he was about the impending destruction of a
whole city of people. He didn't care that God loved these Ninevites, even
though they had been hostile to His chosen people, the Israelites.

4. God Prepared a Scorching Wind

"And it happened, when the sun arose, that God prepared a vehement
["scorching" NIV, NASB] *east wind; and the sun beat on Jonah's head, so that*
he grew faint. Then he wished death for himself, and said, 'It is better for me to
die than to live'" (Jonah 4:8). A "scorching wind" represents a life situation
that takes away our strength and/or causes us to feel defeated. God allows
such things to occur so that we might reach a point of brokenness in which

we will permit Him to transform our heart and straighten our path in life, enabling us to walk once more in His perfect will.

Jonah didn't understand that God wanted to call the Ninevites to repentance because He knew that they were ignorant concerning Him. The Lord tried to make His prophet understand His mercy toward those whom Jonah considered his enemies: "*You have had pity on the plant for which you have not labored, nor made it grow, which came up in a night and perished in a night. And should I not pity Nineveh, that great city, in which are more than one hundred and twenty thousand persons* **who cannot discern between their right hand and their left…?** (Jonah 4:10–11). When we are unable to show mercy toward those who attack us out of ignorance, God may break us so we can feel as He feels and love as He loves.

As long as we continue to resist God, He will pursue us and cause us to come to the end of our own strength. We sometimes forget that "*it is a fearful thing to fall into the hands of the living God*" (Hebrews 10:31). What did Jonah's rebellion cost him and other people? First, I'm sure it cost him a guilty conscience, which takes a great toll on a person. Second, his delay caused him to waste time and opportunities for serving God. Third, he put the lives of all the sailors on the boat in danger. Fourth, he went through the painful process of being broken. Finally, worst of all, he strained his relationship with God. The cost of rebellion is similar for us—a guilty conscience; missed opportunities for obedience and service to God; the placing of our family, business, possessions, and so forth at risk of spiritual, emotional, mental, or physical harm; the experience of brokenness; and, above all, the fracturing of our relationship with our heavenly Father.

No one can rebel against God without paying a high price.

The following testimony illustrates how God comes to us in our brokenness and invites us to be transformed. Alexander's heart was full of hate and pain, and he believed that reacting in anger was the way for him to relate to people and situations. He writes, "Ephesians 4:26, '*Do not let the sun go down on your wrath,*' is a lesson that took me years to learn. More than forty years ago, the spirit of anger took over my life. I was bullied as a child, and the situation became worse after I got eyeglasses. My fellow students would make fun of me by touching my face. I couldn't express my emotions or let go of them, so I kept them bottled up inside me. I hated the idea of people getting too close to my face.

"Like any situation that is not dealt with, my problem with anger grew. Little by little, I started to think that if anyone were to touch my face, I would fight him, hurt him, or even kill him. Many years passed without anyone knowing of this demonic strength in my life. However, when my children were born, God revealed to me that unless I was delivered, the anger within me, which governed the spirit of murder, would become a generational curse. I wanted deliverance, and, one night, in the church that I formerly attended, I received my deliverance. When the pastor began to pray for me and to cast out that horrible spirit, the power of God immediately moved in my life. It literally felt as if something very heavy was being lifted from my shoulders. At that moment, I knew that I had been liberated and that, by God's mercy, the curse had been broken in my children's bloodline. I know beyond a shadow of a doubt that we are free. Thanks to the blood of Jesus, I no longer struggle with anger, and my children will not have to deal with it, either. Thank You, Lord, for my freedom!"

The Breaking Point

Is God getting your attention through the consequences of your sin, through a crisis in your life, or through a sense of conviction in your heart from the Holy Spirit that something is not right in your relationship with Him? If so, what is your breaking point? How long will you wait before responding? Do you want to experience a long process of suffering before surrendering to God? Or, will you make a decision to fully yield to Him right now? The choice is yours! If you return to God, He will receive you.

A person reaches his breaking point when he is ready to surrender and submit to God.

It is often the case that people seek Christ after they reach their breaking point because they know that only a miracle can help them now. The woman who touched the hem of Jesus' garment while believing for healing is an excellent example of someone in this situation. *"And a woman was there who had been subject to bleeding for twelve years. She had suffered a great deal under the care of many doctors and had spent all she had, yet instead of getting better she grew worse. When she heard about Jesus, she came up behind him in the crowd and touched his cloak"* (Mark 5:25–27 NIV).

This woman had definitely reached her breaking point, having suffered from a debilitating sickness for more than a decade. She had tried everything she knew to do, and she had spent all her money, to find a remedy—to no avail. Then, she heard about Jesus. She said to herself, *"If I just touch his clothes, I will be healed"* (Mark 5:28 NIV). This woman was ready to surrender to Christ because He was her only hope. She had no other alternatives. And when she touched Jesus' clothes, *"immediately her bleeding stopped and she felt in her body that she was freed from her suffering"* (Mark 5:29 NIV). And Jesus told her, *"Daughter, your faith has healed you. Go in peace and be freed from your suffering"* (Mark 5:34 NIV). The Scriptures are filled with accounts of people who had reached their breaking point and had no other choice but to surrender to God and seek His help.

You know you have reached your breaking point when your only alternative is God.

As long as you feel you have other alternatives, you will not seek the Lord—and you won't be able to witness God's powerful hand at work on your behalf. However, once you are broken—once you surrender, give up your will, and trust solely in God with no reservations—He will transform your heart and work powerfully in your life. *"For thus says the High and Lofty One who inhabits eternity, whose name is Holy: 'I dwell in the high and holy place, with him who has a contrite and humble spirit, to revive the spirit of the humble, and to revive the heart of the contrite ones"* (Isaiah 57:15).

A broken heart stops resisting obedience.

Purposes and Blessings of Brokenness

"But we all, with unveiled face, beholding as in a mirror the glory of the Lord, are being transformed into the same image from glory to glory, just as by the Spirit of the Lord" (2 Corinthians 3:18). The Christian life is one of continuous transformation. God, in His sovereignty, will initiate and/or use the process of brokenness to further transform you into the image and likeness of Christ, so that you will reflect His character and heart. After you have experienced brokenness and have surrendered to God, you will be a different person—more loving, more humble, and more centered on His purpose for your life. You will not be the same person you were before being broken—but you also will not be the person you will become in the future as you continue to yield to God.

Again, transformation is a process that is to continue throughout our life. If we stop allowing God to change us, we will settle for a reality that reflects only the natural realm and is unable to address our deepest needs and problems. Moreover, if we stop advancing spiritually, we will not only become stagnant but will soon begin to take steps backward.

Once we are aware of the reasons for brokenness and its benefits, we should stop complaining about the things we have had to endure. Rather, we should thank God for them. We sometimes ask ourselves, "Why am I going through this suffering? Could I have disobeyed God?" or "Why did God allow this to happen?" Regardless of the cause of our troubles, if we understand the purpose of brokenness, we can use any difficult circumstance as an opportunity to draw closer to God. When we seek the Lord and yield to Him, He begins to transform us.

There are many blessings and benefits that result from experiences of brokenness. Let us look at ten of the most notable ones:

1. We Will Gain an Increased Sensitivity to God's Presence

Many people wonder why they can't sense God's presence. They don't realize that hardness of heart and/or resistance to being broken by God are the greatest impediments to experiencing His presence. Often, those who respond in a positive way to brokenness by repenting and seeking God can soon perceive His presence. They can clearly hear His voice as their hearts become yielded and tender before Him. I can say beyond a shadow of a doubt that we will experience greater times in God's presence after we have gone through the process of brokenness and have fully surrendered to Him.

2. Pleasing God Will Become Our Highest Priority

Brokenness changes our focus—pleasing God suddenly becomes the most important thing in our life. Doing His will is now our supreme priority, and His purpose is our purpose. We can say, as King David did, *"I delight to do Your will, O my God, and Your law is within my heart"* (Psalm 40:8).

3. We Will Be Led to Spiritual Maturity

"By faith Moses, when he became of age, refused to be called the son of Pharaoh's daughter, choosing rather to suffer affliction with the people of God than to enjoy the passing pleasures of sin" (Hebrews 11:24–25). Moses surrendered his privileges as the adopted son of Pharaoh's daughter—privileges of position, wealth, and luxury—in exchange for the cost of suffering in order to liberate the people of Israel from slavery and to lead them to the Promised Land. Spiritual maturity has nothing to do with earthly fame, prestige, credentials, power, or influence. Rather, it has to do with recognizing God as our Sovereign, relying on Him totally, yielding our heart to Him, and learning to understand and value His priorities and purposes as our own; it consists in learning to be obedient, submissive, and available to our Lord. Moses made a decision to submit to God's will and be transformed in order to fulfill his purpose in life—a life that had been spared from death by God's protection when he was still a baby. (See Exodus 1:15–2:9.) Moses' destiny had been set since birth, yet he had to endure the process of brokenness so that he could attain the maturity required for him to become the deliverer of Israel.

4. We Will Be Enabled to Carry Out Our Purpose and Calling

Every person has been created by God for a unique purpose and calling. No one enters this world by chance. Yet most people don't know the purpose for which they were born. They have not yet received the spiritual insight for it or experienced the spiritual growth necessary to carry it out. Sometimes, our calling unfolds to us over time. Like Moses', our heart must be transformed so that we may recognize our purpose, move forward to fulfill it, and develop the passion and maturity to complete it as the Lord guides our steps.

God already sees our purpose fulfilled before we are even aware of it or begin to pursue it. For example, right now, with His spiritual sight, the Lord may be seeing a certain businessman earning millions of dollars that he will use to advance the kingdom of God. He may be seeing an evangelist winning many souls for Christ, or a pastor whose church has a powerful outreach of healing and deliverance in his city. Suppose the businessman, evangelist, or pastor is pursuing a completely different vocation at the moment but is undergoing a personal crisis or another difficulty. God is allowing that individual to experience brokenness, because He sees beyond the suffering to its ultimate purpose—enabling the person to discern and carry out his true calling and to reflect God's nature, bringing Him glory.

Similarly, when we are in the midst of our own brokenness, God sees His finished work in us; and He sees us carrying out His purpose in the earth. As we go through the process of brokenness, God will remove various obstacles that prevent us from being able to fulfill our calling, so that we are free to carry it out.

5. We Will Know God's Character in a Deeper Way

Brokenness also leads us to experience God and to know Him in a deeper way than we have been able to previously. We will more clearly understand His love and His will. Just as Jonah needed to learn about the vastness of God's mercy, and to emulate it, we need a fuller understanding of the many marvelous characteristics of God's nature. When we understand them and, in response, humble ourselves before Him, He will enable us to reflect those very qualities.

6. We Will Receive a Greater Understanding of Ourselves

Through brokenness, we are led to identify our weaknesses, shortcomings, limitations, and frailties. Through this knowledge, we recognize that we must continually depend on God's mercy and love. Moreover, as God transforms us, we come to a greater understanding of who we are in Christ and how God wants to change us into His likeness.

7. We Will Develop a More Loving, Merciful, and Forgiving Attitude Toward Others

Thanks to brokenness, we begin to see people differently. We realize that they are not better or worse than we are. We let go of our sense of superiority or inferiority and begin to see others from God's perspective. Through the process of brokenness, we are enabled to let go of a judgmental and critical spirit, and to more easily overlook offenses. We develop deeper love for others, extending greater mercy and forgiveness to them in relation to their weaknesses and failings. We no longer "demand"—whether verbally or silently in our own thoughts—that people pay what they owe us or be punished for what they have done to us so they will "get what they deserve." Regardless of the spiritual, emotional, or mental condition a person might be in, we will see him with love, pray for his healing and prosperity, and help meet his needs.

Brokenness increases our love and compassion for other people.

---

8. We Will Develop a Spirit of Meekness

Contrary to what many people think, the biblical concept of meekness is not "weakness." Rather, its meaning is reflected in these definitions: "having or showing a quiet and gentle nature," and "enduring injury with patience and without resentment." Brokenness transforms us into teachable, humble, open, and transparent people. When we have a meek spirit, we no longer need everyone to agree with our opinions. We stop being defensive, so that we are able to hear the advice of others and to learn from them. Leaving behind egocentrism, we are able to work well with others as a team, in order to help other people and to promote the advancement of God's kingdom in the world.

9. We Will Have a New Desire to Grow in All Areas of Life

After going through the process of brokenness and experiencing the healing of our heart and receiving a renewed outlook, we are liberated to become who God created us to be. Accordingly, we desire to grow, mature, prosper, and succeed in every area of our life—whether in relation to our personal development, family life, church/ministry, education, business/work, finances, or another area.

God doesn't exist for us. We exist for Him.

10. We Will Enjoy New Freedom in the Spirit

Last, we will experience greater freedom in the Spirit. We realize that we were formerly in bondage to people, places, and circumstances, as well as to our own prejudices, selfish desires, and other negative outlooks, that hindered us from advancing in Christlikeness through the transformation of our heart. After brokenness, we enjoy a new sense of inner peace and contentment as we yield our own "rights" and "demands" in order to carry out the requirements of God's love. The sinful nature is restrained, and the life of Christ—Conqueror over sin and death—rises within us. Because we have surrendered to Him, He can manifest Himself in and through our life.

Every true sacrifice we make for God is made from the place of a broken heart.

Prayer of Brokenness

Brokenness of heart is a necessary process that every Christian must endure in order to draw closer to God—to know Him better, to please Him in greater measure, and to carry out His will more completely. If we walk around with a wounded heart, never experiencing healing, we will inevitably hurt others, and we won't reach our potential in God.

Have you been resisting the process of brokenness? Have the storm, the fish, the worm, and the scorching wind come, yet nothing has made you yield to God, so that He can heal you, transform your heart, and carry out His purposes through you? Perhaps you feel that you are at your breaking point, that you are at the end of your human strength, and you would like to let go of your burden and find rest in God. Today, you have an opportunity to submit your life to Him, finding peace and wholeness. Pray the following prayer to release your rebellion and resistance and to surrender completely to your loving heavenly Father.

Heavenly Father, I yield my independence, my self-sufficiency, and my pride to You. I want to fulfill what You have called me to do on this earth. Transform every area of my life that is not aligned with Your will. I repent of hindering Your purposes for me and of resisting the transformation of my heart in relation to my [personal development, family life, church/ministry, education, business/work, finances, or another realm]. Forgive me and cleanse me through the blood of Jesus, which He shed on the cross for me. I receive Your forgiveness right now, and I decide, of my own free will, to deny my sinful nature, to surrender to You, and to obey Your will.

I consecrate myself to You and commit to depend totally on You. From now on, no matter what happens to me, I will seek no "alternative" in life but You. Now, I ask You, Lord, to fill me with Your presence. Enable me to sense the reality of Your nearness to me. Pour out Your love and compassion in my heart, so that I can see other people as You see them, and love them as You love them. As You fill me with Your presence, love, and power, help me to lead others to repentance and faith, so that they, too, can draw close to You. In the name of Jesus, amen!

10

The Supernatural Transformation
of the Mind

From the time she was a child, Siobhan had anxiously asked herself, "Am I destined for greatness?" Having earned degrees in biomedical engineering and database development, she had outstanding academic ability and had received recognition and titles. However, she felt driven to succeed, and something was lacking in her life. Here is her story: "I was raised by a Christian mother (and was rarely visited by my father), but everything related to 'religion' was last on my personal agenda. I graduated from high school as one of the top three students in my Caribbean nation. My entire existence was built upon a strong foundation of education and ambition.

"When I was sixteen, I enrolled at the University of Miami with plans to become great at 'everything,' from sports to my scholastic endeavors. My hunger for success was insatiable. I joined academic clubs, social clubs, and athletic clubs—and I designed plans to transform them all. I was busy every second of my life, going from activity to activity. But, at the end of the day, when I would lie down to sleep, I would try to make sense of everything I had done. Regardless of how many trophies I won, how much glory I received, or how much influence I had, I still felt that something was missing. My soul was unsatisfied and empty. I needed 'more'—more plans, more goals, more success, more out of life.

"One Friday night, a friend from school whom I barely knew invited me to attend a youth service. After evaluating the pros and cons, I decided to attend—expecting to gain influence and connections more than anything else. However, what I found that night completely revolutionized my life. It didn't matter how much I tried to analyze it, the experience couldn't be quantified; for the first time in my life, I witnessed the power of God firsthand through healing and miracles. The scientist in me tried to observe, dissect, classify, and replicate the experience, but the only word that seemed to explain what I had witnessed was *supernatural*. This was not an emotional experience, because emotions could never have made bones grow or twisted legs straighten. My purpose had now become clear, tangible, and precise. I felt completely satisfied.

"According to this world's standards, my life had been wonderful, but what God had for me was much better. It was on my way to 'greatness' that I found the One who brought sense and purpose to my life. I had never known the measure of God's grace until I met the person of His Son Jesus. It was then that I understood that my life, the one I thought was 'perfect,' was based on sin and oppression. My family had lived victimized by divorce, anger, adultery, lust, lack of communication, and many other problems.

"Since that day five years ago, I have been a recipient of God's mercy, grace, deliverance, and transformation in every area of my life—but none so powerful as in my soul. The void, insecurities, rejection, unforgiveness, bitterness, pride, and fear of failure that I used to experience were cast out of my life. My soul was restored by the inexplicable power of the Holy Spirit. Many of my colleagues in the scientific world reject my faith, saying that it is 'a leap in the dark.' But, by personal experience, I can say with certainty that my faith in God is the answer to the revelation of Light."

Love God with Your Heart and Mind

A supernatural encounter changed Siobhan's mind-set and led her to the living God, transforming her life. We all need a change of mind-set in order to fulfill what God has planned for us and to live as He intended us to. When we were saved, we received not only the "new man," or a new spirit, with the nature of Christ, but we also received a new mind—*"the mind of Christ"* (1 Corinthians 2:16). Just as our heart has to be transformed by

God to line up with the "new man" within us, our mind must be transformed to align with the *"mind of Christ"* within us. We have a vital part to play in this process, because we are commanded to love God not only with all our heart and all our soul but also with all our mind. (See Matthew 22:37.) Our mind must increasingly become one with God's. Otherwise, we cannot become effective vessels to carry out His purposes.

Throughout this book, we have seen that our beliefs and attitudes are rooted and established in our heart. Consequently, they influence our mind-set and thoughts, prompting our behavior. Additionally, there are ways in which our mind influences our heart and affects its condition. For example, as we have noted, Satan attempts to manipulate our heart by planting bad thoughts in our mind and enticing our sinful nature to rise up in the form of pride, lust, rebellion, and so forth. That is why the manner in which we think and reason, and what thoughts we allow to remain in our mind, are so significant. The apostle Paul wrote, *"For the weapons of our warfare are not carnal but mighty in God for pulling down strongholds, casting down arguments and every high thing that exalts itself against the knowledge of God, bringing every thought into captivity to the obedience of Christ"* (2 Corinthians 10:4–5).

When our mind is aligned with human reason, our focus is on temporal matters, and the impossible remains impossible.

The Original Mind of Humanity

The word *mind* is defined as "the element or complex of elements in an individual that feels, perceives, thinks, wills, and especially reasons," and "the conscious mental events and capabilities in an organism." Our mind is the seat of our knowledge and understanding; it is the intellectual potential of the soul.

We must know what was our Creator's original intent for the mind of humanity, because we cannot comprehend the nature of the transformation we must undergo until we understand His original design. Human beings were made in God's image and likeness; and, in His plan, we were created to believe, think, and act as He does. Humanity's original mind was therefore a reflection of God's—pure, clear, and unlimited in what it could conceive; it worked in conjunction with God's supernatural power. Thus, everything the first human beings did was geared toward manifesting God's will on earth as it was in heaven. Possibilities were the norm to them, because they lived according to the spiritual realm, where everything is possible.

Adam and Eve weren't contaminated by sin at first, so their heart, soul, and body, while living in the natural world, functioned according to the life of the supernatural realm—above and beyond the physical sphere. Their thoughts were filled with revelation knowledge from God, and that is how they were able to bring heaven to earth. All of creation responded to them just as it responded to God, because the Creator had given them dominion over it. As long as they were aligned with heaven, the creation obeyed them because it recognized divine authority.

Adam's mind was designed to be aligned with heaven and to manifest heaven on earth.

Is it possible for us to have that same divine mind today, so that we are enabled to live beyond natural human limitations? Yes, it is possible—as our mind is supernaturally transformed. God's original mandate of dominion has not changed. We can recover God's original intent for us—to live in accordance with the mind He first gave us, which is a reflection of His own mind.

Human beings lost their divine mind-set when they rebelled against God in the garden of Eden. Their spirit was disconnected from the supernatural realm, and their mind consequently became confined to the natural sphere—reduced to a state of limitation and subjected to impossibilities. From that time forward, the natural world became humanity's primary reality. But through Christ's finished work on the cross, everything we lost in the fall has been restored to us, so that we can once more carry out our true purpose. Renewal of the mind must take place in regard to every area of our life—not as a onetime occurrence but continuously, because transformation is an ongoing process for us. Then, when our mind begins to be transformed, we will no longer think in terms of limitations, as the following testimony illustrates.

Andrew was an orthopedic surgeon specializing in surgery of the hand, arm, and shoulder. He knew God and His Word, but he experienced a hunger to know more of God and to see His supernatural power operate today as it did through Jesus Christ. The Holy Spirit led Andrew on a journey in which his frame of mind shifted from the natural to the supernatural—to a place where he found the fullness he had been looking for. Here is his story: "I was raised Catholic but slowly turned my back on the church. I accepted Christ into my heart when I was eleven years old through my mother, who had started to attend a Protestant church. After my new birth, I felt I had meaning and direction in my life.

"At a young age, I had been attracted to the scientific field, and I believed that God had used evolution to 'somehow' create the human race; yet, when I attended college, I began to see that evolution was a theory without foundation. The complexity of creation speaks of a God who is vastly superior to this theory. Ironically, those who do not believe that there is a God always seem to appeal to the infinite. Those of us who do believe in Him know that He *is* 'the Infinite.'

"As this issue was resolved in my heart, I yearned to know the Creator at a deeper level and to have a closer personal relationship with Him. When I was thirty-eight, I attended a church that was filled with God's presence, and I received the baptism of the Holy Spirit. A new world began to unfold before my eyes. At that church, I learned to love the Word of God and to study it in depth. In time, however, a new hunger awakened in me, and I realized that something was missing. As an orthopedic surgeon, I have learned to help people through natural medical means, but the healings that Christ did during His time on earth challenge natural explanation. Because Jesus is the same yesterday, today, and forever, I would ask myself why we didn't see healing in the same magnitude that Jesus commanded during His ministry.

"During that time of searching, I discovered Apostle Maldonado's teachings. When I heard him teach, my spirit was set on fire. He spoke of his book *How to Walk in the Supernatural Power of God*, and I knew that was what I had been yearning for. Reading about that revelation and hearing it preached by Apostle Maldonado has opened up the Word of God to me in ways that are hard to describe. Now I see God powerfully manifesting through signs, miracles, and wonders. I am learning to be a channel through which He can manifest His power on earth. Jesus' life is being revealed in me like never before, and I hear Him more clearly every time He speaks to me. I believe that, in no time at all, I will see Jesus once more restoring everyone who comes for healing."

The Need for a Change of Mind-set, "Structure," and Message

The world around us moves within the framework of certain established mind-sets that resulted from the fall of humanity. Some of its attitudes and outlooks are doubt, insecurity, jealousy, greed, depression, and a fear of death. A change of perspective from a natural outlook to a spiritual one is necessary for the supernatural power of God to manifest through us.

Gaining a new mind-set prepares the way for changes in our "structure." By *structure*, I mean the way in which a person, group, organization, or country functions or operates, or the way in which an individual carries out a particular purpose. For example, a person under the influence of the fall might live according to an oppressive mental structure that keeps him perpetually in a negative state or causes him to experience one personal crisis after another.

Our mind-set guides every action we take. A change of mentality will therefore transform our "structure"—how we conduct our life, and what pursuits we believe are possible. Let me add here that we cannot try to implement a new structure in an organization unless those involved have all experienced a similarly transformed mind-set that has led them to have a new vision for themselves and the organization. For example, if we were to try to change the structure of a church before the people had been taught—and had accepted—its basis in the Word of God, or before they had embraced a vision for change, the result would be only confusion, fighting, bitterness, division, and separation. That is why people must always be taught the Word of God and be given a demonstration of its reality before change can occur.

Finally, as we adopt a new structure, the message we communicate also changes. Each of Christ's supernatural acts was aligned with the proclamation of the gospel of God's kingdom. Therefore, as our mind-set and structure are changed to reflect the supernatural nature of the kingdom, we will go to our families, churches, communities, cities, and nations with the message of a supernatural gospel that transforms lives. Additionally, as we are Jesus' witnesses in the world, we can also help to transform the institutions of our society—whether familial, educational, judicial, legislative, athletic, artistic, or related to another area. Many of these institutions are infused with the mentality and structures of the corrupt fallen nature. We must take the message of God's kingdom to people and institutions in all realms of life, so that the lost will be saved, lives will be renewed, the sick will be made whole, the poor will prosper, and the oppressed will be set free.

A change in mind-set will produce a change in structure. A change in structure will produce a change in message. And a change in message will bring about the manifestation of the supernatural here and now!

The Process by Which the Mind Is Renewed

In the first century, the apostle Paul wrote a letter of instruction and encouragement to the Christians in Rome. At the time, Rome was essentially the capital of the world, a place where political power and commerce were prominent, and where idolatry, violence, and other sins were abundant. Most of the Christians living there had been born and raised in the culture of the Roman Empire; therefore, their mind-set was Roman. Yet, when they accepted Christ and became His disciples, they became spiritual citizens of the invisible realm known as the kingdom of God.

Roman culture, like most cultures and institutions in the world, reflected the mind-set of fallen humanity. Paul wanted to help the Roman believers to put their human culture into perspective so that they could renew their minds by the Spirit of God and begin to live according to a spiritual "culture" based on the nature and character of God.

We, too, live in a society influenced by the fall; and we, too, are spiritual citizens of God's kingdom. The problem is that we often continue to think and behave according to the standards of our earthly culture rather than our heavenly one. As God's children, we must recognize that *"our [true] citizenship is in heaven, from which we also eagerly wait for the Savior, the Lord Jesus Christ"* (Philippians 3:20). We live in the world, but we are not "of" the world. (See John 17:11, 14–16.) Even though we function within the world's system, with its temporal culture and values, we don't "belong" to it; we are members of a realm that has eternal principles and values. Let us learn from what Paul taught the believers in Rome as he explained how they could be transformed to live as citizens of their new kingdom:

> *I beseech you therefore, brethren, by the mercies of God, that you present your bodies a living sacrifice, holy, acceptable to God, which is your reasonable service. And do not be conformed to this world, but* **be transformed by the renewing of your mind,** *that you may prove what is that good and acceptable and perfect will of God.*
>
> (Romans 12:1–2)

Let us examine the various parts of this remarkable passage of Scripture.

1. Present Your Body as a Living Sacrifice

Paul's first request is that we *"present [our] bodies a living sacrifice...to God."* We should present ourselves to Him as if we were a sacrifice on a sacred altar. We won't be able to experience the transformation of our mind in its fullest sense if we do not first become a *"living sacrifice"* to God. We must make the decision to give God our entire physical body—including our mind—because our body is the vessel through which we do everything on this earth.

In the Old Testament, the priest would present an animal on behalf of an individual as a sacrificial offering to God—perhaps an ox, a lamb, or a goat—often to atone for sin. This animal would be presented on the altar after it was killed. Once someone gave an animal as a sacrifice, he no longer owned it, so he could not take it back.

In our case, Jesus was the Sacrifice who died on the cross to pay for our sin and who was gloriously resurrected to give us new life. Spiritually, we have died with Him and have been raised with Him. Therefore, we are to present ourselves to God as a *"living sacrifice"* through a voluntary offering of ourselves for His purposes and His glory. A similar principle of ownership applies when we offer our body to God as applied to the animal sacrifices offered—the sacrifice is a permanent decision.

Because Jesus has paid the price for our redemption, our life belongs to the Lord; it is ours no more, and we cannot take it off the altar. When we present our body to God, it is His from that point on. We no longer determine what we will do with it or where and with whom it will go. Instead, we give God the responsibility of maintaining our body and of showing us to what we should dedicate its use. God doesn't ask merely to "rent" our body but to be its absolute Owner.

The greatest obstacle to moving in the supernatural is having a mind that has not been renewed. And renewal cannot occur until the body is presented as a living sacrifice to God.

Being a living sacrifice involves dying to "self," a process we discussed earlier. This process is painful to our fleshly nature and to our will. But it is tremendously beneficial for us, because God can thereafter make the best use of our life and bring forth maximum blessings of joy, health, and peace for us. We cannot offer our body in sacrifice to sin or to false and destructive mind-sets any longer. We must renounce the fleshly nature and surrender our humanity to God, so that He may transform us into the likeness of Jesus while enabling us to bring His message of redemption and kingdom power to others. God desires that we become His instruments for saving, healing, and delivering those who are oppressed by Satan. Offering ourselves as a living sacrifice, therefore, demands that we make a complete commitment to God, so that He may consecrate us and set us apart for His service. From this moment forward, we present ourselves continually as a *"living sacrifice"* to a holy God who adopts us as His children and makes us *"kings and priests"* in His kingdom. (See Revelation 1:6; 5:10.)

Those who are able to carry something real from God to others have begun with sacrifice—such as fasting, prayer, and seeking God.

The final phrase of Romans 12:1—*"which is your reasonable service"*—indicates that being a living sacrifice is not beyond our reach; it is not impossible. In fact, because we are God's priests, it is one of our functions: *"You also, as living stones, are being built up a spiritual house, a holy priesthood, to offer up spiritual sacrifices acceptable to God through Jesus Christ"* (1 Peter 2:5).

Presenting ourselves as a living sacrifice means totally surrendering to God.

---

2. Do Not Conform to the Mentality of This World

"And do not be conformed to this world…" (Romans 12:2). When we have presented our body as a living sacrifice, we must no longer conform to the world. The Greek word translated *"conformed"* in this verse is *suschematizo*, which means "to fashion alike, i.e. conform to the same pattern." The word indicates an external conformity. We should not allow ourselves to be shaped or formed by the mind-set of the world, as a shoe adapts to the shape of the foot after continued wear.

Again, the world has various values, principles, standards, attitudes, and ways of thinking that are opposed to those of God's kingdom; many of them are based on enthroning "self" and conserving the sinful nature. The world's values are destructive because they focus not on God but on the attainment of prestige, fame, fortune, and fleshly pleasures, and the pursuit of success at all costs. This is generally the mentality of the culture we live in, and Christian people are being pressured to conform to it. For instance, we are being pushed to assent to the idea that there are many paths to God; and, if we claim that Jesus is the only way to God, we are called narrow-minded. In another example, we are being pressured to accept the belief that homosexuality is a legitimate lifestyle and that any belief contrary to that is outdated. The world wants us to follow its pattern, but we must not. The apostle James wrote, *"Do you not know that friendship with the world is enmity with God? Whoever therefore wants to be a friend of the world makes himself an enemy of God"* (James 4:4).

The Greek word for *"world"* in the above passage is *aion*, which means "an age" and, by implication, "the world." God deeply loves the people of this world—so much so that He came to earth to die for them. Yet He doesn't love the mind-set of the world, because it is controlled by the evil one. (See 1 John 5:19.) Any area of your life that is not transformed according to the nature of Christ has been conformed to the world and needs to be renewed by the Holy Spirit.

Do not allow yourself to conform to the fallen world's mind-set, values, and behavior; rather, let it be the other way around. Help to bring the gospel to all the "subcultures" of the world—the arenas of education, politics, sports, science, business, economics, the media, the arts, and so forth. The message of the gospel of the kingdom is able to transform not only you but also other people in your sphere of influence, by the example of your lifestyle and by the power of God working in and through you.

Any area of your life that is not transformed according to the nature of Christ has been conformed to the world and needs to be renewed by the Holy Spirit.

---

3. Be Transformed

"…but be transformed…" (Romans 12:2). The Greek word translated *"transformed"* is *metamorphoo*, which means "to transform (literally or

figuratively "metamorphose")," or "to change into another form." I believe this word indicates dying to one way of life in order to be reborn into another—a process similar to what happens to a caterpillar inside a cocoon when it is transformed into a butterfly—a new creature. The transformation of our mind is a supernatural process, because it is a work carried out by the Holy Spirit. It does not produce merely an external or temporal change. It effects a total change of character and behavior in the person who surrenders to God with all his heart, soul, mind, and strength.

The transformation of the mind is supernaturally accomplished by the Holy Spirit.

---

4. Renew Your Mind

"...*by the renewing of your mind*" (Romans 12:2). The Greek word translated "*renewing*" is *anakainosis*, meaning "renovation" or "renewal." Note that one cannot "renovate" or "renew" something that never previously existed. When Paul wrote of "*the renewing of your mind*," he indicated that the mind had an original state from which it had moved away—the mind the first human beings had in Eden before they sinned. So, again, when we renew our mind, we come into alignment with humanity's original mind-set. That is why renewal is such a powerful key to understanding and carrying out God's will. The reason God tells us to renew our mind is so that we can return to His purpose for us. He wants our mind to reflect His mind, enabling us to think and even function as He does. This is why we must surrender our mind to the Holy Spirit for transformation.

Renewal has to do with thinking and living differently. The renewal of our mind enables us to return to the mind-set with which God originally created us.

Consequences of Failing to Renew Our Mind

Some people don't imagine that the process of renewal applies to them, because they think they are doing fine just the way they are. It is usually easier for us to see where other people need to make improvements in their life than it is for us to identify the changes we need to make. The truth is that we *all* need to renew our mind—continually—because we always must be advancing spiritually. Otherwise, we may experience the following consequences:

+ *Our circumstances will be our primary—or only—reality.* We will conform to our problems—whether sickness, pain, debt, depression, or any other trouble—even though they are temporal facts and not eternal realities.

+ *We will lack clear direction for our life.* When our mind is not renewed, we cannot commit to believe in God and His Word wholeheartedly. We will be spiritually indecisive, unable to conclude who we were meant to be, what we should believe in, and what we should be doing. We must know where we are headed in life, just as an airplane pilot sets his course by a fixed destination. When we don't understand our purpose as God intended—or if we can't or won't commit to it—we will lack clear direction for our life, and this uncertainty will cause us anxiety and leave us in a vacillating state of mind.

+ *We will be spiritually vulnerable.* When we have difficulty committing to God's Word and His purposes, as emphasized in the previous point, our vacillation causes us to be spiritually weak and vulnerable. If we truly believe in something, we will commit to it, and we will be decisive in matters related to it. We cannot exercise faith with a mind that is not made up about God and His promises. Do we believe in them or not? We must decide. The enemy is searching for minds that still have not determined what they believe about God or have not yet become established in their beliefs, because those minds are open to receive other options and therefore can be deceived and enticed to doubt God's Word.

+ *Our mind/thoughts will conform to sin.* We may begin to mentally assent to the idea that certain sins are acceptable, so that our mind is in agreement with practices that go against God's nature. If "self" retakes its lost position of supremacy, it will be harder for us to see things from a spiritual point of view because we will be slipping into a fleshly state of mind. Consequently, we might start to call an obviously sinful practice a mere "weakness," or we might claim that we have the right to participate in a particular sin because it makes us "happy." We will gradually accept various sins as the norm, compromising the godly principles by which we used to live.

+ *Our behavior will conform to sin.* If we mentally conform to sin, we will eventually "become" sin in the sense that it will shape and dominate our lifestyle. Adapting to sin causes a person's conscience to be seared and his eyes to be blinded to the truth. For example, if a person conforms to the idea of adultery in his mind, he will probably become an adulterer by his behavior. Likewise, if someone conforms to the idea of addiction, he will likely act in such a way that he will become physically addicted. It is dangerous for someone to allow himself to become conformed to the false mentality of this world, because he will then begin to live according to a deception that ultimately leads to spiritual death. Frighteningly, at that point, he may not even be able to see his destruction coming, because sin will have taken over his heart and mind. On the other hand, if an individual allows the Holy Spirit to transform him, he will become a true child and imitator of his heavenly Father, with the right to inherit all His blessings and to see all His promises fulfilled in his life.

+ *We will experience spiritual dryness.* When we stop renewing our mind, we may cease experiencing the daily "showers" of God's presence that keep our spirit fresh and alive. This is because we start to gain an interest in earthly things that cannot provide life for our spirit, and we manifest a spiritual dryness that slowly parches the life of the Spirit within us. Under these circumstances, we need to return to God and receive a fresh infilling of His Holy Spirit.

One evidence of a spiritually dry condition is when people who once had a living faith turn "religious," having only the letter of the Word rather than the Spirit of it. (See, for example,

2 Corinthians 3:6.) "Religious" people are often characterized by spiritual stagnancy and a resistance to change. Some of them employ every available argument they can think of against change, as well as any possible means to stop it from occurring. As a result, they do not receive God's power, and are they unable to see or to demonstrate His miracles.

When people are in a spiritually dry state, their perspective and even their lifestyle may begin to change for the worse. For example, they may be more critical of others, attend church only occasionally, cease living in the revelation of the Spirit, and stop progressing to higher levels of faith. Such people no longer operate according to the beliefs they once had or the anointing they once received. If we are not careful, such dryness can be our spiritual undoing.

♦ *We will return to false mind-sets and habits, and we will regress spiritually.* If we begin the process of renewing our mind in the Holy Spirit but then halt our progress, we will likely retreat to our previous ways of thinking in line with the world's mind-set. Again, this outlook reflects only a natural, temporal perspective. Consequently, we will return to our former sinful habits, thereby breaking our fellowship with God and with our brothers and sisters in Christ and regressing spiritually.

In addition, when we cease to renew our mind, we may start to see our circumstances in a different light from when we were living in faith. Before, we would have viewed negative traits in others and difficult situations in our life as opportunities for God to manifest His love, grace, and power, but now we will see them only as "flaws," "faults," inconveniences," "problems," "difficulties," and "crises." When our circumstances become our reality, we will speak more about our problems than we do about God, and we may construct a stronghold of doubt and defeatism in our mind that is difficult to tear down.

The mind of faith is not "ignorant," as some people believe; rather, it has a supernatural knowledge that goes beyond human understanding.

+ *We will lose our kingdom relevance in the world.* Let me illustrate this point with a simple analogy: Generally speaking, technology has advanced with each new century of human history; currently, it seems to advance every few years. Most people eventually incorporate new technology into their daily routine, so that their life keeps pace with the various scientific developments of society. Similarly, as we continue to be renewed in spiritual knowledge, and as we incorporate that knowledge into our character and lifestyle, we will better understand the ways in which God is manifesting His kingdom in our contemporary world, and we will remain spiritually relevant. But when we stop being transformed and go back to false ways of thinking and sinful practices, we will lose our spiritual relevance and cease to know, or to participate in, God's fresh revelation.

+ *We will experience recurring issues and frustrations.* People who are stuck in a fallen mind-set will repeat the same mistakes and failings and will continually deal with similar problems and obstacles, no matter where they are or with whom they associate. They—not others—are the cause of their own difficulties, but they can't see that fact, because their mind is blind to it. We cannot walk in the Spirit and operate in the supernatural when we have a carnal mind that is totally opposed to the mind of God and always doubts and questions Him.

Recurring issues and problems in our life can indicate that we are trapped in a carnal mentality.

---

5. Prove the Will of God

"*...that you may prove what is that good and acceptable and perfect will of God*" (Romans 12:2). The Greek word translated "*prove*" is *dokimazo*, which means "to test," with the implication of "to approve"—in other words, "to attest," or "to affirm to be true or genuine." When our mind is renewed, we will understand the will of God, which is "*good*," "*acceptable*," and "*perfect*" for us. From the above conclusion to Paul's entreaty in Romans 12:1–2, we recognize that, in order to discover God's will, we must first present our body as a *"living sacrifice,"* making ourselves totally available to Him.

God's will is a reflection of His nature and qualities, and one of His greatest characteristics is His supernatural ability. Therefore, to manifest the supernatural is to be in alignment with an aspect of His will. Some evidences that we are in His will are the supernatural healings and miracles and the instances of supernatural provision, guidance, peace, and/or joy that are manifested in and through our life. When we pray, *"Your kingdom come. Your will be done on earth as it is in heaven"* (Matthew 6:10), we are asking that the dominion and will of our heavenly King be exhibited and carried out in our midst. God wants the reality of His supernatural realm to invade our life, and He wants His will to be manifested through us as a result of the transformation and renewal of our heart and mind.

Consider how God's will is demonstrated in heaven. Everything there is complete and eternal; no one experiences limitations due to time or space; and there is no iniquity, sickness, lack, fear, or sadness. In heaven, the redeemed experience true life, never-ending peace, perfect health, and an abundance of all good things. Therefore, if we live according to a transformed heart and mind, with access to the heavenly realm, we can bring God's will—including all these elements—to earth.

When your mind is continually renewed, you will know God's will and walk in it.

As our mind is renewed according to the *"mind of Christ"* (1 Corinthians 2:16), we become truly useful to God. If we operate outside the purposes of His mind, it will be a rare thing for God to use us, regardless of how "available" we make ourselves to Him. The Lord will not be able to work through us if our thoughts and/or our behavior are in conflict with the mind of Christ.

But when we renew our mind, we become a powerful instrument for God's kingdom. This explains why our mind is the place of ongoing spiritual battle. The enemy will try by any means possible to stop us from renewing our mind. He will scheme to make the world's culture and ways seem comforting and appealing; he will attack us with *"the lust of the flesh, the lust of the eyes, and the pride of life"* (1 John 2:16). He tempted Jesus in the same ways, but Jesus was loyal to His Father's heart, mind, and kingdom purposes. We offer ourselves to that which we enter into agreement with our heart and mind. Often, our thoughts reveal where we have placed our loyalties—either with God's ways or with the ways of the flesh and the enemy.

A renewed mind is essential to bringing the reality of the kingdom of God to others.

Let us now look at three striking testimonies that demonstrate God's supernatural ability to transform the human mind. In these cases, He performed miracles to heal people supernaturally from physical and mental disorders of the brain. The first testimony is of Yanaris, who was born premature, weighing only two pounds. The doctors determined that part of Yanaris's brain was missing, and he was diagnosed with mental retardation. As he grew, he had trouble sleeping, was unable to learn to read or write, had a very short attention span, was quick to become bored, and had problems with his memory—to the point that he would forget things within seconds. He was given prescribed medication, and he was dependent on his mother and other adults for everything. In school, the other children made fun of him. He instinctively defended himself, but his self-defense turned into anger, frustration, bitterness, and depression. He grew up to be a violent and abusive young man.

Tired of his situation, Yanaris began to ask God to help him to be "normal." Then, he attended a youth conference hosted by our ministry. I preached at one of the sessions, and, at the end of the session, I purposed to demonstrate, by way of signs and miracles, what I had preached. Yanaris ran to the altar, and I laid my hands on his head. Yanaris testifies that he felt the fire of God burn throughout his body—and he also began to have a bad headache. When he went home, the pain in his head was still there. The following day, he was taken to the hospital to be examined. There, doctors discovered that his brain was now whole! Jesus had created the part of his brain that had been missing!

The doctors told him, "Yanaris, we don't know how this is possible, but your brain is complete. You are now able to live a full life without any problem." With joy, Yanaris jumped, shouted, cried, and praised God. He embraced and kissed his mother and danced from pure happiness. Now he is an independent man. He finished high school and, in a short time, went from being a waiter to being one of the best chefs at the Marlins stadium in Miami. He is happy and very grateful to God for the tremendous miracle that was given to him. When he shares his testimony, he says, "Parents, do not accept mental illnesses in your children. The supernatural power of God and His great love for humanity have no limits. Nothing is impossible for Him! If He recreated part of my brain, He can do great things for your children."

The next testimony is of Safi, a young man who was well-educated but lived with internal conflicts that he couldn't understand. Eventually, he was diagnosed with schizophrenia—a mental illness that only the supernatural power of God can cure. Here is his story: "When I was fourteen years old, I attended a school for gifted children. I would complete three hours' worth of homework every night, but then I would spend all my free time in the ghettoes and lower-class neighborhoods. As a teenager, I was arrested several times for minor offenses. However, I graduated from high school and was awarded a scholarship to attend the university. By then, I was stealing from every type of business.

"My first schizophrenic episode was of demons raping me. This experience led me to question my sexual orientation. Later, I would hear voices making racial comments toward black women when they passed by me, and I thought it was my own thoughts. In an effort to calm myself, I started to drink. I had no idea what schizophrenia was, so I didn't understand what was happening to me. I started to see demons with huge knives, stabbing people. The demons threatened to cut my loved ones if I didn't attack or hurt someone else.

"One Mother's Day, the demons came at me stronger than ever. They told me they were going to hurt my mother if I didn't go out and hurt someone. That morning, I went out and stole from about ten people in just under an hour, threatening them with a knife. The police were looking for me, but I just kept robbing people. Finally, I went to rob an elderly woman, and, as I looked into her eyes, I heard a voice that said, 'You'd better not do it.' I let her go and surrendered to the police.

"I was put in prison, where I fought the correctional officers, so I was placed in solitary confinement. When I found out that I was facing life in prison for the crimes I had committed, I broke down. I asked for a Bible, but they said I wasn't allowed to have anything in solitary confinement. After a few weeks, during which I caused no further incidents, I was returned to the regular prison. I made friends with two men whom God used as 'angels' to guide me in the right path. I started to read the Bible, to pray, and to attend the church service held at the prison.

"I was discharged from prison a year later because I had been diagnosed as schizophrenic prior to my arrest and didn't have any other crimes pending. I was given five years' probation and was released on my own recognizance to live at a halfway house. I returned to the university and joined the Christian club and the business clubs, where I met my mentor.

"Now, four years later, I serve in the church and have scholarships to go to leadership conferences in Washington, D.C., Poland, and Israel. I never violated my parole, and I was released two years early. Today, God continues to work in me, and His mercy is eternal. I am a free man! God set me free! Through His grace, He has shown me that I can be a totally restored man—free of 'voices,' attacks, anger, and chaotic behavior."

The third testimony is of Antonio, who was diagnosed with attention-deficit/hyperactivity disorder and Tourette's syndrome when he was seven years old. Tourette's syndrome is a neurological disorder that manifests in bizarre thoughts or ideas, compulsive speech, and involuntary movements, including obscene words and gestures and the repetition of words. Antonio also suffered from sleep disorders, including sleepwalking, nightmares, and insomnia.

Antonio's mother says that her son was treated with various drugs but made no apparent improvement. Seeing her child in this state drove her to desperation. She reached a point at which she simply got sick and tired of the situation and decided to take Antonio to the early-morning prayer meeting at our church. I was ministering that day, and I laid my hands on Antonio, declaring his healing in the name of Jesus. As an act of faith, his mother stopped giving him the prescribed medications. Let me emphasize that no one told her to do this; it was her own choice, as an act of faith, because that is what she felt God was leading her to do.

A few days later, she received a call from the school where her son attended. Antonio's teachers told her that he was showing noticeable improvement in his schoolwork. He had passed all his exams with excellent grades, and the teachers were surprised. They thought his mother had increased the dosage of his medications, and they told her they would even be moving him to a gifted class. When they discovered that Antonio was no longer taking the medications, they couldn't believe it!

Today, Antonio is fully functional. He can play with his fellow students, is well-behaved in class, earns good grades, and is able to participate in family gatherings. His grandmother, who was a doctor of psychiatry in Cuba, opposed the decision to stop administering Antonio's medications, but when she saw her grandson's improvement, she was amazed by the supernatural power of God. She has stopped believing in psychiatry and is now totally involved in the vision of our ministry. Both the mother and grandmother want to learn how to take the supernatural power of God to children who have been abandoned and/or who suffer with illnesses similar to those Antonio had.

Since God is able to perform creative miracles and tremendous healings that transform people's minds, as He did for the young men in the above testimonies, He can surely renew our mind through the Holy Spirit, so that it reflects His own mind.

The Importance of Renewal of the Mind

Let's review the following truths about the renewal of our mind:

+ Unless we renew our mind and cast off our fallen, limited mentality, God will be able to do little in us that is new.

+ As we renew our mind, we begin to perceive, "see," and "hear" the spiritual realm.

+ As we renew our mind, old and limiting structures that do not bear fruit for the kingdom will fall away. Jesus said, *"No one puts new wine into old wineskins; or else the new wine bursts the wineskins, the wine is spilled, and the wineskins are ruined. But new wine must be put into new wineskins"* (Mark 2:22). I believe that the *"new wineskins"* Christ talked about refer to changes in mind-set, in structure, and in message. Again, we cannot use a new structure while we still maintain our old mentalities based on the fallen nature. Yet the transformation of the mind produces a change of structure and message that reflects a living gospel—which, in turn, produces the manifestation of the power and presence of God and revolutionizes our life as the *"new wine"* of the Holy Spirit flows in and through us.

No transformation can take place without true repentance.

+ When we become established in the continual renewal of our mind, God is able to trust us with His anointing, His supernatural power, and the experience of His glory. Living according to the mind of Christ leads to powerful demonstrations of His will and purposes.

+ The renewal of our mind assures that the deliverance, healing, or other supernatural manifestation we may receive from God will remain. No transformation is permanent without a change of mentality; there must be a comprehensive renewal from the inside out. Transformation cannot be counterfeited for very long; it cannot be maintained if it is not genuine.

When we renew our mind, we become a more usable and powerful instrument of God.

+ The renewal of our mind is the beginning of success. When we break away from a defeated, negative, limited mentality in order to enter into the victorious, positive, limitless mind-set of the kingdom, we will prosper in every aspect of our life, just as our soul prospers. (See 3 John 1:2.)

+ Renewing our mind, or establishing God's thoughts within us, causes us to continually experience new spiritual challenges, and it demands increasingly greater surrender to God and sanctification in Him. Renewal must be an ongoing "rhythm" in our spiritual life. If we lose that rhythm, we will no longer flow in the supernatural but will slow down until we finally return to functioning according to a natural state. To keep from losing this rhythm, we must rise to meet these challenges and demands through faith, always obeying God immediately and fully, and retaining what we have gained spiritually in Him.

No transformation is permanent without a change of mentality.

+ When our mind is renewed, we have access to God's imagination. The false arguments and mental processes of the fallen human mind-set produce a limited vision. The reason we often ask, "How can this be?" in relation to God's promises is that human reason alone can't understand the things of God. The fallen mind has a vast imagination, yet it is still limited, and it is unable to comprehend the marvelous plans, ideas, and thoughts of God. Yet, when our mind is renewed in Christ, we are able to think according to the outlook of heaven, and we realize that doubting God's Word is merely a waste of time.

You know that your mind has been renewed when the "impossible" becomes logical to you.

How to Continuously Renew Your Mind

The transformation of your mind comes as a result of humbling yourself before God and acknowledging that you have lived according to a mentality that is contrary to His mind-set—one that is limited to the natural world and unable to believe in His power, much less manifest that power to heal sickness, remove heartache, and set free those who are in bondage. The transformation occurs when you truly hunger to see God's presence manifest and His supernatural power and grace operate for His glory—in your life, in the life of your family members, and in the life of your church, city, and nation. For the transformation of your mind to occur, you must regularly do the following:

1. Immerse Your Mind in the Revelation of God's Word

Revelation leads to a new experience with God. Our mind begins to be renewed when the Holy Spirit reveals to us a truth from God's Word, and the renewal is complete when we obediently put into practice the revelation we receive. When Noah had a revelation of God's purpose, his mind-set changed, and, in obedience, he built an ark in the middle of a desert—even though it had never rained before. When Peter had a revelation of Jesus as the Messiah, his mind-set changed, and his life was established on a course that led him to be a principal leader through whom Christ established His beloved church.

Without the revelation of the Word, we cannot experience transformation.

2. Meditate on the Word

The Lord commanded Joshua, "*This Book of the Law shall not depart from your mouth, but you shall* **meditate in it day and night, that you may observe to do according to all that is written in it.** *For then you will make your way prosperous, and then you will have good success*" (Joshua 1:8). In some religions, to meditate means to "empty" the mind of all thoughts, but that is not what biblical meditation means. In fact, emptying our mind can be a dangerous practice, because it lowers our spiritual guard and opens the door for demons to influence us. We know that the enemy doesn't wait for an invitation to enter—he searches for an opportunity to take over the territory of our mind and heart. (See, for example, Matthew 12:43–45.)

To meditate in a biblical sense means to spend time reading, studying, and thinking about the truths of God's words—including the prophetic words written in the Bible and those given to us directly by the Holy Spirit as revealed knowledge and wisdom—and considering how to apply them to our life, for the purpose of filling our mind and heart with God's revelation. Every person in the world practices "meditation" in the general sense of focusing his thoughts on particular things; the question is, on what is he reflecting? For instance, when we worry about something, we are meditating in a negative sense, filling our mind with doubt, anxiety, pessimism, and other destructive attitudes. The Scriptures give us clear guidelines for what we should be thinking about. Paul wrote, *"Whatever things are true, whatever things are noble, whatever things are just, whatever things are pure, whatever things are lovely, whatever things are of good report, if there is any virtue and if there is anything praiseworthy—meditate on these things"* (Philippians 4:8).

If we don't purposefully take time to meditate on God's Word, our mind can be dominated by temporal, carnal thinking. For example, if we allow fearful thoughts to remain in our mind for a long period of time, a fearful mentality can become established in us. Yet, if we meditate on biblical truths that assure us of God's faithfulness, trustworthiness, and promise of help in time of need, we will have His peace. *"You will keep him in perfect peace, whose mind is stayed on You, because he trusts in You"* (Isaiah 26:3).

To meditate in a biblical sense means to spend time reading, studying, and thinking about the truths of God's words and considering how to apply them to our life.

---

3. Seek Supernatural Experiences with God

As we increasingly align our mind with the mind of Christ, we will have encounters or experiences with God that cause us gradually to disassociate ourselves from the thinking of the natural realm in order to move into the supernatural realm and to think in supernatural terms. This doesn't mean that we will become disconnected from reality, turn "mystic" or "odd," or begin to deny reality or the existence of the natural world. We will continue to use our natural mind, our common sense, and our five physical senses to function under natural conditions. However, our spiritual senses will be awakened to see, hear, and perceive God; and we will learn to live in such a way that these senses are continually on full alert and totally functioning, enabling us to know God better, to confirm His will, and to discern when and how He wants to move supernaturally in our world. We will walk in the assurance that God is always carrying out His purposes, just as He reveals them.

That is how we can go beyond human reason and logic, thinking and living above natural limitations. In the supernatural realm, there is no room for doubt, because everything is possible with God! We are always ready to be a vessel through whom God can manifest the reality of His kingdom and bring His supernatural power to this world—here and now—to meet people's present needs.

In the New Testament, Saul's encounter with the glory of Jesus (see Acts 9:3–4) transformed his outlook on God and renewed his life, so that even his name was changed—to Paul. His mind-set, his "structure" of living, and the message he proclaimed were all transformed. Paul had been an "old wineskins" religious man and a persecutor of the church, full of hate, and blind to how God was working through Jesus and the church. But when his mind was transformed by his supernatural experience with Christ and his subsequent study of the Scriptures with the illumination of the Holy Spirit, he was able to see the reality of God's kingdom and to work to bring that reality on earth as it is in heaven.

Supernatural experiences are an aspect of our inheritance as children of God and citizens of His kingdom; often, such experiences are the only way many people can understand certain spiritual truths and thereby change their outlook. For example, we don't really know what it is like to be born again until we have a genuine salvation experience, with a knowledge of the forgiveness of our sins and the indwelling presence of God's Holy Spirit. Many leaders in the church today are trying to prevent people from having experiences with the power of God, because they are afraid that such encounters are either deceptions of the enemy or manufactured events. We must, of course, exercise spiritual discernment regarding supernatural experiences. However, we must also realize that we are being deceived if we *do not have* genuine encounters with God and His supernatural power, because then we are living below the reality God intends for us.

The gospel messages that produce the most powerful changes in people's lives are those presented by individuals who have experienced what they preach. Receiving a revelation of any kind from God is a supernatural experience. If we try to preach any aspect of the gospel without having received revelation about it through the Holy Spirit and/or without having experienced it, our message will lack authority and substance.

Our encounters with God—or lack of them—govern how our mind thinks. If we experience the reality of His kingdom, and then renew our mind accordingly, we will never again be the same or think in the same way. For example, after we have experienced the baptism of the Holy Spirit and spoken in other tongues, our spiritual mind-set changes. Likewise, our perspective alters after we receive a healing, a miracle, a prophetic word, or any other supernatural manifestation.

Knowledge is not truly yours until you have an experience with what you know.

---

4. Pray to God and Commune with Him

"Pray without ceasing" (1 Thessalonians 5:17). When we pray, we can experience communion with God as we spend time worshipping Him, listening to His voice, and receiving His direction through the Holy Spirit. We are always changed in some way when we enter into a relationship with another person. It is the same when we spend time in God's presence—we become more like Him, and we are better able to understand His heart, His mind, and His ways. As we develop an ever deeper relationship with Him, we can increasingly pray according to His will—for the advancement of His kingdom on earth as it is in heaven.

5. Align Your Mind with the Mind of Christ

As an act of our will, we need to pray to the Lord, "Let Christ's mind be fully formed in me. I purposefully set my mind on what is 'above'—especially on You, Lord, our unlimited God! I will think about what is true, noble, just, pure, lovely, of good report, virtuous, and praiseworthy. I will bring all my thoughts into alignment with the mind of Christ, so that they are 'captive' to Him. In Jesus' name, amen!" (See Colossians 3:1–2.)

Prayer for Transformation of the Mind

Is your mind being transformed so that the supernatural power of God can move in your life? The purpose of this transformation is to establish Christ's church, which the enemy—through "religion" and false philosophies—seeks to undermine and destroy. When your mind is renewed, you can flow in accordance with the "river" of the Spirit—spontaneously and with freedom. Rather than quench the Holy Spirit (see 1 Thessalonians 5:19), you will give Him His rightful place in your life, acknowledging the One who sent Him—God the Father—and the One in whose name He was sent (see John 14:26).

Dear friend, I sincerely believe that this is the time for you to begin to renew your mind—or to advance to a greater level of transformation. It is time for you to let go of a mentality that limits you in fulfilling God's purposes, one that has kept you trapped in a repetitive cycle of thinking, preventing you from experiencing abundant life and seeing God's power manifest here and now. I invite you to pray the following simple but powerful prayer. I know of innumerable testimonies of people who have prayed this prayer and have experienced a total transformation of their mind—and their life.

Heavenly Father, thank You for the revelation You have given me through Your Word about how my mind can be renewed. Today, I want a radical change in my life. I repent of living according to the mentality of this world and of gratifying the sinful nature. I renounce the negative influences of the world, including "religion" and the limitations of human knowledge and reason. I want Your mind, Lord. I want Your way of thinking. I want Your supernatural mind-set. I surrender my mind and my thoughts to Your supernatural power, so that they can be exchanged for Your mind and thoughts. Please renew my mind, so that I can become a useful instrument in Your hands for Your kingdom and can take this revelation to other people who are trapped in the same condition I have been in. "Here I am, Lord; send me!" In the name of Jesus, I thank You for hearing me and for activating Your supernatural power over my life—here and now. In Jesus' name, amen.

If you are suffering from a physical or mental disorder, like the young men we read about in the testimonies earlier in this chapter, I pray that God's supernatural power would fill you right now and make you completely whole, in the name of Jesus! Receive your healing by faith and begin to thank God for working a miracle in your life. All things are possible with God!

11

A Heart After God's Own Heart

At the beginning of my ministry, God gave me this prophetic word through Apostle Ronald Short: "I will give you a heart with the fire of Jeremiah and the speed of Elijah, and a heart after My own heart, just like David's." This word impacted me greatly, because, for a long time, I had asked myself, *Is it possible to have a heart after God's own heart? Are we born with such a heart, or is transformation required to obtain it?* That was when I first understood that such a heart is gained through a supernatural transformation by the finished work of the cross. I knew that although I didn't yet have the heart described in the prophetic word, and that developing it would not take place overnight, I would go through a process that would enable me to receive it.

My desire has always been to have a heart after God's heart. And, by the grace of God, I have seen the above three characteristics increasingly develop and manifest in my life. The "fire" of God is always in my heart, burning endlessly for Him, for His kingdom, and for people's souls. (See Jeremiah 20:9.) Furthermore, every endeavor I am involved with accelerates in terms of growth and the fruit it yields. Third, I have a heart that passionately seeks God's presence with holy fear and a desire to please Him; and, by God's anointing, I also have a disposition for spiritual warfare and conquest over the enemy, just as God gave David.

The Lord has led me through a process of supernatural transformation of the heart that continues to this day. Once, I had no passion to seek God;

but after I received Jesus as my Savior and Lord, He kindled that passion within me. At one time in my life, I had neither the attitude of a conqueror, nor was I courageous; but after God delivered me of fear, I was able to develop those qualities. What I am today is due to the supernatural grace of God. I am a living testimony that He can thoroughly change the heart of a man. It *is* possible to have a heart after God's own heart!

David's Heart Versus Saul's Heart

The prophet Samuel announced to Saul, the first king over Israel, *"But now your kingdom shall not continue. The Lord has sought for Himself a man after His own heart, and the Lord has commanded him to be commander over His people, because you have not kept what the Lord commanded you"* (1 Samuel 13:14). God had desired to work with and through Saul, but the king repeatedly disobeyed His voice. He would filter God's clear instructions by acting according to what seemed reasonable to his human intellect. Saul pretended to seek and to serve God, but his heart was set on his own agenda. His intentions and motivations toward the Lord were not genuine—he merely practiced a religious ritual.

For example, Saul seemed to treat the ark of the covenant not as the holy dwelling place of God's presence but as a "good luck charm" in battle. He would seek God only when he faced difficulties. But even then, he again did not obey God's commands, because he always ended up doing what he had already planned to do in his heart. Of supreme importance to Saul were his position and his preeminence in the eyes of the people. He walked so far away from the Lord that he ended up consulting a witch. After this incident, Saul and his son Jonathan died on the battlefield.

Although Saul was God's anointed king, he ended up a failure because he didn't allow God to guide him, and he didn't follow His counsel. We must all examine our heart to make sure it doesn't have any of the characteristics of Saul's disobedient heart. If it does, we should diligently seek God's forgiveness and the transformation of our heart so that we may learn to hear and obey God and take responsibility for growing in Christlikeness. Likewise, we must not follow any leader who has a heart like Saul's; otherwise, we may be destroyed along with him.

God rejected Saul because of the king's continued disobedience, and He raised up another man—David—to be king, instead. While Saul held on to his rebellion and did not allow God to form him, David had a heart after God's own heart. David's good character had been established long before he was called to the throne; as a youth, he had spent much time worshipping God, meditating on His Word, and delighting in Him. To receive God's acceptance, and to avoid His rejection, we must allow Him to form our heart to be like His own.

This truth is what a man named Abedef came to recognize. He thought he would conquer the world with his athletic abilities, until a personal crisis led to the transformation of his heart in Christ. The following is his story. "From the first day I arrived in the United States from Haiti, the only thing I knew, experienced, and breathed was basketball. I remember returning home with body aches and black-and-blue marks as I struggled to become a professional player. My high-school years were devoted to attaining success and fame as I dreamed about how I would finally be able to bring my family out of Haiti's poverty.

"Basketball was my idol—it was what I adored and what I lived for; it was everything I knew and loved. It was my 'drug,' the vehicle for my exceeding pride and arrogance—on and off the court. Although I didn't use illegal drugs, have promiscuous sex, or drink alcohol, I would become impatient and would verbally unload my anger on my family. Then something terrible happened: While practicing for a championship game, I suffered a meniscus tear and was rushed to the emergency room, where the doctors told me I would not be able to play basketball for at least three months. That meant the end of my season. Consequently, I fell into a deep depression. I lay on the hospital bed, crying, until I exclaimed, 'If I can't play basketball, what reason is there for me to continue living?' Then and there, I decided to take my own life.

"That same day, a friend whom I had not seen for years called me and said, 'I haven't heard from you in a long time. Why don't you come to church with me?' I didn't want to go to church, because I thought I would hear a boring message and would leave the same way I had come in. My friend insisted until I agreed to go with her to a Bible study in someone's house. There, the power of God greatly impacted me. Halfway through the teaching, the leader said to me, 'You can be healed of your condition. God will heal you.' Although I felt a bit skeptical, I said, 'All right; I surrender. I want to see God heal me!' The leader prayed for me, and I felt heat travel throughout my entire body.

"The next day, I started to play basketball again! My trainer couldn't fathom what was happening. The doctors didn't understand it. But God did much more than that. He changed my heart and showed me my true purpose in life. I no longer depend on basketball. I don't need any idols. I need God and His eternal promises. I was set free from depression and was able to finish my last basketball season. All the hunger I'd had for the sport was transferred to a desire to serve God and to preach His Word. Now people admire me not for who I am but for what the Lord has called me to do. My dream was to play in the major leagues, but now I am finally on the right path. My destiny was not basketball but serving God."

"A Man After My Own Heart"

"[God] *raised up for them David as king, to whom also He gave testimony and said, 'I have found David the son of Jesse, a man after My own heart who will do all My will'"* (Acts 13:22). David is the only person named in Scripture whom God the Father specifically referred to as having a heart after His own heart. You may wonder, "How could David have been a man after God's own heart if he became an adulterer (see 2 Samuel 11:1–5), a murderer (see 2 Samuel 11:6–17), and a man who spilled much blood (see, for example, 2 Samuel 8:1–6)?" If we look at David from a human perspective, it makes no sense for God to consider him a man after His own heart; therefore, we must look at him from God's perspective.

What led God to forgive David, remove his sin, and preserve his kingdom? David had slept with Bathsheba, the wife of one of his soldiers, impregnated her, and then arranged to have her husband killed. But God knew David's innermost heart. He knew David was sensitive to Him and that he had allowed Him to greatly mold him in the past. Moreover, whenever David sinned, he was quick to genuinely repent, because he loved God passionately and recognized that he had deeply offended Him. (See, for example, Psalm 51.)

I am not saying that God ever tolerates sin or agrees with it. But, again, He sees our heart; and He considers us according to our finished state in eternity—as having the righteousness of Jesus and a transformed heart and life. Perhaps you have had a major failing, as David did, and you think it is the end of your relationship with God or even your life. Yet, if you will repent, He will restore you and lead you to the destiny to which He called you before the beginning of time. The Scriptures say, *"He who covers his sins will not prosper, but whoever confesses and forsakes them will have mercy"* (Proverbs 28:13). God expects you to repent of your sin and to believe that you have been completely forgiven in Christ. Then, He wants you to allow Him to continue to transform your heart.

Divine grace is not a license to sin but rather the supernatural means by which we receive a heart that is pure and clean, and through which we can draw near to our heavenly Father. Therefore, whenever we fail, we should immediately go to God for forgiveness through Christ. *"Let us therefore come boldly to the throne of grace, that we may obtain mercy and find grace to help in time of need"* (Hebrews 4:16). If our heart has not been transformed, so that we fail to understand God's grace by supernatural revelation and do not repent, we will abuse that grace, dishonoring the precious blood Christ shed for us. We must experience the transformation of our heart!

Alex is the owner of a prestigious international legal firm that deals with cases in the United States, Canada, Panama, and Honduras. Yet he experienced deep grief. When God began the process of transforming his heart, he received new joy and spiritual freedom. Here is his story: "My wife and I lived through a very difficult crisis—we lost two of our children. One died at age twenty-eight and the other at age thirty-three. Personally, I believe the death of a child is the hardest blow anyone can experience. In this condition, I attended a meeting at King Jesus Ministry, which made a great impact on me spiritually. God told me that I had to make a change, that a new season was coming for me. I experienced a peace that I had never felt before.

"From that day, God has dealt with my heart, and our life has changed 100 percent. He has prospered me as a man, as a father, and as the priest of my home, and He has removed my deep grief over the death of my children. Furthermore, He has prospered me in a supernatural way. My legal firm has grown greatly, and I truly believe that the Lord has given me a gift that I didn't have before. We have invested in many things and now own several construction companies, community development companies, and pharmaceutical companies, as well as a film production company, and we continue to grow. God has made me influential in order to impact my city for Him; but, most of all, He has built up my wife and me and given us hope, so that we can provide our grandchildren with guidance and purpose."

God gives us His supernatural grace to live a holy life.

Characteristics of a Heart After God's Own Heart

The only way to have true success in our journey through this world—success that will last for eternity—is for our heart to be in the right place. How did David merit being called "a man after God's own heart"? How did he capture the heart of God? The following are the major characteristics of a heart after God's own heart.

1. A Heart After God's Own Heart Passionately Seeks God's Presence

One of the virtues of David's heart was that he was passionate about God. He wanted to know God, to love Him, to dwell in His presence, and to receive direct revelation from Him. He sought to please God and to serve Him with his whole being. David wrote, *"O God, You are my God; early will I seek You; my soul thirsts for You; my flesh longs for You in a dry and thirsty land where there is no water. So I have looked for You in the sanctuary, to see Your power and Your glory"* (Psalm 63:1–2).

David was always "thirsty" for God—and his thirst impelled him to seek the Lord's presence continuously. Psalm 42 provides another vivid image of a heart that is thirsty for God: *"As the deer pants for the water brooks, so pants my soul for You, O God. My soul thirsts for God, for the living God"* (Psalm 42:1–2). Such a thirst for God cannot be manufactured. It manifests in a person's life during a sincere, continuous quest to experience His presence.

David was consumed by this quest. He sought God's face every day, and even during the night. (See Psalm 63:6.) And, each time he was confronted with a crisis, he would look to God for help, because he totally depended on his relationship with the Lord. The more we love God, the more we will desire Him; and the more we know of Him, the more we will want to learn of Him—always more. "More" of God will never be enough for us!

A lack of spiritual thirst will produce spiritual dryness, which will yield only legalism, religion, and spiritual death.

---

2. A Heart After God's Own Heart Passionately Worships God

David was also passionate about worshipping God. He wrote, "*One thing I have desired of the LORD, that will I seek: that I may dwell in the house of the LORD all the days of my life, to behold the beauty of the LORD, and to inquire in His temple*" (Psalm 27:4). I believe David altered the history of worship by establishing a pattern of praise and worship for Israel that was observed by God's people from Old Testament times through the practices of the New Testament church—and his influence continues to impact us today. From David's writings in the book of Psalms, it seems as if he lived thousands of years ahead of his time—as if he lived according to the grace released by Christ's death on the cross and in the power of His resurrection. (See, for example, Psalm 16:9–11.)

Generally, David did everything in his life from a position of worship, because he had received the revelation of how worship affects the heart of God. He knew that worship greatly pleases Him! If we had a revelation of this truth, we would worship God more. We must understand that, like the exercise of our faith, our worship of God develops and matures the more we practice it.

Let us now explore the effects of worship on God's heart and on our own heart.

Our Passionate Worship Opens God's Heart to Us and Our Heart to His

Our genuine, passionate worship of God opens His heart to us while softening our own heart, because it is an act of voluntary submission and obedience to Him. Obedience is one of the greatest acts of worship. If we have a heart that is hardened and unwilling to submit to God, our "worship" will be rejected by Him, and He will close off His heart to us. Authentic worship makes us more sensitive to the Lord, leading us to recognize our true spiritual condition so that we will surrender to God, repent, and allow His Holy Spirit to operate the needed transformation within us.

When you are a genuine worshipper, your life is submitted to God in everything—He takes first place over everyone and everything else.

Our true worship will reveal God's presence, so that we will often tangibly sense it. A true worshipper knows how to respond when His presence manifests. There are times in a church service when the spiritual atmosphere is so full of joy that shouting, applauding, and dancing are the best response. But there are also times of worship that are so holy that a joyful shout would seem out of place. Those are moments in which our approach should be to merely wait in reverent silence.

True worship means the King is present.

We must be careful to watch our attitudes during worship and not allow ourselves to become listless, bored, or angry as our mind wanders to dwell on temporal matters. Our mind-set toward God should be that of attentiveness, love, reverence, and gratitude. As in any other personal relationship, our attitudes toward God will define the quality, intensity, and duration of our interactions with Him.

The highest level of worship is to "become" worship. In other words, our entire life should be an expression of worship to God.

Our Passionate Worship Leads to Intimacy with God

Many people today avoid intimacy with other people. They are afraid of getting too close to others because they don't want their own faults, weaknesses, and failings to be exposed. A true worshipper doesn't fear going before the presence of God, regardless of his current spiritual condition, because he knows that God loves him deeply and wants the best for him. Such an individual passionately desires to be close to the Lord so that his heart may be transformed by the Holy Spirit, enabling him to carry out the purposes of God's own heart.

What touches the heart of God? What pleases Him? What moves Him? What makes His presence manifest? The answer to all these questions is a relationship of intimacy with Him. True worship may be compared to a "romance" with God. For example, when we begin a time of worship by praising God and thanking Him, it is as if we are in the "courting stage" of our relationship with Him. As the Scriptures say, *"Enter into His gates with thanksgiving, and into His courts with praise"* (Psalm 100:4), and *"Let us come before His presence with thanksgiving"* (Psalm 95:2).

We "romance" God through our praise, thanksgiving, and worship, by which we develop intimacy with Him.

After praise and thanksgiving, worship represents the "marriage" of our relationship with God. The Bible uses analogies of the sexual relationship between a husband and wife to describe the depth of the intimacy between God and His people, which is a reflection of their mutual love and faithfulness. (See, for example, Ephesians 5:30–32.) Today, many people think of intimacy in terms of a casual sexual relationship, such as many couples seem to engage in today. But the intimacy I refer to is a union that is pure, within a covenant relationship, in which each party manifests deep respect and tenderness for the other and seeks to give to the other.

Worship from a believer whose heart is obedient, and who expresses his love for God with messages of trust and devotion, will set the tone for intimacy, thereby beautifying the atmosphere for unity, or spiritual oneness, with God. We must offer God our undivided attention so He will experience our genuine love, allowing the moment of intimacy to manifest. When we set everything else aside to seek God, He will give us His undivided attention. When this happens, we can then say that we have experienced a relationship of mutual love with God through worship.

When we worship God, we give Him our absolute and undivided attention, and in return we receive His undivided attention.

In contrast, if our attitude is wrong and our actions are thoughtless during a time of worship, we will cause God's presence to leave before this unity can occur. Unfortunately, after receiving what they need from God—such as healing, provision, or another miracle—some people abruptly cease worshipping Him. Their worship was never really genuine—they were moved to worship God not because of a deep love for Him but merely because of self-interest or a sense of desperation over their troubles. True worship that leads to intimacy with God and brings transformation to our heart occurs when we die to self, lose our awareness of this world and its problems, and focus only on Him—for His own sake.

We must worship Him with a sincere heart until His presence comes! Lose yourself in God until you are one with Him. Similar to the sexual act in marriage, our worship should not be merely a "quick" experience, because that will neither please God nor satisfy our heart. Therefore, when you go into God's presence—when you enter into eternity with Him—take time to commune with Him as you would with a beloved spouse.

God reveals His presence to us when His heart is pleased.

Our Passionate Worship Leads to "Conception" and New Life

When our relationship with God is stagnant, we will not be able to manifest new life in Him. We cannot really know God or fulfill our purpose on earth if we are not true, passionate worshippers. It is during the intimacy of worship that we "conceive" how God wants us to carry out His purposes, plans, and vision. Moreover, when our worship is lifeless, we will merely be going through a religious ritual, and our spiritual womb will become "barren." Our worship should "birth" salvations, healings, miracles, deliverances, visions, dreams, revelations, and heart transformations as the fruit of our intimacy with God. During my times of worship, the Father has revealed many of the truths I write about in my books. He has also given me the creative ideas I have implemented for the expansion of His kingdom, as well as my vision to impact the nations for Christ.

The main purpose of worship is intimacy, and the purpose of intimacy is to conceive and produce new life.

Our Passionate Worship Causes God to Make Himself Known

When God's people worship Him wholeheartedly, He will reveal Himself to them. Many Christians go to church just to hear the Word preached, and they never join in during the praise and worship portion of the service. I believe this shows a lack of reverence for God. A number of believers seem to have lost the revelation that Jesus is our King and High Priest and that we are called to prepare an atmosphere in which He can manifest His presence, speak to His people, and perform supernatural miracles, healings, and deliverances.

As we worship God, He gives us revelation of His mind and heart.

Our worship cannot be monotonous, mechanical, or repetitive if we want God to reveal Himself to us. Rather, it must be heartfelt and intimate. The Lord wants to show Himself as the Almighty, the Healer, the Deliverer, the Provider, the One who baptizes with supernatural power—the One who is our All in All. God is eternal, and there is always a new aspect of His nature for us to discover. We must not become spiritually complacent or cease progressing in our capacity to worship Him, because we will miss out on His revelation.

Our Passionate Worship Leads to Personal Transformation and Corporate Revival

When we enter into God's presence during worship, our heart is changed to become what He originally intended it to be, as a reflection of His own heart. And, as we progress in the process of transformation, we are able to manifest the realm of heaven on earth through the grace and power of the Holy Spirit. When this occurs, our churches and communities will experience revival.

We must understand that revival will cease if we no longer allow our heart to be transformed. Our relationship with God will be contaminated, and we will see a reappearance of "religion" and a return to a natural, temporal mind-set. If we want to maintain God's presence in our life and sustain a spirit of revival, we cannot allow our love for Him or our worship of Him to grow cold! I believe that much of the church today has no passion for God's presence, and, as a result, we have a church without power.

Unless our worship of God is genuine, His presence will not come; and, without His presence, we cannot experience transformation.

Our Passionate Worship Enables Us to "Carry" God's Presence Everywhere We Go

The presence of God is an "atmosphere" that a true worshipper carries wherever he goes. We can "transport" the essence of heaven to others, so that God is glorified as He bestows His presence and power to transform people's lives.

The following testimony from a Venezuelan pastor reveals what can happen when a person begins to seek God wholeheartedly. Here is his story: "I was born into a dysfunctional family. My father abandoned us when I was only four years old. I suffered from loneliness, lack of love, slander, and instability, and I was rebellious and angry throughout my childhood and teenage years. At a young age, I moved to the United States, where I eventually studied forensic science and psychology. Even though I went to school and worked nonstop, nothing filled the void in my heart, calmed my anxiety, or satisfied my ego. I attended several churches but never experienced any change. My heart was hardened.

"For more than twenty-five years, I worked for the greatest oil and energy companies in the world, where I became greatly influential at every level. By all appearances, it seemed that I had total control of my life. I was a good businessman, and I had substantial education, knowledge, fame, and wealth. I was independent, enjoyed the pleasures of life, and had famous friends—but nothing seemed to be enough. All my marriages were characterized by fights, manipulation, lack of communication, and division.

"When my present marriage was on the verge of divorce, I began to ask God for supernatural intervention. My wife used to watch the program *Tiempo de Cambio* (*Time for Change*), hosted by Apostle Guillermo Maldonado, and I, too, began to watch it. By this time, the war in Iraq had begun, and the corporation for which I worked had assigned me to that part of the world, assuring me that the building designated for the Red Cross would not be in danger. However, the day I was supposed to travel, I heard an audible voice say to me, 'Don't go.' I obeyed, and, four days later, I saw a news broadcast showing images of the Red Cross building being bombarded. That voice saved my life!

"Sometime later, my wife and I visited King Jesus Ministry, and I felt I had arrived home. Everything in our lives began to change very rapidly. We started attending the church and covenanted for the projects of the ministry. Because of the vision God gave us through our spiritual father, we experienced a total turnaround. God restored our marriage and finances. He delivered us from unforgiveness, anxiety, fear, the spirit of independence, rebellion, egotism, hardness of heart, past wounds, sickness, false mental structures, religiosity, lack of communication, passivity, and more. He has filled us with His supernatural love, grace, and favor. We have become pastors, and we participate in the global spiritual movement that influences every stratum of society."

In worship, when we exalt Christ's finished work on the cross, honor God's name, and extol His glory and majesty, He brings His power and presence into our midst here and now.

3. A Heart After God's Own Heart Is Obedient and Submissive

Unless we have a heart after God's own heart, it will be difficult for us to obey His will—and we may even turn rebellious, as Saul did. In chapter 7, "The Obedient Heart," we talked about the fact that Saul's "obedience" went only halfway. But David fully followed God's will. In one of his psalms, he wrote, *"I delight to do Your will, O my God, and Your law is within my heart"* (Psalm 40:8).

A complete dedication to God's will was also a main characteristic of the heart of Jesus, who was called the *"Son of David"* (see, for example, Matthew 1:1). *"Jesus said to [His disciples], 'My food is to do the will of Him who sent Me, and to finish His work'"* (John 4:34). And God said of Jesus, *"This is My beloved Son, in whom I am well pleased. Hear Him!"* (Matthew 17:5).

We can declare the lives of Christ and David "successful" due to the fact that they each had a heart after God's own heart and they each fulfilled their divine purpose, completing all the work God had called them to do. In addition, both left a kingdom inheritance for future generations. Jesus and David established a pattern for us by demonstrating what it means to have a heart that continually follows after God. Both had a heart that adored and worshipped the Father *"in spirit and truth"* (John 4:24) and was willing to obey Him beyond its own strength, through the power of His divine grace.

We cannot have a heart after God's own heart if we have not learned to fully submit to, and obey, His will. Again, total obedience means doing whatever God says, wherever and whenever He says to do it, and however He wants it accomplished. Are we able to say that God can do anything He wants in and through our lives? Are we willing to obey Him always? The

Lord seeks a generation through which He can carry out His purposes for this momentous time in human history.

A person with a heart after God's own heart allows God to do whatever He desires through him.

---

4. A Heart After God's Own Heart Is Quick to Repent of Sin

When the prophet Nathan confronted David about his adultery with Bathsheba and the murder of her husband, David immediately recognized his sin, humbled himself before God, and repented. *"So David said to Nathan, 'I have sinned against the LORD.' And Nathan said to David, 'The LORD also has put away your sin; you shall not die'"* (2 Samuel 12:13).

As we saw earlier, one of David's virtues was that, whenever he failed God, he was quick to repent. He had a tender heart and a passion to be in God's presence. When he repented of the above incident, he prayed, *"Create in me a clean heart, O God, and renew a steadfast spirit within me. Do not cast me away from Your presence, and do not take Your Holy Spirit from me. Restore to me the joy of Your salvation, and uphold me by Your generous Spirit"* (Psalm 51:10–12).

Our true repentance always brings us back to the presence of God.

There are people who refuse to repent because they love their ego or fleshly pleasures more than they love God, and sin has hardened their heart. Consequently, they begin to feel that their ungodly behavior is acceptable and within their rights. Yet when a person genuinely repents of his sin, he can then produce fruit that is characteristic of a heart after God's own heart.

The sin that we refuse to repent of is the sin that will mold our character.

Is there any sin in your life that you have not repented of? One important reason we must dedicate time to reading the Bible is that, in the Scriptures, we discover what pleases God and what displeases Him. If we have an ongoing, daily relationship with God, His Spirit will continually reveal to us His will. If you have experienced the conviction of the Holy Spirit with respect to any sinful attitude or behavior in your life, repent of it right now so that your heart can remain a heart after God's own heart.

It is impossible to repent if we don't acknowledge our sin as sin.

At the beginning of my Christian life, I was taught that when I sinned, I was not to hide from God but to repent and go before Him immediately, confessing my wrongs. However, in time, I began to develop a mentality of sinfulness, because I was focused on my sins rather than on God's grace. I was constantly aware of my weaknesses, so that I could not enjoy my Christian life. I needed to receive God's revelation on this subject. That is when the Holy Spirit led me to understand the processes involved in the transformation of the heart and the renewal of the mind. I comprehended that God had given me His supernatural grace so that I could experience a clear conscience, having a heart that not only repented of sin but also desired to live in holiness, integrity, and righteousness before Him. I learned that I am continually being transformed by God's Spirit and that I should not expect myself to have yet reached perfection. And I realized that I may still sometimes sin and fail God—but also that God has changed my heart so that I no longer sin *as a lifestyle.*

Today, every time I enter God's presence, I repent and ask Him to remove all sin, transgression, and iniquity that might be in my life. I do this even when I am not aware of any explicit sin. I wash my humanity in the blood of Christ every day as an element of the process of transformation. Now, every time I feel conviction for sin, it is not the result of a guilty conscience on my part but because the Holy Spirit is prompting me to repent in order to change my heart. Therefore, whenever He convicts, I repent immediately and experience His forgiveness and grace so that I may move forward in the life and power of God. *"If we confess our sins, He is faithful*

and just to forgive us our sins and to cleanse us from all unrighteousness"
(1 John 1:9).

> We can overcome the strength of sin by repenting of our sin
> immediately and by accepting God's forgiveness and grace on our
> behalf. Otherwise, we will establish a repetitive cycle of sin
> in our life.

---

5. A Heart After God's Own Heart Has the Quality of Innocence

David prayed to the Lord, *"Let the words of my mouth and the medita-tion of my heart be acceptable in Your sight, O LORD, my strength and my Redeemer"* (Psalm 19:14). David was not innocent of sin—as none of us is. However, he desired that his thoughts and words would be fully acceptable to God, enabling him to live in a state of innocence before Him.

Jesus told His disciples, *"Be wise as serpents and harmless ["innocent"* NIV, NASB] *as doves"* (Matthew 10:16). There is a difference between inno-cence and ignorance. Innocence means not knowing what God doesn't want us to know. Ignorance means choosing not to know what God *does* want us to know, which is equivalent to disobedience. I believe that when God commanded the first human beings not to eat of the Tree of Knowledge of Good and Evil, it was because He didn't want them to have personal, spe-cific knowledge of evil. However, they wanted to have the knowledge that God had forbidden them, and, as a result, they fell from grace.

Jesus also emphasized, *"Unless you are converted and become as little children, you will by no means enter the kingdom of heaven"* (Matthew 18:3). Here Christ was referring to the innocence of a young child's heart. A child's heart isn't hardened, because he hasn't yet experienced the disap-pointment and emotional pain that many teenagers and adults have known after being mistreated by others—feelings of hurt and betrayal that lead them to hold on to offenses. That is why it is easier for a child to trust in God's goodness and promises than for many adults. Such a nature of in-nocence is one of the characteristics of a heart after God's own heart.

We need to recover a heart of innocence—one that is not hardened and that trusts in God and believes in Him 100 percent. If you have lost that quality due to past hurts and offenses, so that your faith has been undermined, today is the day for your heart to return to innocence. Ask God to forgive you for hard-heartedness and to restore your heart. Then He can manifest His grace and power in and through your life.

6. A Heart After God's Own Heart Has the Attitude of a Servant

David was a true worshipper of God who had the heart of a servant. For example, when he was merely a youth, he offered his services to single-handedly strike down the giant Goliath, who was part of the Philistine army attacking Israel. David volunteered out of devotion to God, as His servant, because the Philistines had *"defied the armies of the living God"* (1 Samuel 17:36), and no one else in God's army was doing anything about it. David said with holy confidence, "[God] *will deliver me from the hand of this Philistine"* (1 Samuel 17:37). And God did.

Our service for God should never be disconnected from our worship of Him. The book of Isaiah describes the heavenly beings called the seraphim, who are special angels of God. In the Old Testament, the Hebrew word translated *"seraphim"* (Isaiah 6:2, 6) means "burning." The prophet Isaiah related the appearance of the seraphim: *"Each one had six wings: with two he covered his face, with two he covered his feet, and with two he flew"* (Isaiah 6:2). I believe that the wings that cover the faces and feet of the seraphim represent worship and reverence of God, while the wings with which they fly represent service to God. The seraphim have four wings dedicated to worship and two dedicated to service. Similarly, we should devote ourselves first to worship and then to service, in order to keep these two aspects of our relationship with God in proper proportion in our life.

Our worship of God should always be our first priority; then, as a result of that worship, we will render a life of service to Him. However, we must also recognize that worship alone—without service—is hypocrisy. As Jesus said, *"You shall worship the LORD your God, and Him only you shall serve"* (Matthew 4:10). His statement reinforces the idea that worship should always be followed by service.

Unless our service is born of worship, we will often perform it mechanically, and it will not be characterized by God's presence and power.

7. A Heart After God's Own Heart Fears God and Seeks to Please Him

One of my greatest holy fears is that I will stand up to preach but God will not be with me because my disobedience will have caused Him to grieve. Consequently, I continually ask the Lord to give me a heart that holds Him in reverence, so that I will always seek to please Him, and so that the most important pursuits of my life will be to reflect His heart and to obey His Word.

The apostle Paul wrote, *"For do I now persuade men, or God? Or do I seek to please men? For if I still pleased men, I would not be a bondservant of Christ"* (Galatians 1:10). Sometimes, when we try to please other people, we end up dishonoring and displeasing God. To avoid doing so, we must be sure that we have not elevated other people above Him in our heart.

The "fear of God" refers to reverence and respect for Him.

The Scriptures say, *"Do not grieve the Holy Spirit of God, by whom you were sealed for the day of redemption"* (Ephesians 4:30), and *"Do not quench the Spirit"* (1 Thessalonians 5:19). It is sad but true that many churches and ministries systematically violate these Scriptures. Each time the Holy Spirit wants to move among the people, He is suppressed by the erroneous attitudes and actions of church leaders who are afraid of what people might think or do. Then we ask why there is no movement of the Holy Spirit in our churches, or why God doesn't manifest His supernatural presence and power in our midst with miracles, signs, and wonders.

The Holy Spirit doesn't manifest on our terms but according to His own terms. In the Scriptures, the Holy Spirit is depicted as a dove. A natural dove is sensitive to sound and sudden movements. God uses the dove as a symbol of His Spirit because He, also, is very sensitive, especially in relation to the condition of our heart. We must treat Him with reverence, respect, tenderness, and spiritual knowledge—hence the necessity of knowing God's nature. If we are rude and unthinking in our relationship with Him, and if we do not concern ourselves with pleasing Him, we will "scare" away God's presence—we will *"grieve"* or *"quench"* His Spirit—and He will not move in our lives.

Our resistance or indifference to God is a clear sign that we are displeasing Him.

"*The fear of the* LORD *is to hate evil; pride and arrogance and the evil way and the perverse mouth I hate*" (Proverbs 8:13). During the time that King Saul persecuted David, David had opportunities to kill the king, but his fear of the Lord—including a respect for His delegated authorities on earth—kept him from doing so. David said, "*I will not stretch out my hand against my lord* [Saul], *for he is the* LORD'*s anointed*" (1 Samuel 24:10). Many believers who lack the fear of God in their heart end up judging various leaders in the church. As a result, these believers often experience various troubles, such as sickness, failed marriages, and rebellious behavior in their children. To avoid grieving God by judging other believers, especially His delegated authorities, we must develop a heart like David's—a heart after God's own heart—with a healthy fear of the Lord.

Knowing God produces a reverential fear of Him; the more we know of God, the more we will develop a profound respect for Him.

---

8. A Heart After God's Own Heart Loves God Deeply

David's psalms are filled with expressions of his deep and enduring love for God. For example, in Psalm 18:1, he prayed, "*I will love You, O* LORD, *my strength*," and, in Psalm 31:23, he urged God's people, "*Oh, love the* LORD, *all you His saints! For the* LORD *preserves the faithful*."

Love is the essence of God. (See 1 John 4:8, 16.) He manifests all the characteristics of love, such as patience and kindness. He never manifests attitudes that are contrary to love, such as envy, boastfulness, pride, rudeness, and selfishness. (See 1 Corinthians 13:4–5 NIV.) The love of God goes above and beyond human comprehension and reason, because it is supernatural, unconditional, and unlimited.

Anyone who has a heart after God's own heart will be filled with His love. Our love for God is a response to the love He first gave us. (See, for example, 1 John 4:19.) Our love comes from Him, because He pours out His love into our hearts by His Spirit (see Romans 5:5) when we are born again.

In the Old Testament, human beings received the mandate to love God, but they struggled to fulfill it because they were living under the law and had not received the indwelling Holy Spirit, as we have. We must understand and receive the truth that God loved us first and that we can love Him in return because of His powerful work of grace within us.

The reason we must first *be* loved *in order to* love is that we cannot give what we do not have. We need a revelation of the love of God that has been given to us so that we can, in turn, give His love to others. I needed this revelation after I had children. When my oldest child was four years old, he would come to me seeking affection and hugs, but I didn't know how to give them to him, because I had never received affectionate love during my own childhood. Because such love was not "in" me, I couldn't give it to him. It was then that God filled me with His own love, so that I was able to love my dear son.

God loved us first so that we could love Him and other people.

We should never boast about how much we love God but about how much He loves us. His unconditional love is the solution to many of our needs, such as a lack of identity, feelings of rejection, low self-esteem, and other emotional obstacles that prevent us from having wholeness of heart.

We are commanded in the Scriptures to love God (see, for example, Mark 12:29–30), and this command is not optional. As we have seen, we demonstrate our love for God by our obedience to His Word. We cannot say that we love God and then freely violate His commandments! We won't fully obey the Lord unless we develop a genuine, deep love for Him, because authentic love for God aligns us with His purposes, motivating us to keep His commandments. *"Whoever keeps [Jesus'] word, truly the love of God is perfected in him. By this we know that we are in Him"* (1 John 2:5). Love doesn't compromise when it comes to God's principles; it doesn't sin by abusing others. Love will always be the right motivation for everything we do. If we love God, we will guard our heart to keep His commandments; as a result, obedience will become a natural part of our lifestyle.

When we have genuine love for God, we are motivated to obey Him, because real love always seeks to please Him.

To love God is to have a desire to please Him with every aspect of our life—including our thoughts, our words, and our actions. Accordingly, we are grieved when we offend Him. Love always wants to please its beloved. Christ lived His entire live for the purpose of honoring the Father and fulfilling His will—not to be "seen" by others doing good deeds. When love is our motivation, people will see our heart rather than the works of our hands. My motivation for doing the Father's will comes from my love for Him. His love and His presence in my life compel me to offer my life in service to Him to accomplish His purposes. As my love for Him deepens, I become more effective for Him, and I feel complete.

Genuine love must dwell within us if we are to demonstrate that love to others.

Is it possible for us to love God with all our heart? Of course we can! But we must make a decision to love God and to receive the love that He has poured out into our heart by His Spirit. To experience God's love, we simply have to believe that He has given it to us—and accept it! I am never satisfied with just seeing miracles, signs, and wonders manifested, because my chief passion is to know God and to love Him more each day. When we love Him, our greatest desire in life is to experience the manifestation of His presence; then, He gives us everything else that we need, because His love couldn't give us anything less.

When we love God, our greatest desire in life is to experience the manifestation of His presence.

In the following testimony, a woman named Vilma explains how the love of God transformed her heart after she had experienced years of abuse and rejection. "I was born and raised in a Muslim home in Albania, never knowing who Jesus Christ was. Throughout my childhood, I never received any love, and the abuse and rejection I suffered led me to be depressed.

"My father never loved my family. In my country, people don't speak up for themselves, much less on behalf of women. My mother had been forced to marry my father—a violent man who used to beat both of us, who never worked but would steal our money, and who often didn't even come home. He would frequently take a gun and lock himself in a room with my mother, and I never thought she would come out of that room alive. He would shout at her, accusing her of being a prostitute and claiming that he would rape me in front of her if he wanted to. He never accepted me as his daughter, saying that I owed him everything.

"When I was eleven years old, my mother decided to leave Albania to seek a new life away from him. That was when we came to the United States, penniless and without any clothes except what we were wearing. I felt as if I had the weight of the world on my shoulders, to the extent that I became cold and emotionless. My mother was unable to show me love, so I began to look for it elsewhere. By the time I was eighteen, I had a boyfriend, and I thought that surely he would love me—surely someone in this world would love me! But it was not so. He would tell me that I was fat and ugly and that all he wanted from me was sex. I became addicted to pornography. I no longer cared about anything. I was so depressed that I vomited every day. Finally, I decided I would join the adult entertainment industry. I thought that if no one was going to love me, I would at least gain something out of sex—money, cars, homes, and anything else I could get my hands on. Yet, when I was typing out my application/contract, my computer froze and turned off. God had other plans for me that night.

"I felt so desperate that I ran out of my house in my pajamas and went to a church that was always open for prayer. That night, I gave my life to God and later began to attend a church where I received Jesus as my Lord and Savior. However, I continued to place my boyfriend above God and stayed with him for five more years, until I finally ended that relationship. But I continued partying, drinking, and taking drugs.

"One day, while at home, I prayed, 'Lord, please send me Christian friends. I am tired of this life.' A few months later, while browsing a social network on the Internet, I saw some pictures a friend had posted of a House of Peace. I called him and began to attend those meetings, and my life began to change. During a deliverance retreat, I was set free of unforgiveness, sexual immorality, depression, abuse, hatred, and rejection. I was able to feel my heavenly Father saying that I was His precious possession, that He had always been my Father, that He would never leave me, that He knew me and loved me more than I could ever understand. I felt His words penetrate my heart. I experienced God's love, and He was able to mend my broken heart. For the first time in twenty-five years, I was called 'daughter' and not 'prostitute.' For the first time in years, I was able to cry out, 'Abba, Father, I need You.'

"Now I sleep in peace. Evil spirits used to torment me at night, but now I feel God's presence. The night before my water baptism, my mother, who had been a devotee of the Islamic religion, decided to be baptized together with me. Ever since that time, I have seen the supernatural power of God in my life. My broken heart was healed, and my faith was renewed. Now I am happy, focused on the things of God, and enrolled in nursing school. My desire is to be a missionary in the medical field in India and to take the gospel of Jesus to Albania."

Prayer to Receive a Heart After God's Own Heart

As we conclude this chapter, let us ask ourselves some searching questions. If we will be truthful when answering them, our answers will reveal the current state of our heart as it is being transformed to become a heart after God's own heart. Answer the following questions as honestly as you can: "Do I regularly seek God's presence?" "Have I become a passionate worshipper of God?" "Am I learning to be obedient and submissive to God in all things?" "Do I repent of sin quickly and wholeheartedly?" "Has my heart been restored to innocence?" "Do I have an attitude of willing service for God?" "Do I have a reverent fear of the Lord, and do I desire to please Him in every area of my life?" "Do I love God deeply with all my heart?"

We cannot reflect God's true nature unless our heart continues to be transformed into a heart after His own heart—so that we think as He thinks, feel as He feels, and love as He loves. My family members and I, as well as each of the leaders who help to carry out our ministry, have experienced the transformation of our heart, and we continue to do so. We burn with the desire to have a heart after God's own heart so that we can please Him, demonstrate our love for Him, establish His kingdom on earth, manifest His supernatural power, and see lives transformed by His grace. If anything inspired me to write this book, it was the great need that God's people have today to experience a supernatural transformation that will give them a heart after His own heart. If you are willing to pay the price necessary for this to take place, I invite you to pray the following prayer:

> Heavenly Father, thank You for bringing me this revelation that I need a heart after Your own heart. I want to be a genuine worshipper of You. I desire true intimacy with You, born out of mutual love and respect. I want to serve You as the direct result of my passionate worship of You. I desire to please You and to fulfill Your will for my life in everything I do and wherever I go as a carrier of Your presence, glory, and power to others.

> Transform my heart by removing from it everything that displeases You and by filling it with all the qualities of Your nature. Transform my mind and my lifestyle so that I may honor You with every decision I make and with every step I take. Grant me the supernatural grace of Your Spirit, so that everything I do will be according to Your strength and not my own, and so that my life will be a living and holy sacrifice to You that will burn until I take

my last breath on this earth. My heart belongs to You. My life belongs to You. My chief desire is to please You always. In the name
of Jesus, amen!

12

Conformed to Religion or Transformed by His Presence

After we accept Christ as our Savior and receive His own nature within us as the *"new man"* (Ephesians 4:24), we are called to experience the progressive transformation of our heart. We do not "sit out" our salvation, waiting to go to heaven or for Jesus to return. Instead, we purposefully and progressively move to higher levels of spiritual maturity as we die to "self" and the sinful nature. We must allow the same anointing from God that saved us to change our heart—a heart that has been corrupted by sin, egotism, wicked desires, perverse passions, emotional wounds, wrong motivations, and many other evils.

Each person experiences transformation in a unique way, because God's work in each of our hearts is distinct and special. The process is not always easy, and it can be painful; however, after we come through it, we will see supernatural fruit and other manifestations of God's power in our life, confirming that it was worth it all! (See Hebrews 12:11.)

Our Lives Are Tangible Evidence of the Supernatural

The world wants to know that it is possible to experience genuine change, because transformation is what it desperately needs. Our lives must provide tangible evidence to other people that God is real and that they can have a spiritual relationship with Him that includes supernatural demonstrations. Many things in our world today are being "shaken"—the global economy, nations, leaders, religious institutions, and even the physical world. For example, there seems to have been an increase in natural disasters, such as earthquakes and tsunamis, and in upheavals in nature, such as drought and changes in weather patterns. Many people are frightened and uncertain about their lives; they sense a lack of stability all around them—literally and figuratively—and they want to find out what is real, what is constant, and what can bring them true purpose in life. If they don't see supernatural transformation in us, they will not come to our churches, because they don't want just "more of the same." They want something that can genuinely address their deepest needs.

We must comprehend that the transformation of our heart is not for our benefit alone but also for the sake of those who do not yet know the God of heaven—the God who came to earth in the person of Jesus Christ to die on the cross to free them from sin and bondage. And now that Jesus has returned to heaven, He has sent *us* to set them free (see Mark 16:15)—He has sent us to be carriers of divine healing, deliverance, and transformation, just as He brought divine healing, deliverance, and transformation to people when He walked the earth. Jesus applied the following prophecy from Isaiah 61:1 to Himself:

> *The Spirit of the* Lord *is upon Me, because He has anointed Me to preach the gospel to the poor; He has sent Me to heal the brokenhearted, to proclaim liberty to the captives and recovery of sight to the blind, to set at liberty those who are oppressed.* (Luke 4:18)

When we understand our vital calling as Jesus' followers, we will seek to remove from our heart everything that hinders us from fulfilling that calling.

Christ's special anointing—after announcing the gospel—was to address matters of the heart.

Traps of Conformity to Religion

We have seen that one of the chief hindrances to our transformation is conformity—conformity to people, ideas, environments, and situations that are contrary to God's nature and ways. Traps of conformity are all around us, and we often are unaware of their hold on us—especially traps of conformity in regard to religion. Many people have altered the practice of Christianity so that it has essentially become another religion rather than a relationship with the living Christ. Christianity has been structured according to a human mind-set, so that faith has become formalized and modified; and, under these conditions, people are no longer edified. For these reasons, let us review various types of conformity to religion while examining our own heart in relation to them. We must regularly search our heart for the presence of such conformity in order to avoid being ensnared by these traps.

1. Wanting to Please Others Above God and to Avoid Controversy

Many pastors today preach a "gospel of conformity"—a watered-down version of God's message of salvation and transformation—because they are more concerned with pleasing other people than with pleasing God, and they want to avoid controversy. They want to make people "feel good" rather than challenge them to increasingly reflect the likeness of Christ. These pastors promise blessings but leave out the prerequisite of repentance; they offer grace without pointing out the need for obedience and for developing a holy fear of the Lord. Consequently, the power of the supernatural is absent from their churches, because the people have conformed to human egotism and self-indulgence.

By trying to please people, certain leaders have watered down the gospel, thus departing from the true nature of the church.

If the above scenario describes your situation—whether you are a pastor, a worship leader, or another believer—your heart can still experience supernatural transformation, as the following testimony confirms. After reading one of my books, Pastor Donald, of Paraguay, South America, was convicted to cancel the preaching engagements he had made in accordance with his personal agenda and to surrender his church to the Holy Spirit, allowing God's presence to flow freely in his services. He exchanged his religious, traditional mentality for the mind-set of God's kingdom. This decision initiated a tremendous breakthrough in regard to everything that had been stagnant and infertile in his church. Since he surrendered to God, hundreds of people have been healed and delivered through his ministry. Families have been restored, creative and financial miracles have taken place, and his congregation has grown from 200 members to 1,500 in less than a year.

Pastor Donald says, "People used to ignore my church, even though I would use all means of communication available to promote it. Now, they come from every province in Paraguay, and even from other countries, because they have heard that miracles, healings, and deliverances take place there. They come because they are attracted by the supernatural power of God. Thank God that many people who used to be in bondage to illegal drugs, crime, idolatry, and other sins are now being saved and becoming leaders and evangelists who take the supernatural power of God wherever they go. I am happy and motivated, because I can say that now we are truly a Christian church in revival. Apostle Maldonado has helped me to understand that 'religious' pastors are the greatest obstacles to God and to their churches. The people greatly need the love of God and His supernatural power, and it is our duty and responsibility to allow the Holy Spirit to work in our congregations, just as we are responsible for identifying and training others to do the same."

A leader cannot guide people into the presence of God unless he has already gone there himself.

2. Having an "Appearance" of Religion and the Supernatural

Many churches have the outward appearance of being Spirit-filled, but they lack the power of the Holy Spirit and supernatural manifestations.

"Having a form of godliness but denying its power" (2 Timothy 3:5). God's truth is the highest level of reality. In contrast, a "form" of godliness is a mere outward appearance that has no relation to reality. When the truth of the gospel is preached, we no longer have the form of godliness but the reality of it.

We have a form of godliness when we aren't living according to true faith but are merely going through the motions, or the "mechanics," of faith. We may sing praise songs, give offerings, listen to the sermon, and so forth, but because the reality is not present, we don't enter into God's presence and become transformed, receiving His life and power. When we have merely a form of godliness, nothing changes in our life. We continue to have the same dysfunctions, emotional needs, sicknesses, and so forth. And we keep trying to deal with them according to human methods.

Churches that operate according to a form of godliness do not actively or openly practice the gifts of the Spirit; in fact, the exercise of these gifts is often discouraged. In addition, miracles, signs, and deliverance from demon-possession are never—or rarely—witnessed. Many of these churches claim to want more of God, but they are cutting off the flow of His Spirit.

These churches have been structured in such a way that their services have a time limitation and are focused on man-made plans rather than God-made plans. As a result, the people no longer practice waiting on God. They go to church without expecting to see supernatural manifestations, and they leave without having experienced any spiritual renewal. Their mind has been programmed to merely hear a message designed for the intellect and/or the emotions but not to promote a transformation of their heart.

When we don't wait on God, we take over His role; consequently, we fail to do what He is doing and to say what He is saying.

We must never become complacent about the condition of our heart, because we are all vulnerable to fall into a religious mind-set. Conformity to religion does not occur only in "traditional" or "mainline" churches. It occurs even in churches where supernatural signs and wonders are manifested.

It occurs wherever people's hearts become indifferent or rebellious. When people are in this condition, and God's presence *does* come among them, they want to maintain the appearance and reject Him, because they have been existing for so long without His reality! When I preach and bring the reality of God to a church that has been living according to mere appearance, its condition is exposed. Many people feel intimidated when this happens, and they may reject my message. When Jesus spoke God's truth to the people in the synagogue of His hometown, the people rejected Him because their hearts were exposed, and they did not want transformation. (See Luke 4:16–30.) But when God's reality touches us—and we respond to Him rather than resist Him—we will be set free.

You can't continue to practice a mere appearance, or "form,"
of godliness when the reality of God comes to you.

---

3. Abandoning the Supernatural to Return to Religion

A number of believers have seen, heard, and experienced the power of God but have not allowed it to have a lasting effect on them. They have witnessed miracles, signs, and wonders, and they may even have been used by God as His instruments for ministering these blessings—but then they eventually returned to religion and tradition. They may have begun to accept lukewarm spiritual attitudes as the norm, or they may have backed off from the supernatural because they experienced the rejection or persecution of others, so that now they tolerate a lack of God's presence and power in their lives.

Their heart did not experience a genuine transformation or "metamorphosis"—one that clearly demonstrates a "before and after" of spiritual growth and maturity. Perhaps they were merely "spectators" of God's deeds, and when they got tired being "entertained," they left in the same condition in which they had come. Or, maybe they became offended by something someone said, or by a certain supernatural manifestation. Whatever the reason, many of them went back to churches that are spiritually powerless, lacking the manifest presence of God. Some returned to the church they had previously left when they were hungry to experience the supernatural.

I would never give up participating in the fresh outpouring of God's Spirit over a simple offense! If we turn back after witnessing the blind see, the deaf hear, and the dead raised to life, then we have not been transformed.

This is what happened to the Israelites whom God delivered from slavery—those who saw the signs and wonders He performed on their behalf in Egypt and in the desert. Rather than experience transformation, their hearts remained cold and hard. A similar thing occurred in relation to many of Jesus' followers. In John 6:66, we read, *"From that time many of His disciples went back and walked with Him no more."* These disciples had seen the arrival of God's kingdom through Jesus Christ—with its signs and miracles—yet they left the Lord because they were offended by one of His teachings. They called it a *"hard saying"* (John 6:60). They heard something from Jesus that seemed too difficult for them to accept, and they preferred to follow their human reason and pride rather than continue to follow the Son of God.

Similarly, today, a person whose heart has not been transformed won't be able to tolerate certain words of revelation given by the Lord. Have you been offended by a "hard saying" of Jesus? We must allow God to confront us with the true condition of our heart and to challenge us to undergo transformation, so that we will continue to follow our Lord, regardless of the cost to our "self" and the sinful nature. God transforms our heart through supernatural means—His Word, His presence, His glory, Jesus' finished work of the cross, and His resurrection power—bringing about permanent change. Let us always move forward with our Lord as He transforms our heart!

The religious spirit always opposes the move of God and the flow of the "river" of God.

---

4. Holding On to Former Moves of God and Old Methods

There was a time when the people who have become "old wineskins" were "new wineskins." (See Mark 2:22.) They are what we might call the "old guard"—those who cling to the practices they have always followed and who function in the same way they have for years. These people became "old wineskins" because they stopped seeking spiritual renewal; they ceased to perceive how God is working today, so that they "leveled off" in their walk with God, conforming to the past. Many of them developed an "I have arrived" mentality; some have not yet progressed beyond the experience of their new birth in Christ, never imagining that there is more for them to receive from God or to do for Him. Yet they are often the first to attack those who are advancing to higher levels in the Spirit.

We should respect the wisdom of those who are older, and it is our duty to learn from those who have come before us. Yet if someone is a true "father" of the new generation God is raising up, he should be able to transfer a "double portion" of his anointing from God (see 2 Kings 2:9–15), rather than criticize, discredit, or try to destroy the current move of the Spirit.

Many of the churches led by "old wineskin" pastors used to be places where people were saved and transformed, but now they have become religious establishments where tradition is valued more than the supernatural, where rules have priority over grace, and where human structures quench the move of the Holy Spirit. God is always bringing us something fresh. We are living in a new spiritual season that can be understood only by supernatural discernment, and that perspective will come to us only by the transformation of our mind and heart. If we want to keep moving ahead to the next plan God has for this generation and for this world, we must be flexible and prepared to receive what He is doing today—and what He will do tomorrow.

Change is the enemy of the "old guard," but everything that doesn't change will eventually die.

5. Missing God's Fresh Moves—or Rejecting Them When They Manifest

Some people in previous generations prayed to God for an outpouring of the Holy Spirit and a visitation of His glory. They begged for a revival. Some even prophesized that it would come. But, when it arrived, they rejected the way in which it manifested, saying that it didn't come from God.

They began to accuse those who were involved with it of unorthodoxy. None of us can declare that a divine move isn't genuine just because we don't understand it. Our criticism of it may indicate that we are spiritually stagnant, living according to a form of religiosity that stifles the life of the Spirit and His work in our lives.

Are you ready to let God do things His way, or do you have a certain agenda for what you want Him to do—and how you want Him to do it? What if God has been answering your cry for revival, but you have not recognized it? There is always another level of His glory to experience! We cannot personally define how the next move of God on earth should take place. All we can do is surrender to God so that He can show us what is coming.

In the name of "order," the religious spirit tries to stifle the move of the Spirit.

---

6. "Touched"—but Not Transformed

There is another aspect of conformity to religion that afflicts some who have already experienced the supernatural—that of being "touched" by God yet still failing to be transformed by Him. The expression "touched by God" refers to our feeling His supernatural power in some manner. For instance, when someone is touched by God, he may experience intense emotions that cause him to weep or laugh. He may fall down, or "be 'slain' in the Spirit." However, there is a problem if the person comes away from that experience without having been released from any of his wrong attitudes or false ways of thinking—for example, indifference, rebellion, disobedience, or hard-heartedness. The individual may have been touched in his emotions and in his physical body, but the experience never reached his innermost being.

If we fall under the presence of God, it simply means we have made contact with His power. This experience is wonderful, but it doesn't necessarily indicate that we have opened ourselves up to God during that encounter in order to be changed. When no transformation is evident after we have had such an experience, then we have not allowed God to operate in our heart. The following are some examples of people in the Bible who were touched but not transformed.

In the Old Testament, Pharaoh witnessed signs and wonders from God through Moses, but he continually hardened his heart and would not set the Israelites free until he was forced to in the end. (See, for example, Exodus 7:14–25; 14.) In the New Testament, Jesus' disciple Judas spent three-and-a-half years with Christ; he heard all His teachings and saw Him perform many miracles—even the raising of the dead—but he did not open up his heart to be transformed by God. Instead, in a pursuit of greed and self-interest, he betrayed Christ—and ended up destroying himself. (See, for example, John 12:3–6; 13:2, 21–30; Matthew 27:3–5.) Ananias and Sapphira were believers in the early church. They were likely among Jesus' followers at Pentecost, and they had seen the signs and wonders that had accompanied the proclamation of the gospel. Yet, motivated by greed and hypocrisy, they tried to deceive the church by feigning the degree of their generosity. They, too, were touched but not transformed, and the corruption of their heart led to their deaths. (See Acts 5:1–11.)

Continuous Transformation

Only when we are exposed to higher levels in the Spirit—realms of faith, anointing, glory, miracles, provision, and more—and when we respond to those revelations with an open heart, will we understand that God is greater than everything we have seen and heard to this point. I have witnessed God supernaturally heal the blind, deaf, mute, and lame; create new bones and organs; raise the dead; and even control the weather. I have seen many transformations take place in people's lives: drug addicts have left their addictions, agnostic intellectuals and atheists have come to faith in Christ, churches have grown from hundreds of members to thousands in a short period of time, and so forth. I could list many other such miracles and works that God has done in my ministry, as well as the ministries of my spiritual children.

Yet I still hunger for God's presence. I still seek transformation daily. I know there are dimensions of His glory that I have not yet seen and that I will enter only if I keep my eyes on Jesus while being transformed into His image—His heart, His mind-set, and His glory. (See Philippians 3:12–14.) We must wait on God so that we may hear His voice and follow His direction. Then, He will bring a change of season in our life that will lift us out of our dry spiritual state to receive the Wellspring of living water.

To enter a greater dimension, we must die to what we know and to what we have accomplished up to this point.

Many people are afraid to submit to a supernatural process they aren't familiar with and don't understand. They fear losing control, and they fear losing themselves in God. In the following testimony, a pastor named Edgar from Bolivia shares how his life was transformed when he surrendered his will, stopped doing things his way, and began doing things God's way. "As a new graduate with a bachelor's degree in theology, I was named pastor of a two-hundred-member church. I began with great momentum, but all my plans failed over and over again. The members would attend Sunday services, but they refused to commit to God and His work. Desperate for change, I saw Apostle Maldonado on television and immediately identified myself with his word, his personality, and his anointing. I traveled to Miami to King Jesus Ministry with the intention of asking for financial help, but nothing happened as I had planned. The word I received in the conferences confronted me, and I realized that I had many religious paradigms; thus, everything was strange to me. I used to think that the changes I had made in my church had been enough, but then I found myself in another level of revelation.

"I had gone to Miami with a beggar's mentality—to ask for help—but the ministry's response was this: 'We don't help with money. Here, we lead you to your purpose. We don't give you the fish; we give you the fishing rod.' This concept revolutionized my spirit! God broke through my beggar mentality and my religious paradigms and transformed my heart. Two years later, I came under the spiritual covering of the ministry. While we worked on the transition from the pastoral to the apostolic, my own church began to change. We established an apostolic, fatherhood government. We adopted the vision of King Jesus Ministry, and each teaching and impartation we received from our spiritual parents pushed us from level to level and equipped us with powerful kingdom tools.

"We are not the same! The prophetic word we received from King Jesus Ministry was foundational. It gave us direction and activated us to advance. Our congregation went from 300 people to 4,500. We identified and formed leaders (sons and daughters of the house) and sent them to establish new ministries. We were once a passive, dying church, but today we are impacting our city and our surroundings. The demonstration of supernatural power in our ministry has become a regular occurrence. We continually see powerful miracles.

"In the beginning of my ministry, I couldn't get a movement going, but today, we host monthly crusades—supernatural evangelistic programs that are carried out on the streets and in people's homes—and people are being won to Christ, discipled, and activated into leadership. We have learned to pray, to intercede, and to do spiritual warfare in which break-throughs begin to take place and in which we win battles. Our finances, which had been barely enough to pay for our basic needs, have increased 900 percent. We have more than 25 pastors and leaders working full-time at the local level. We started construction of an orphanage without any outside help. We have television and radio programs—an impossibil-ity for most churches. We purchased land and built a church for 6,000 people—debt free!

"The greatest problems we faced when establishing the vision were the betrayal, defamation, lack of understanding, and isolation by other pastors in our city, but they could not prevail when they saw the evidence of the fruit produced by our ministry. This is supernatural acceleration, break-through, and multiplication! God has transformed our mind and heart, and everything that used to be impossible is now a reality."

Many pastors who have turned from religion and conformity to enter God's supernatural movement have lost up to half their congregations. But after they made the transition, God brought in many new people in only a brief period of time—people who were in love with Jesus; who were hungry to see change, the movement of the Spirit, and the manifestation of divine power; who entered into the supernatural realm of transformation and expansion. Today, the numbers in these pastors' congregations are double or even triple what they used to be.

Many people resist entering into God's glory because to do so means exposure and change.

God's works are limitless. To talk about God is to talk "big" and to think "big"—to think of multitudes of people belonging to Him, always growing and maturing under His direction and care. God blessed the human race with the potential for multiplication. He told Adam and Eve to *"be fruitful," "multiply,"* and *"fill the earth."* (See Genesis 1:28.) He gave Abraham the great vision that his descendants would be as innumerable as the stars in the sky. (See Genesis 22:17; 26:4; Hebrews 11:12.) Jesus commissioned His disciples in the power of the Holy Spirit to make new disciples in Jerusalem, Judea, Samaria, and onward to the ends of the earth. (See Acts 1:8.) God's mind-set is one of continual growth, multiplication, and expansion, and He calls us to have the same mentality. Many church leaders make statements such as, "I may not have quantity, but I have quality." We should have both!

One of God's smallest creations is a seed that has the potential to grow into a great tree. Everything God creates has the potential to grow and to multiply.

Keys to Transition from Conformism to Transformation

There are times when God will allow us to feel dissatisfied or discontent because He is leading us to seek something more in Him than what we have yet seen or experienced. Consequently, we begin to hunger and thirst for something new, something greater, something stronger, and we start looking to Him more and reaching for higher levels of His glory.

Are you feeling uncomfortable with the spiritual level at which you are functioning—one that you have perhaps been "stuck" in for a long time? Does your spirit cry out for transformation? If so, don't be afraid of undergoing change, because God is the One who has placed this desire within you. It is as if your spirit is in labor, getting ready to birth new spiritual fruit.

Transitions are birthed in the midst of spiritual dissatisfaction and frustration. The spiritual hunger inside you is evidence that God is calling you to a greater dimension.

Please understand that, during this time of transition, you may feel as if you don't fit in anywhere. Others may misunderstand you and your motivations, because they do not share your spiritual hunger—the spiritual desire that burns in your heart. You may feel alone for a time, but then God will connect you with other people who have the same hunger for transformation and expansion. When you come out on the other side of this experience transformed, you will be ready for the new dimension of the glory of God that He wants to bring to your life and/or ministry.

That is what happened in the life of a man named Moises from Mexico. The following is his testimony: "Six months after coming to know Jesus Christ, I became a youth leader and then the national secretary of youth. I attended a seminary and became an evangelist. I preached at healing campaigns in Latin America and the United States, where I planted three churches. But I reached the point at which I knew there had to be more—I needed something new and more powerful in God.

"During a conference, I met Apostle Guillermo Maldonado. What I experienced at that conference was a supernatural transformation that impacted me so deeply that I requested his spiritual covering to take this transformation to my church in Mexico. In my thirty-one years in ministry, I had never experienced anything like it. When I entered this supernatural move, changes began to take place. We went from 800 members to over 3,000 in only a few months; and the conversions and miracles multiply daily.

"We purchased land and built an auditorium. We established a ministerial school to prepare new ministers. We participate in community outreach programs that help homeless children, and we bought land to assist with this purpose. We support pastors who are experiencing financial need. Our intercession and spiritual warfare have released miracles, multiplication, and breakthroughs. With the transformation of our heart, we have entered into the 'new' of God where the supernatural has brought acceleration and growth to every personal and ministerial area."

Transformation begins when we expose our true heart to God in order to be changed into our true identity in Christ. When we are transformed into His image, Christ will live in us, and the world will see Him through us.

When you have used up all of your resources but still find yourself in the same place, transformation is necessary—and urgent!

Has your Christianity somehow changed from being a relationship with Christ to being a religion—a trap of stagnancy and spiritual dryness? If you are willing to break through that reality in order to transition to a higher level of spiritual reality, then put into practice the following keys, which will enable you to cooperate with the Holy Spirit as He performs this work in you. Open up your heart to God so that you may be transformed by Him. He has only good things in store for you—above and beyond what you can now imagine. (See Ephesians 3:20.)

1. A Spiritual Diet of "Solid Food"

Many believers have not progressed from "milk" to "solid food" in their knowledge and understanding of God's Word. The milk of God's Word contains only the fundamentals of faith and doctrine. *"Anyone who lives on milk, being still an infant, is not acquainted with the teaching about righteousness. But solid food is for the mature, who by constant use have trained themselves to distinguish good from evil"* (Hebrews 5:13–14 NIV).

The "meat" of the Word is our "solid food." Unless we progress in our spiritual diet from "milk" to "meat," we may experience spiritual "starvation." We need specific nourishment from the Word for each stage of our spiritual growth. It is only as we advance from basic doctrine to the deeper spiritual truths of the Scriptures and God's revelation that we will be able to continue to grow and to mature, being continually transformed into the image of Christ.

2. The Activation of the Fivefold Ministries

"And [Jesus] Himself gave some to be apostles, some prophets, some evangelists, and some pastors and teachers, for the equipping of the saints for the work of ministry, for the edifying of the body of Christ, till we all come to the unity of the faith and of the knowledge of the Son of God" (Ephesians 4:11–13). Christ established the five spiritual offices—known as the "fivefold ministry"—listed in the above passage. He gave them to His church as "agents of change" to perfect His people. Jesus invests Himself in the leaders He has appointed so that they, in turn, can invest themselves in others. When the church functions under the structure of the fivefold ministry, believers are enabled to receive revelation from God from each of the spiritual offices. In that way, they can partake of the balanced diet of "solid food" they need in order to be transformed into the image of Christ.

In fact, every believer should share what he has received from God with others, especially his fellow Christians. This keeps our spiritual lives fresh and current. We can't just "fill up" on revelation knowledge and wisdom, spiritual anointing, and ministry gifts. When we fail to "empty" what we have received into the lives of others, we eventually become spiritually stagnant, having a selfish, religious mind-set.

I impart the vision of our ministry as I preach to believers in churches around the world. I also train their leaders to become vessels in God's hands that will "empty" themselves into the lives of others. These leaders are manifesting genuine demonstrations of God's supernatural power and grace. God is continually revealing His presence and power in new ways, prompting people to seek Him and to experience the ongoing transformation of their heart.

If you are a pastor, and your local church does not yet fully function according to the fivefold ministry, I encourage you to begin establishing relationships with other Spirit-filled leaders and outside ministries who can support you in the offices in which you are lacking. Then, your people will be able to grow spiritually in a comprehensive way. As always, you and your members must desire transformation, or you will not allow the anointing of these five ministries to be effective in changing you.

3. Breakthroughs in Regard to Your Environment

Jesus healed a certain blind man in an unusual—but prophetic—manner. (See Mark 8:22–26.) To begin with, Jesus took him by the hand and led him out of town, so that the restoration of the man's sight took place outside his normal environment. Couldn't Christ have healed him within the town? Of course! But I believe there was an "atmosphere"—such as unbelief—in that town that would have prevented the manifestation of God's power to supernaturally heal. After Jesus had healed the man, He told him, in effect, "Don't go back to town—go directly to your house." Why did He say that? I think the reason was to keep the man from losing his healing by returning to that atmosphere.

Our environment may be keeping us from transitioning into a new dimension.

Is there anything in your environment—spiritual, physical, emotional, intellectual, or another realm—that might be hindering you from experiencing the transformation of your heart and mind, making you unable to receive revelation or to demonstrate the supernatural? Our environment can greatly influence us to conform to false ideas and attitudes that prevent us from being transformed. As we have noted, many people conform to the stagnant doctrine of their religion or their particular church denomination, or to other erroneous beliefs that are promoted by their culture, embraced by their family members, or adhered to by their close friends. Some people conform to negative circumstances, such as sickness or poverty; others conform to emotional bondage, such as fear or depression. In all these cases, those who are trapped in conformity must break through their oppressive "environment," or "atmosphere"; otherwise, they can never become what God has called them to be through the finished work of Christ.

Breakthroughs in regard to environment can be accomplished only by the Spirit of God, but they are initiated as we make the decision to surrender our life completely to God. If you have allowed yourself to conform to others' false beliefs because you don't want to offend them or make them feel "uncomfortable," or because you are afraid of what it will cost you to stop conforming, you are accountable to God for your lack of response to Him. If you know that you must break through an environment that is spiritually stifling to you, don't delay! Make the decision today, take the risk, and push through the atmosphere that is preventing you from reaching new levels in Christ.

The following testimony, from a man named Eduardo, shows what can happen when an individual leaves his environment in obedience to God and surrenders his life to the Lord. Here is his story: "I grew up in a dysfunctional home. My father abandoned my mother when I was only sixteen years old, leaving her with seven children to raise by herself. By the time I was eighteen, I was drinking and having promiscuous sex. I was also irresponsible and a liar.

"I reached a point in my life where I questioned God, asking Him if He was even real, because my family members and I lived such chaotic lives. I asked Him to allow me to raise a family of my own, if He really did exist. He spoke to me in dreams and said that I should leave my family. I didn't understand His request then, but I still left my country of Colombia and journeyed to the United States.

"When I was thirty-eight, having a great void in my life, I received Jesus as my Lord and Savior. When I went to the altar, I immediately felt as if the great weight I had carried all my life had been physically lifted off me—a spiritual burden of unforgiveness, lies, and adultery that hadn't allowed me to live in peace. When I confessed and received Christ, I felt free and full of joy, and the fear of death that had followed me for years was lifted from me. In its place, the love of God entered my heart. I thank God because He took my life of torment, falsehood, and death and exchanged it for one of joy, peace, and love. I understand that I have a purpose to carry out on this earth.

"After twenty years, I can testify that God is faithful. He gave me the family I asked for, and together we serve the Lord. I thank Him for King Jesus International Ministry, where we have been educated in God's Word and where God has raised us up as pastors to carry His Word to the ends of the earth."

Each time God calls someone for an unusual purpose, He calls him out of his usual environment.

---

4. Continual Supernatural Encounters with the Presence of God

Perhaps the greatest obstacle blocking a move of God in the life of an individual or group is the idea of having "arrived." As we have seen, many people have a difficult time accepting the fact that there is something for them spiritually beyond what they have already known and experienced in God. They believe they have seen, learned, and done it "all." What a mistake! To think in such a way is to overlook the truth that God is infinite in power and in creativity. There is much arrogance in such a mentality. How can we preach about an eternal, sovereign God—the Creator of heaven and earth—and then imagine that there is nothing more we can learn from Him or experience in His presence?

This mind-set is typical of the spirit of religiosity that comes to deceive Christians and stop them from growing spiritually and multiplying a harvest of fruit for the kingdom. If we are unwilling to progress to new dimensions in God, then we cannot say that we live by faith. When we already have something, we are living by "sight" rather than by faith.

The answer is to continually seek supernatural encounters with the presence of God. There are some people who have never sensed the nearness of God or witnessed any of His manifestations. In one of the countries where I ministered, a woman approached me and said, "Pastor, I have been a Christian for over fifteen years, but I have never experienced the presence of God." I have heard the same comment from various pastors and other leaders. This leads me to wonder what form of Christianity they have been living.

Sadly, it seems that what they have really known is religion—human tradition that speaks of merely a historic Christ and/or follows a series of rites and practices lacking true life and the power to transform. Countless ministries and churches have been founded on doctrines and theologies that have never changed anyone's life. The most they manage to do is provide some information or entertainment or offer a setting where people can get to know one another and benefit from their association in certain ways. But those functions are identical to the ones we would find at a social club or a trade association.

Transformation is not possible outside the presence of God.

Why follow a belief system that doesn't produce genuine, significant change in your life? Once we experience the presence of God, we are inevitably transformed in some way. And, after we have been transformed, we inevitably manifest the effects of that transformation—we can't help but radiate the change.

As I wrote earlier, the world wants to see genuine transformation take place in us, because that is what it needs. We must provide living evidence for people to see that supernatural encounters with God are real—and that they can experience them! We owe the world supernatural encounters with the presence and power of God. Accordingly, we must preach a complete gospel—a gospel of both Word and power (see, for example, 1 Corinthians 2:4), a gospel that continually produces spiritual knowledge and supernatural experiences in keeping with what has been preached.

Our God is always bringing us new revelations of Himself, new levels of supernatural power, and new dimensions of His glory with the manifestation of His presence. Therefore, it is essential for us to understand and accept the fact that we don't know "everything" about God—"we know [only] in part" (1 Corinthians 13:9), as the apostle Paul declared. The best approach for us to take is to be open, humble, and expectant before God, always seeking to see, experience, and receive something new from Him beyond what we have known to this point.

Regardless of how much revelation we have already received, God always has more for us! We must be transformed and renewed by His glory through continuous encounters with His presence, from which the new life of His Spirit flows!

Some of our heart issues can be dealt with only when we are in the presence of God. Our changed heart is a sign that we are moving "from glory to glory."

Prayer for Moving from Conformity to Transformation

I believe it is time for us to make a decision. The era in which we live demands committed Christians who are totally surrendered to God and to His will. We cannot bring about change in this world by presenting people with messages that merely give them information or entertain them, or by promoting various rules and religious formalities. We must therefore access the supernatural power of God that can transform people's hearts and circumstances; otherwise, the "Christianity" they follow will be just another religion, subject to the present corruption of this world. Our world is collapsing under the weight of the fall, and people's only hope of salvation and deliverance is Jesus Christ. Our part is to *be* transformed *in order to* help transform others.

The purpose of Jesus' lordship over us is to transform our heart, so that He may manifest His life through us.

Sons and daughters of God, what is your decision? Will you remain stagnant in your religion and conformity, or will you break through your current environment to become "new wineskins" capable of containing the "new wine" that Christ is pouring out upon this generation? Will you join the "old guard," never participating in the great new manifestation of God's glory on earth, or will you continuously seek encounters with the presence of God that will lead you to experience a radical change of heart so that you can reach out to others with His grace and power?

It is time for us to surrender our heart, our family, our work, our talents, our past experiences, and our calling to Christ, so that He can become Lord and Master over our whole life. When He does, He will take responsibility for everything that concerns us. This is the only way we can experience a true transformation of our heart so that it may be filled with new life—the very life of God.

If you want to make the decision to be transformed by God's presence, please pray the following prayer:

> Heavenly Father, I come before Your presence with an open heart—not hiding anything from You or pretending to be "spiritual." I recognize that I have lived according to a religious mind-set, with patterns of conduct and deficient "structures," or methods, of ministry and service that have left me spiritually stagnant. I ask You to forgive me for ignoring and/or rejecting the supernatural. Today, I make the decision to break away from the environments that hinder me and to begin seeking Your presence wholeheartedly, because I am hungry and thirsty to know Your transforming power!
>
> Come to me, Lord, and show me the areas in my life that need to change. I don't want just a "touch" from You—I want a complete transformation of my heart. I want to think as You think. I want to believe as You believe. I want to do what You do. Change my heart and my life. Open my spiritual eyes and ears so that I may see and hear the move of Your Spirit and follow it, regardless of human opinion or any other temporal, earthly influence. I want You to dwell within me and to enable me to become useful and relevant in service to Your kingdom. Thank You, Lord, because my transformation begins today! In the name of Jesus, amen!

About the Author

A postle Guillermo Maldonado is a man called to bring God's supernatural power to this generation at the local and international levels. Active in ministry for over twenty years, he is the founder of Ministerio Internacional El Rey Jesús (King Jesus International Ministry)—one of the fastest-growing multicultural churches in the United States—which has been recognized for its development of kingdom leaders and for visible manifestations of God's supernatural power.

Having earned a master's degree in practical theology from Oral Roberts University and a doctorate in divinity from Vision International University, Apostle Maldonado stands firm and focused on the vision God has given him to evangelize, affirm, disciple, and send. His mission is to teach, train, equip, and send leaders and believers to bring the supernatural power of God to their communities, in order to leave a legacy of blessings for future generations. This mission is worldwide. Apostle Maldonado is a spiritual father to more than 100 pastors and apostles of local and international churches as part of a growing association, the New Wine Apostolic Network, which he founded.

Apostle Maldonado has authored many books and manuals, a number of which have been translated into several languages. His previous books with Whitaker House are *How to Walk in the Supernatural Power of God*, *The Glory of God*, and *The Kingdom of Power: How to Demonstrate It Here and Now*, all of which are available in Spanish. In addition, he preaches the message of Jesus Christ and His redemptive power on his international television program, *Time for Change (Tiempo de Cambio)*, which airs on several networks, thus reaching millions worldwide.

Apostle Maldonado resides in Miami, Florida, with his wife and partner in ministry, Ana, and their two sons, Bryan and Ronald.